THE HISTORY OF
SWIMMING

THE HISTORY OF
SWIMMING

A MEMOIR

KIM POWERS

CARROLL & GRAF PUBLISHERS
NEW YORK

THE HISTORY OF SWIMMING

Carroll & Graf Publishers
An Imprint of Avalon Publishing Group, Inc.
245 West 17th Street, 11th Floor
New York, NY 10011

AVALON
publishing group incorporated

Library of Congress Cataloging-in-Publication Data is available.

ISBN-13: 978-0-78671-723-1
ISBN-10: 0-78671-723-8

9 8 7 6 5 4 3 2 1

Printed in the United States of America
Interior design by Maria E. Torres
Distributed by Publishers Group West

For Tim, For Jess

BOOK ONE

FRIDAY

CHAPTER ONE

M y twin brother Tim wrote these paragraphs the night he had a nervous breakdown, seven years ago, our senior year at the same college. He had stayed up all night finishing a paper on Richard Henry Dana's novel *Two Years Before the Mast*, about a boy who goes off to sea, and this was a sort of preface to his paper:

"The History of Swimming"

My older brother taught me to swim when I was five years old. Edwin, who was nicknamed "Porky" by my father, led my twin brother Kim and me to the water one Sunday morning near Easter. He promised we would not drown if we did what he said.

Porky held his arm across the water's edge and told us to fall over it until we felt the water. I stared at the pool until my twin leapt over Porky's arm

and into the water. Kim turned back around to me, smiled, and I followed. We shared an adventure in space.

In adolescence, I forgot how to swim but spent a great deal of time yearning for the water. At Boy Scout camp, I panicked when a water safety instructor told me to run to the water's edge, strip, and save a pretend drowning victim. I am still amazed by the speed at which the water becomes a razor's edge.

With this story, I go swimming every night for a new adventure in space. I am surprised that time and memory have taught me to swim again.

I've read and reread those paragraphs countless times over the years, but they've never seemed as foreboding as they do now. Tim writes, *"With this story, I go swimming every night for a new adventure in space,"* but which "story" does he mean? The novel he had just finished reading—*Two Years Before the Mast?* The anecdote he had just told, about being taught to swim by our older brother Porky? Or the paper itself, the one he had written for his "Literature of the Sea" class?

I keep thinking it's that, the actual paper, that holds the key to his breakdown. I read it once, years ago—before I was looking for clues—but it's disappeared since then. I doubt it even made it out of Tim's dorm room at graduation; I can imagine him leaving it there, hammering it into a wall like an angry edict from Martin Luther, a warning about the dangers of thinking too much about the past to the incoming freshman who would inherit the room and all its secrets.

Maybe Jim Gray, the English professor for whom it was written (a Vietnam vet who once told me the experience of war was like one long, unrelenting rock concert), still has a copy of it. Not filed neatly away, able to be retrieved at a moment's notice, but never completely

out of mind, either. Just like me, Jim's always looking for that one clue in it that might unlock the mystery of Tim's breakdown; he's always thinking maybe he could have prevented it, had he only known. But known what? That's the real mystery.

In *Two Years Before the Mast*, a boy goes to sea to find himself. It's the basic plot of practically everything: somebody goes somewhere—New York, Louisville, Africa, the moon, fill in the blank—and discovers, for better or worse, wondrous, strange things about himself. What did Tim discover about himself, reading that book? And did he write about it, leave a map in those words, written seven years ago? *"With this story, I go swimming every night for a new adventure in space. I am surprised that time and memory have taught me to swim again."* I keep reading those sentences, but all I can see are separate words, nouns, no verbs, themselves swimming in my mind and refusing to *do* anything: night, adventure, space, time, memory, surprise. Little words, big ideas. Scary things. I keep thinking I'm just on the verge of understanding, but then the picture falls apart. The images don't form a logical story, even though I *think* I remember the separate images he conveys: being taught to swim by our older brother, the humiliation of Boy Scout camp, the sadness of Easter (maybe that's just my memory).

Who knows?

Who knows (and who the fuck cares—except me, right?) what Tim meant in that goddamn preface. It was written ages ago, long before either of us could have predicted what would happen in the years to come. So *why* do those few, mysterious paragraphs keep tumbling over and over in my head right now? Because they keep my mind off the thing at hand? Because they're so beautifully written? Because I think there might be hidden clues in them?

All of the above.

My twin brother Tim is missing, really missing this time, and I have no idea where he is. For the first time in my life, I think he might be dead. I don't know if I can live without him, even though I don't think I can live with him anymore, either.

⌒

The first call came around noon today. Joyce, the secretary where Tim worked, called to see if I knew where he was, or rather, in her not-wanting-to-scare-me-but-beginning-to-get-pissed-off way, if I had "heard from him" this morning. He hadn't shown up, hadn't called in, couldn't be reached. Joyce sounded like she wanted to say more—call me paranoid, but I'm an expert at hearing things that aren't there—but knew this wasn't the time.

I tried to stay calm and asked if this had happened before.

She said nothing, and in that silence, I knew it had.

I'd been expecting a call like this; I'd known something was going to happen, sooner rather than later. Tim was following a familiar pattern: any time he had to face a major change—and he was supposed to move to a new apartment tomorrow, or rather, escape his old one, with me helping him—he would disappear, usually on a drinking binge. There would be no apology or explanation when he resurfaced, only anger; usually directed at me, because he refused to direct it at himself.

Things had been too strange lately. Things had been too strange the last seven years. We had lived apart most of that time. I had migrated from college in Texas to New York, moved in with a lover, gone to grad school, gotten a coveted job finding scripts and books for a semifamous TV star to turn into movies. Tim had moved to Louisville, Kentucky, and social service, one of JFK's Volunteers in

Service to America. He discovered drinking in Louisville, and long-distance abuse toward me over the phone. Drunken calls late at night, telling me how I had failed him. How I had become a New York snob. How we had been cursed by our childhoods (that part probably true).

But on occasion, there was also long-distance love over the phone and through the mail. We'd blithely make long, rambling phone calls to each other in our lean and hungry postcollege years, no clue how we'd pay for them, just certain there'd be some way once the bill came due. It was the kind of enchantment, or luck, or blessing that had followed us through most of our lives: things always seemed to work out, at the very last possible moment. (It was the same way we'd gotten through life to that point—no clue, no map, just a vague hope we'd find a way by the time we got there—wherever "there" was. Let it be said the Powers twins coasted through life with a certain charm, but nothing a parent could call "real life skills.") We'd exchange magnificent letters, more from Tim than me; his crafted over long periods of time and written in different inks: this one from work, that one scribbled on a bus, another from home late at night. Letters that treated his drinking as a joke, a punch line. "I'm sitting here in a bar, writing this letter. No, don't worry, it's 8 A.M., but I've only had a few drinks."

But the drinking, or the cursed childhood, or the absence of a map took control, and things in Louisville became more difficult for him, until everything "crashed and burned," his frequent description of things. He moved to New York, where I had already lived for several years, and we didn't have the soften-the-blow cushion of long distance anymore. Things got worse for him. He started losing small things: phone numbers, keys, Citibank cards. Then bigger things: jobs, apartments, boyfriends. Finally, he attempted suicide. I had

gotten to the point where I literally stopped breathing whenever the phone rang, afraid of what might be on the other end of the line: Tim, the police, a hospital, the morgue.

End of the line, indeed.

But none of it was worse than this: no phone call at all, his complete disappearance. Even with his suicide attempt a month or so ago, when he tried to hack off his hand, there was something to do, an action to take: sew him back together. After his breakdown in college, he used to say he'd let it happen so he'd have the luxury of being put back together again, like Humpty Dumpty. But now, what if there was nothing left to put back together?

With that one phone call from Joyce in his office, all the panic I'd stored up over the last seven years came flooding over. "Maybe he's just not picking up for me. Why don't *you* try calling him?" she sneered, then hung up.

Well, fuck you, too.

And my little brother.

My little brother by all of five minutes.

There were a dozen useful things I could have done just then, but my brain had stopped—one phone call and bam, it just froze—and all I could think about was the little orange pumpkin on my desk.

⌒

I had brought it back from the country the weekend before, the first bit of decoration in my new office at a new job. I had brought back miniature pumpkins for the whole staff of four. For a while, they were the only bit of color in the plain white rooms we had just moved into, where I worked the phones and did lunches, begging agents to let me see their "female-driven" projects first, before

actresses who could actually get the movies made saw them. (Once, when I had to go to my boss three times in as many weeks to say a bigger TV star had beat us at optioning the books we wanted, she said, "If I have to hear that bitch's name one more time, I'm going to scream." So much for camaraderie among female stars of a certain age, and a certain talent.)

I had bought the pumpkins at the last minute, as my boyfriend Jess and I headed back to our apartment in Brooklyn after a weekend trip to Connecticut. The little pumpkins weren't even officially from New England; I got them at a roadside stand just before the New York turnpike, set up for weary travelers who, stuck in Sunday return traffic like ourselves, had put off buying their rustic mementos until it was almost too late. I thought Tim, who had been staying at our apartment that weekend, would like some farm-grown apples or fresh-pressed cider—he was Mr. Fruit and Vegetables, always had been, since childhood; I was Mr. Cookies and Cakes—and I got those for him too, as well as a pumpkin to carve for Halloween, never thinking a sharp knife was the last thing I should be putting in his hands.

But by the time we got back to our apartment, our weekend get-away euphoria was gone; we were tired and cranky from the drive, the traffic and exhaust of New York. The same dread I used to get every Sunday night about going back to school on Monday was gripping my gut, but now, it had transformed itself into the dread of the happy face, the high-pitched, happy voice, I'd have to put on for Tim. The walking on eggshells. The discovery of some new calamity. And, like time and tide, he didn't disappoint.

We got home, and the big iron gate that was the entrance to our ground floor apartment was open and unlocked, and I knew Tim had fucked up. The bolt was turned but hadn't caught in its slot; a

sloppy mistake, typical of Tim thinking he'd done what he was supposed to, but hadn't done at all.

My face clenched, I went barreling in, already yelling his name,
ready for war, even as Jess tried to pull me back. And even before
I saw Tim sprawled out on the coach, I smelled him: beer cans and
empty popper bottles, porno tapes stacked high and unwound on
the coffee table. He was still asleep, in a drunken blackout, even
though it was six or seven in the evening; his consciousness was
buried under boozy dreams and too many cum shots. But hearing
me, it took him no time at all to come alive and fly off the
couch—fully clothed, fully awake now—and know why I was so
mad. It took us no time at all to start screaming at each other, no
time at all for him to grab his things and run out of the apartment,
his final "Fuck you" ringing in my ears. That or the clang of slamming the metal gate behind him; it was hard to tell which was
louder.

At least this time, he remembered to close it.

I chased after him, begging him to come back, at the same time I
wanted him to go away and never return.

When is a pumpkin not just a pumpkin? When you just gave it to
your twin brother, who's now running down a dirty New York street
with a hangover headache and no shoes. When your twin brother
turns around one last time, not to say he's sorry, not to beg the
heavens to explain why the twin boys who used to love each other
so much now hated each other, but to hurl the pumpkin at you,
splattering its rind and seeds all over the sidewalk.

Oh, yes, Mr. Sondheim was right: a weekend in the country.

Fucking baby pumpkin.

I twirled it in my fingers, fingered its serrations like rosary beads, as I tried calling Tim from my office. The message on his answering machine was his regular one, Tim in happier times, not drunk, and I already wondered if it would be the last record of his voice I'd ever hear. I spoke through the machine, hoping that if he heard me, who had seen him through the worst and still not abandoned him, no matter how much I had felt like it, he might pick up. But there was no answer, for me or anybody else, so I went to his office, just a few blocks away from mine, to see if I could figure out anything more in person.

Tim works for Frank, a director who once made important "films," but now makes "movies." Bad ones. And even those he had trouble financing. Tim was Frank's lackey, reading scripts and running errands for his socialite wife. The company had just set up shop, like my employers, but unlike ours, their walls were already covered with posters that were a retrospective of the director's career, as if to remind him he had once had one. Of course, Tim, not Frank, had the job of schlepping around and getting all those posters framed. There wasn't enough money to make movies, but there was enough to buy big, expensive frames. (And really, was there that much difference between me and Tim and our jobs? I had an expense account and a business card that said "Director of Development"; he had no card, no title, but we both schlepped home books at night and on the weekends, to wade through for other people. Mine came in the form of hundreds of loose pages of manuscripts that practically dislocated my shoulder with their weight. Tim bought his off bookstore shelves, already published, too late to really play the game, but we were both doing the same thing: reading, the thing we'd taken refuge in since childhood.)

Frank's secretary, Joyce, had always been gracious to me, intrigued by the mystery of twinship, asking the same first-meeting questions people always ask: Can you read each other's minds?

(We can't, not really, but in the breath he takes before he says hello on the phone, I can hear his life.)

Do you know what the other one is thinking?

(I don't know when he feels a specific pain, but I know he's *in* pain.)

Can you feel when he's sick? Can you "mind-read" where he is all the time?

(I don't know when he leaves his house, but I know he is not there now.)

Did you ever try to fool each other's girlfriends?

(Maybe it was the fact that we are fraternal, not identical, that saved us from that one; more likely it was the fact that anyone could tell we didn't have girlfriends.)

Now, all that polite curiosity was gone, and Joyce wanted to hold me accountable for Tim. His absence had screwed up her day, and she needed someone to blame; it might as well be me. To her, at that moment, we were the same person, interchangeable, even though we weren't identical.

In our looks, and certainly in our voices, there is the hint of kinship—that gap between our two front teeth, from the Perkins side of the family, the barest touch of a Texas accent—but Tim has always been taller than me, maybe because he stands up straighter, with light blond/brown hair to my darker locks. Our late grandfather called Tim "Blondie" and me "Brunie." Tim always has a tan, no matter what time of year; I don't like the sun that much, and have the "pasty-white skin of the stay-at-home," the only phrase from the Boy Scout Manual that has stayed with me all these years. I look

small, even frail. People always assume I'm the little brother, not the older, by a big fucking five minutes. (When we'd go to the movies every Saturday as children, the popcorn lady would say to Tim, "Now, don't bring your little brother next week. The movie's too grown-up for him." "Just give me extra butter and shut the fuck up," I felt like saying back to her, sailor-mouthed at six.)

"Look," Joyce said. "Is this a joke?" No preamble, no "I'm sorry," no "I hope he's alright," no "I can't imagine what you're going through."

"Just give me extra butter and shut the fuck up," came back to mind, but I held my salty tongue.

She pointed to Tim's desk, piled high with papers, scripts, receipts, old *New York Posts* and *Daily News*es, the packs of gum the director needed to keep from smoking, probably even a change or two of clothes.

I didn't know if the mess was the joke Joyce meant, or something else. She just kept staring, pointing with her head, hands on her hips like the proverbial little teapot (I expected her to say, "Tip me over and pour me out"). Did she want me to clean it up? Is that what all this was about? He hadn't been hired for his neatness; surely she'd figured that out by now. There's a picture of him in one of our college yearbooks, sitting in his dorm room, which was overtaken by papers, books, records, dirty clothes, and, so help me God, a vacuum cleaner. What that was doing there—it had certainly never been used—I never could figure out. Tim should have pasted copies of that picture on his résumé: "Here, this is who I am: smart, but a mess. It's a package deal. Take it or leave it."

"Look," she said again. Alright already, I'll clean it up. I went over to the desk and finally saw what she meant. Excavated from the rubble was his Day-At-A-Glance calendar. Joyce had flipped to

today's page, where Tim had written, in the spidery, almost old-fashioned calligraphy that was his trademark, "Swimming."

He'd also written, in the pages leading up to it, that familiar phrase that made my stomach seize up: "Crash and Burn." He'd written it so often he even came to abbreviate it C&B.

"What's that mean? Crash and Burn? Swimming?" She shook her teapot head again. "I don't know how much longer Frank's going to stand for this."

I looked at the page again; there was something else about it, something more than those foreboding words "swimming" and "crash and burn" in all their isolation. Was it the relative blankness of the pages earlier in the week that was so strange? Monday through Wednesday were completely empty, unlike most of the previous weeks, which were filled with appointments written in different colors of ink—"red/blue/green," said very fast, the punch line to a joke I remembered from grade school. No erasable pencil for my brother, no sir. Thursday night, the night before this, he'd written "Something with Peter G." around 6:45. Tonight, Friday, he was supposed to go out with "Dan M." (No last names for my brother, either. It's not me protecting the innocent, that's just the way he wrote them.) On the next day's page, Saturday, he'd written "Moving to Weehawken, NJ" with big stars around it, like the light bulbs on a movie marquee, the same icon he had drawn in high school and college on special letters to special friends.

I would have called those people, Peter and Dan—I knew who they were—but it wasn't the appointments, who had last seen him when or where or who was supposed to see him, that meant something. It was the date, the end of October.

I closed my eyes—not easy to do under the watchful, judgmental glare of the ever present Joyce—and tried to think. And again, all that

came to mind was pumpkins. Orange. Late October. Days before
Halloween. Early sunsets, dark, jeweled nights. And then something
started taking shape. I pushed harder and tried to make my mind
zero in on something specific. The smell of fall, my favorite season.
("I praise the fall; it is the human season," the poet Archibald
MacLeish once wrote.) College. Rehearsing for "The Faust Project."
Standing by some bushes, talking to Tim.

And there it was.

Swimming.

I suddenly knew.

If not the exact anniversary of his breakdown, it was certainly
around the time he had left school, near one of the fall holidays, Halloween or Thanksgiving.

When he had gone "swimming" in time and space.

In the weeks before his breakdown, that fall of our senior year, Tim
had been reading *Moby-Dick* for his "Literature of the Sea" course;
"Moby's *Dick*" we'd yell out with a cackle, across the din of the cafeteria, then stretch our arms as far apart as they'd go, a visual of
Moby's dick that left nothing to the imagination.

That was when we *were* talking to each other. More often than
not, in those days, we weren't: we'd pass each other and stare, a challenge, angry over some unspoken slight. Those silent looks were our
favorite weapons then, much more than words. Strange: the boys
who were so much better with words than anything else—people,
cars, emotions—couldn't use them with each other, at least at that
strange juncture in our lives.

And I couldn't figure out why we weren't talking. Tim seemed to

have undergone some sort of sea change that summer and fall. He'd come back from a summer spent with our college's theater troupe, off in the Hill Country near San Antonio, and he was different. Strange. Moody. I'd ask him why, and he'd just give me what I'd started calling his "Pip look."

Pip was Melville's servant boy who went underwater and came back—what? Dead? Alive? An unholy, visionary mixture of both? An almost beatific look would come into Tim's eyes whenever he talked about Pip, which was often, as if they had both lain witness to the same thing. Maybe Atlantis, maybe God, but whatever it was, Tim couldn't wait to see it again. And those of us who hadn't seen it, whatever it was, weren't worth talking to.

Tim was Pip that fall.

My last conversation with him, before his breakdown later that night, took place by a row of bushes surrounding the campus's central administration building. It was early evening, and I, self-important little college actor that I was, was racing off to a rehearsal for *The Faust Project,* our attempt to be avant-garde, when I ran into Tim. Literally. I was playing Faust and mumbling my lines to myself, wondering how in the world I could convince an audience I had seen hell—later, it would be so easy—when I bumped into him. He blurted out that he didn't have time for me, didn't have time for anything. I said something nasty in return, and we stood there, wondering who was going to have the last word.

That's what it always came down to in those days: who would have the last word.

For those few, silent seconds, I remember picking at the waxy leaves of that hedge, getting their rich green and chartreuse pulp underneath my fingernails, as if I needed to dig my nails into something, to keep from digging them into my own skin, or Tim's.

Several walkways radiated out from where we stood, like spokes from a central hub, and we could have taken any one of them to escape each other. But for some reason, we didn't. Maybe we were bonded, for those few minutes at least, by memories from our childhood: the feel and smell of waxy leaves, the sight of street lamps on timers, flickering on and off as falling nighttime teased us, then finally took hold, in those waning days of summer; the last days of childhood, when we would try to squeeze every last second out of the darkness before we had to go in for the night.

Now, Tim smiled first, a little cautiously, like dipping his toes in water to test the temperature, then began telling me about a painting that my dorm room neighbor had been working on: a mystical, almost otherworldly depiction of two naked bodies, neither male nor female, their hills and valleys beckoning to the acolyte. As Tim described it, he was overtaken by the Pip look—that inscrutable set of his eyes and mouth, his brow and the brain behind it, that harkened back to some wondrous, strange thing that only he had been chosen to witness.

I was surprised by Tim's description of my neighbor David's painting; I didn't even know they were friends. I'd taken to nightly chats with David as study breaks (I had a little crush on him) and had never heard him mention the painting, or even knew he painted, because he was a bigwig in the music department. I told Tim I'd have David show it to me. Tim half smiled as he walked away; the missing half of the smile was a mystery I was supposed to solve.

Later that night, I was at the *Faust* rehearsal when Tim "broke down," unreachable even if he had tried to reach me. I've always needed to think he did. (Did his breakdown happen in a single minute, an hour, a night, or did it take the twenty-odd years of our lives to gather force and strike?) Ironically, after that night's rehearsal,

I'd been talking to my friend Ken about his own sister's breakdown. He'd charted a whole world, at that time unknown to me, of lithium, therapy, nerve synapses, auras. When I saw Ken recently in New York, he said, "Everyone always thought you'd be the one who'd go nuts; I always knew it was going to be Tim."

Gee, thanks.

Inadvertently, I was told on the phone the next morning by one of Tim's professors that something had happened. Dr. Hinkle assumed I already knew; I didn't. That was the first time I've ever felt the panic on a phone call that has been a frequent visitor these past seven years.

Tim wrote this that very first night my father brought him home:

"Time At Home"

I stopped crying after midnight and told my father about a friend at school.

"His name is Michael. If boys are pretty, then Michael is such a pretty boy."

My father stared out the window of thehouse where I was born.

"Last summer, he went across the United States and spent only $30. Can you imagine that?"

My father counted streetlamps from the window and reached for a cigarette on the table.

"Michael met so many people on the road. They bought him dinners and gave him places to stay."

My father drew the shades. He stubbed out his cigarette in a cup of cold coffee and said, "I think, son, if I were not such a scarecrow now, I could make the trip for $20."

My father kissed me goodnight and walked down the hall to his bedroom. I got up from

the couch and heard the clock strike from
the courthouse square:
  It is no time / To make your father cry.

                        ⌒

It is no time to make your brother cry either, but that is what I was
on the verge of doing, when Joyce brought me back to the present
and said Frank wanted to talk to me.

I was intimidated by Frank's fame and always worried about whether
I sounded intelligent and witty in his company. "Company" was hardly
the word for it; presence was more appropriate. But at the same time that
I felt awkward around him, I was privately dismissive about the com-
mercial comedies he was now making, and angry at him for causing so
much of Tim's unhappiness. (That's right, Kim: blame everybody but
Tim. Blame everybody but yourself.) Tim felt differently about Frank's
movies each time he saw them, depending on how he felt about Frank at
the time. When Frank was nice to him, the movies, even the bad ones,
were works of genius the rest of us failed to understand. When Tim was
mad at Frank, and I had finally figured out something nice to say about
the movies, Tim thought they were a mess, and was I out of my mind?

Frank was the kind of person I deepened my voice to talk to.

The first and only thing he asked, was if Tim had cut his wrist the
month before: the scar, the roll of gauze bandage he had passed off
as covering a burn. . . .

Frank knew.

Maybe he had tried the very same things in his life.

I told Frank the truth, even as I knew Tim would be furious at
me for doing it. And even though Frank said he was worried and

wanted to find Tim and get him help, he seemed determined to let me know he wasn't going to tolerate his behavior much longer. It was a threat, an ultimatum. Not only did I have to worry about Tim's whereabouts, but what might happen to his job when—if—he was found.

At one point—maybe the only point of real kindness in the short conversation—Frank shook his head and said, "Oh, Kim." Nothing more, but I understood. He had been a child like us—nervous, sensitive, not sure of his way—and maybe he still was, even though he couldn't let it show anymore. He knew what could make a sensitive boy disappear, but not how to find him. That would be up to me, and he didn't envy me the task.

He wished me good luck, and our meeting was over.

I took the calendar on Tim's desk on my way out.

Joyce saw me do it—she opened her little tea spout and started to say something, to protest, "We paid for that, it's ours"—but the pain and fear in my eyes silenced her for once.

Maybe the calendar would help me find my brother, wherever he was swimming.

CHAPTER TWO

Bad things had always happened to us in connection with water and swimming, even though they gave us so much joy. When we were five, the same year Porky taught us to swim, Tim broke his leg in a little plastic wading pool in our backyard. Our father had placed the portable pool at the bottom of a swing set slide so we could whoosh down its hot metal and into the water in the pool, still frothy from the green rubber garden hose that had filled it up. But Tim's knee had somehow buckled under him on the way down, or when he hit the water, and he landed on it in a twisted position.

No one believed his pain, though, and that very same day, he was forced to go on a family outing to the lake. In his agony, he wouldn't play with me, running in and out of the ebbing tide. (Does a lake have a tide? It does now, in my scrambled memory.) I made fun of

him for being "a scaredy-cat of the water." When my parents finally realized something was wrong, they took him to the doctor.

Tim's leg was broken, of course. I could have told them that.

I knew.

Twins know.

My father, who could be said to have been responsible for the accident in the first place, even though he put the wading pool there for our pleasure, proudly rigged a homemade wheelchair for Tim out of a folding chair and a furniture hand truck from the store where he worked and paraded him around our neighborhood as grandly as he had wheeled us around in our double stroller when we were first born.

Another time, when our mother was driving us home from summer swimming lessons after the first or second grade, we were in a wreck, our mother ramming our car into one that had stopped suddenly in front of us. That morning in swim class, a hysterical mother had made the teacher jump in to save her little girl, who was straggling behind in the water. "My baby! My baby! She's drowning!" She wasn't; she was just slow. Tim and I, entertainers at an early age, had been doing imitations of that for our mother—at least *she* hadn't been the one screaming and embarrassing us—when metal slammed into metal.

In our wrecked car, with whiplash, she drove us to the emergency ward. We were fine (terrified, guilty perhaps, but not hurt), but that memory kept us both from swimming for many years afterward.

Whatever one of us did, the other did, too.

We both got scared of the water for a while and quit swimming, connecting it in our minds to an inevitable disaster.

In the fourth grade, I broke my right arm jumping across a water-filled drainage ditch at the end of our block, a contest with the

neighborhood boys to see who could jump the furthest and land completely dry on the other side, without their feet touching the water. I was determined to win. To beat the other boys, I would use a graceful, balletic leap I had learned from the dance books I checked out on weekly trips to the library. Style over substance.

Without a drop of water on me, I landed on the other side with my right arm held straight out against the earth; I saw my forearm literally fold in on itself at impact. I clamped my left arm on top of the now-hinged right arm to flatten it out, then held both arms tightly against my stomach as I walked the half block home, crying, my eyes closed. Neighbors out on their porches asked if I needed help. The other jumpers trailed behind me, too afraid to come up close, as if they'd be blamed, but dogging me with questions nonetheless: "You okay? What's wrong? You shouldn'ta put your arm out like that."

Our mother—now the hysterical one, when I showed her how I could bend my arm in three places—took me to the same doctor who had swathed Tim's leg in gauze and warm plaster a few years earlier. I still remember the warmth of getting that cast put on, the wooziness from the pain shot the doctor gave me. Tim was the first person to sign my cast, as I had been the first to sign his.

I sometimes even *think* I remember our birth: me, swimming around in our mother's womb, then shooting out first—not because of any great courage, but because Tim chickened out at the last minute, a scaredy-cat of dry land *and* of leaving the comforting water of the womb. "Come on out, it's great on shore," I call back, more to convince myself than a statement of fact. I'd say anything to have Tim follow me, even though I don't know what waits for us in the outside world. Tim does, though, and that's why he wants to stay inside; he's a lot smarter than I am, even in the womb. The heart

knowing more than the eye can see, as he would later write. He just smiles and defers, politely but adamantly, and I dig in again: "Whatcha waitin' for? *Come on.*" I lead the way, and Tim finally, nervously follows.

He should have stayed in.

Twins know.

Hoping, praying Tim would answer his door in person even if he wouldn't pick up the phone, I left Frank's office and took a cab to the apartment where Tim was staying, his third in as many months. Notice I don't say "his apartment": nothing connected to Tim was his; everything was temporary, on loan, this apartment more than others. He had moved from sublet to sublet during his two years in New York, but something always happened, and he would burn yet another bridge behind him while he found the next place to pitch camp. I had found him the current apartment by going through my address book and calling everyone I knew, ending with my friend Liz, who needed a roommate—and whose last name began with W. By the time I got to her, I'd reached the end of my patience with Tim, and the end of the alphabet. When she said, "Now don't be offended, but I have to ask: does he use drugs?" I almost laughed but stifled myself; if I told the truth, he'd be homeless. "Oh, no ma'am, he doesn't touch the devil's weed. Oh, yes ma'am, he's so blotto he can barely stand up. But does anybody really think alcohol is a *drug*?"

The apartment was way up and over on the Upper East Side, huge and fortresslike, with different wings branching out from a gigantic concrete courtyard, like some militaristic, Fascist building from the '30s. Big and anonymous, a perfect setting for Tim to disappear in.

Of course, that's not why he picked it; there was no "picking" involved, no choice. But it fit, nonetheless.

A set of exterior stairs zigzagged up the outside stucco walls to each floor, and I heaved up the four flights to his apartment, actually welcoming the strain in my thighs because it gave me something to focus on besides the buzz in my head, the ricocheting thoughts that Tim was dead. "Twins know," I wrote earlier, but now I'm not so sure. I knew he was gone, but not where. I thought he was dead and didn't, at the same time. That's the other thing twins do, or don't: they don't—they *can't*—think their other half is gone forever.

His metal door, at the top of the stairs, wasn't ominously open; there were no scratches or gouges on it, no streaks of blood, as I'd feared. I knocked softly at first, then pounded it with the side of my palm, then the knuckles, then switched back to the side of my fist, harder, deeper, madder. "Tim, come on. PLEASE. Open up. It's me. It's alright. *Please.* Just open the door." There was still no answer.

I went back downstairs to see if the super could let me in; maybe he'd seen my little show, seen how serious this was. But once I found him, he insisted Tim didn't live there, more with sign language and grunts than English. I tried to explain how Tim was the new roommate of Liz W's, the girl in 43R—maybe he just hadn't met him yet?—but he retaliated by showing me a black binder with tenants' Polaroid pictures in it. Liz herself was so many generations removed from the original tenant she wasn't even pictured; there was no way Tim was in it. I went from zero to sixty in no time flat and yelled I'd call the police if that's the only way I could get in.

He grunted some more.

I took that as his "go ahead."

At the nearest pay phone I could find, I dialed 911 for the first time in my life.

"I want to report a possible missing person."

"Possible." That must mean I still had hope, even though I don't think I did.

"Why do you think the person is missing, or in trouble? Has he been sick, or depressed?"

"He has tried to kill himself before." Somehow I knew to be very precise, very careful, not use contractions; I knew to take the operator's lead and follow the same careful, calm, spelled-out script she was reading. If I matched my rhythm to hers, maybe she'd help me faster. I made my voice and words sound even and steady, even if my heart wasn't.

"Yes, he has tried to kill himself before."

"Okay, good. That's what I needed to know. Now we can get to work." *We* can get to work; she would make it a team effort. *He* has tried to hurt himself before; that was the key that unlocked everything. (And if he *hadn't* tried to hurt himself before—would she have hung up on me?)

Get to work we did, this angel I envisioned as a big black woman, the fat dangling from her upper arms belying the strength she called on whenever she got a distress signal from a little white boy like me. She told me to wait for the police, so I did, standing behind the columns in front of the apartment complex, dreading what we'd find once we got inside.

⌒⌒

I had been in the apartment only once before. Tim had had some kind of trouble with his contact lenses, his eyes had become infected, and he'd missed work—again. I was taking him money—again—to go to a doctor.

The apartment was a mess, cramped and overheated. I had found Tim there, crumpled like Pinocchio after his strings had been cut, just as they had been cut when our father retrieved him from school and carried him home the night of his breakdown, along with a single green trash bag crammed with the few things worth keeping. Now I, not my father, had been forced into the role of Gepetto, old before my time, and Tim was the little wooden boy, knowing he'd done wrong. His eyes were squinting, his face red and chapped, but whether it was from crying or a broken thermostat, I didn't know. He was in his closet of a bedroom, sitting on a lone mattress on the floor, piled high with more green trash bags, his version of a suitcase ever since college.

He pulled himself up and tried to rush me out of the apartment but, as if overcome by the heat, gave up and collapsed into a chair. I had seen the mess; the damage was done; we might as well stay. I was embarrassed for my friend Liz whose apartment this was, and she wasn't even here to see the mess. I couldn't help but think she hadn't been there in weeks, or she'd have already kicked him out, drugs or no drugs. I had seen her wear velvet dresses and jaunty little hats with pearls and gloves; a person who dressed like that surely couldn't live in a dump like this.

Tim kept asking if I loved him, if I was mad at him.

The truth would have killed him.

It was killing me.

The job was too big. Restoring the apartment, restoring Tim. I couldn't do either one of them anymore.

~~

The police finally arrived. Sean was Irish, with a sort of "faith and begorrah" accent, red hair, pale skin, and even paler blue eyes; Dave

was an Italian hunk. Neither of them talked very much as we walked across the courtyard to the stairs; it was all "another day, another dollar" to them; this kind of thing happened all the time, they said. They seemed to know already the broad strokes of my story. Maybe my big black angel from the phone had told them, right before she said be extra nice to him, this little white boy who's lost his twin brother. In my head, I was already apologizing, embarrassed at how messy the apartment would be, embarrassed that we were twins, embarrassed that they would think I was like Tim.

I assumed they'd have some sort of universal key to get us in, but they were no better equipped than I was. They jiggled the doorknob, peered around the balcony-like landing to see if there was a window they could climb through, all the things I'd already tried.

Maybe *they* could force the super to let us in.

We trotted back to him and I repeated my story, to this man who was so proud of his archaic Polaroids, his precious little black book. But the police made no difference: the super didn't even *have* a key. There were two locks on each door, and only the tenant had the key to the top one. Tim's roommate Liz had one, but she was nowhere to be found. We'd have to get a locksmith, and come back the next day.

All four of us—the cops, the stupid super, *and* I—were shocked when I said it didn't matter when we got in, because we'd still find the same thing: nothing, or Tim's body.

I actually said that.

The police took me back to their station house. Sean asked if Tim was having girlfriend problems. I played word games and said he didn't have a girlfriend, worried they'd quit searching if they knew he was gay, or I was. But no, they were sure he'd show up, he must have had a fight with a friend or his boss, gone somewhere to sort

things out. When I said I wanted to fill out a missing person's report, they said I was jumping the gun and would have to wait.

They didn't get it: Tim was gone.

I knew.

Twins know.

What would the rest of the conjugation be? Twins *had* known?

⌒⌒

Our mother—a tiny, high-strung woman of forty, her dark bangs cut straight across her forehead like Joan of Arc's and already flecked with gray—had discovered there were two children on the way just a few weeks before we were born. We were so little, weighing only three pounds each and folded in on each other, that the doctor had thought she was carrying only one child with some sort of echoing heartbeat.

Two babies, not one, so late in life, twelve years after her first child.

Maybe that's when, and why, she started going crazy, a school-teacher whose life was already swarming with unruly kids.

Maybe that's when, and why, our father—a self-taught Yankee transplanted to the South, with dreams of building a ranch house just like the Ponderosa on *Bonanza*—started drinking.

Porky, already twelve when we were born, was given the perk of naming us, to make up for the lack of attention he was getting. He started work on our names with fierce concentration, in that last stretch of weeks before we were born. But in the end, his choice was easy: he would name us after his two best friends, both male, who stood next to him in the marching band in which he played both trombone and tuba: Kim, who had been named after Rudyard Kipling's *Kim*, and Joe Bob, the default Texan, Southern Baptist

name. Thank the God of Small Favors our parents weren't native Texans: Joe Bob wouldn't do. Porky could keep him as a friend, but not as their son's name. So Porky stayed with Kim, and for Joe Bob, substituted Tim, based on nothing but its rhyme.

In later years, after I learned the story of our naming and had forgiven Porky for the curse of growing up in Texas with the name Kim, I wondered how the left-out Joe Bob felt, when he first saw us: did he know how narrowly he had missed out on becoming part of the family legacy, or was that a surprise Porky had been planning but never got to reveal?

Many years later, in our adult years, I made videos of some old Super 8 home movies for Christmas presents for Tim and Porky. In them, Tim and I rolled around in our cribs, two blobs of flesh in diapers; Porky took one look at the babies on the screen and said it was impossible to know which of us was which then. I took one look at the blobs of flesh and said it was no trouble at all. I knew who I was. So did Tim. I was the one on the right, Tim on the left.

Twins know.

Twins had known?

Have I said that already?

⌒

It was night by the time I got back home to Brooklyn. Jess, a theater costume designer, was out of town on a job, as he so often seemed to be in those days, during my moments of crisis with Tim. The only thing to do was start returning the phone calls that had stacked up during the day, answers—or not—to my SOS's. First, the easy ones: "Dan M," who, according to Tim's Day-At-A-Glance, was supposed to have drinks with Tim that night. I'd called him earlier in the day

to let him know what was going on, but he still hadn't heard any-thing from Tim. Then "Peter G," who'd had Tim over for dinner the night before. Even though I was intimidated by him, by his success as a playwright—who *didn't* intimidate me, besides that stupid super at Tim's apartment?—I was also mad at him: did he say or do some-thing to make Tim go running into the night, and disappear? But polite Southern boy that I am, I didn't say any of that and let him do the talking. He told me he knew Tim had a crush on him, and that meeting his lover for dinner in their chic downtown apartment "could have been painful."

No shit, Sherlock.

My brother carries his belongings in trash bags, and you have nice furniture, and a lover who's a doctor, to rub in his face.

No wonder he ran away.

"This is all my fault," Peter said again, almost wanting me to agree.

"No it's not," I said, even though I thought it was.

"If only I had . . . I should have known what was going on. I should have stopped him."

"It's okay. Really." An exhalation of silent tears came out, that I took back as quickly as I inhaled. "Where the fuck is he?"

"He needs help, Kim. He really does."

What I said: "I know."

What I *wanted* to say, but didn't, too afraid of offending someone: "Tell me something I don't already know. You're supposed to be so fucking smart, with your plays and everything, tell me something I don't already the fuck know. 'He needs help.' Jesus."

Before I actually *did* say any of that, I got off the phone.

I had put off calling Porky until now; I always put off calling my to-the-point older brother, holding down his fancy government job in Washington, until I absolutely had to. But he wasn't home, so I

told his lover, Steve—yeah, three gay brothers, film at eleven, stay tuned—what had happened. Trying to share, maybe even keep me on the phone so I wouldn't do anything rash, Steve told me of a girl from his office, a girl who seemed to have no problems. A week ago, she'd jumped in front of one of those spotless, graffiti-free Washington subway trains and killed herself. Steve must have wondered why he was telling me that at exactly the same moment I did, because the air went dead. Then he recovered and said he'd have Ed—he'd never gotten used to the family nickname of Porky—call as soon as he got in.

When Porky did call, an hour or so later, I finally let everything come spilling out: "Tim is dead. I know it." And then, a weird P.S. to follow that: "I hate him. I hate him!" I screamed and raged against Tim, finally had the high school hissy fit that had been simmering in wait for years and a day, this day: the abuse, the destruction, the drinking, the being my brother's keeper. I knew the Bible said I was supposed to do it, but I couldn't anymore.

Porky said he'd fly in tomorrow if necessary. And why wouldn't it be? What was going to change? On the other hand, what was he going to do? Help me search a city he hated, rarely visited, and barely knew, even though his baby brothers lived there, struggling to stay alive? It would be far easier if Tim were lost in Paris, a city Porky loved and flew to at the drop of the hat, a city whose name was stamped on every single inserted page of his bulging passport.

I hung up, now as pissed off at Porky as I was at Tim.

Pissed off at a dead person. You couldn't get much angrier than that.

Only to Jess, on the phone, did I confess my guiltiest secret: that I had already prayed to God that Tim didn't feel any pain when he died.

Because dead was the only answer to where Tim was.

I couldn't make any more calls.

I couldn't tell the story one more time.

I couldn't keep asking the same questions, and getting the same answers: "No, I haven't seen him."

"No, I don't know where he is."

"No, but I'm sure he'll show up, he always does."

"No, he won't, not this time." That would be me talking.

But I couldn't not do *something*. A missing person's poster. I could do that . . . and the minute I thought of it, the memory of a sad, desperate family I had once seen came to me, frantically handing out makeshift flyers with their little girl's picture on them, at a mall in Texas. But instead of that poor white-trash family, now it would be me handing the flyers out, white trash myself but trying to cover that up. Instead of a cute little blond girl in a Sears photo on it, there would be a twenty-eight-year-old man who used to be blond, curly blond, when he was a laughing, happy baby. I have the pictures. I can prove we used to be happy.

I went to my file cabinet for a picture and began sorting through them: Tim in his many phases—bearded or clean-shaven; wearing glasses or contact-lensed; playful or serious; artist, or young scholar, in his atelier. But there was a problem: we were together in nearly all of them. It was the twin curse; you don't even get a picture to call your own. I'd have to cut them in two, like an angry divorcee banishing any trace of the former husband, and take in just half to the police.

In that assortment of old family photos, I could literally trace the timeline, the history, that had brought us to this day.

The earliest: a picture of the three sons taken when Tim and I were less than a year old; it went on our family Christmas card the year we were born. Tim and I are propped up on either side of Porky, on the couch in the living room. Centered by a creaky old air

conditioner behind him, Porky wears pressed chinos, a pullover sweater with a patterned shirt underneath, and a medallion on a chain. Tim is on the left as I look at the picture, propped up against Porky on some kind of book—the Dallas phone book maybe, or a thick recipe book, Daddy's lone souvenir from his stint as a cook in the Army—to keep from sinking into the devouring cushions of the sofa. I am nestled in Porky's arm, on the other side. We're both dressed in soft white cotton—striped T-shirts, diapers, baby booty socks, and we're surprisingly fleshy for the skinny, sickly little babies I've always been told we were at birth. Amidst all that billowy white, our eyes are the darkest value in the picture. We're both looking off to one side—is it to our mother or father in the wings, trying to goo-goo and gaw-gaw a sign of life out of us, in the brand new house that signaled a fresh start?—but Porky is looking straight ahead, into the camera.

Click, the next picture: our third birthday, we're dressed identically, on a lakeshore in Vermont, our father's country. An aunt has made two cakes, both in the shape of little lambs who graze on pastures of dyed green coconut. In separate high chairs, we coo and stroke the lambs with our pudgy little fingers and smile for the cameras.

Click, our fourth birthday, back home in Texas: we're in color-coordinated shorts and Banlon shirts, Tim's rust orange, mine green, banging our fists into jelly bean cakes of our own design—white-frosted cakes with multicolored jellybeans stuck in the icing. I remember picking out the yellow and green jelly beans to eat, and leaving the rest.

Click, our fifth birthday: we're climbing on an old army tank memorial at Finch Park, where a nearby picnic table is covered with a paper tablecloth—Batman that year—that's weighted down by cupcakes and presents. Our kindergarten friends are there; the next

year, Tim's first-grade teacher will write on his report card, but really about the both of us, "The twins' popularity speaks for itself." Later, in high school, when I feel I have no friends, I will quote that line and laugh, to keep from crying. Later, in New York life, Tim and I will both quote that line, and skip straight to the crying.

Click, our seventh birthday: wait, there's no picture of that, but I'll describe what it would have shown: me, with seven wasp stings whelping my uncovered arms and legs, after I had gotten out of our car when I wasn't supposed to and played in the bushes at the post office the day of our birthday, while our mother was inside on an errand.

That's the last picture she could have been in; she would be dead by the time we reached our eighth birthday.

What pictures—without her—would come next?

Me, an eight-year-old four-eyes in thick black glasses, literally not able to see anymore. I was terrified of having the school nurse come in for routine eye checks; I faked being able to see the blackboard by asking classmates, as long as possible, what was on it. By then, it had become the nurse's witch hunt to get me into glasses. When I finally got them, Tim did, too. Like I said, whatever one of us did, we both did: we both went blind at the same time. Driving us home from getting the glasses fitted, my father asked how I was adjusting to them. This was my all-knowing answer, from my eight-year-old mouth: "Now I can see far too well."

Daddy thought it was cute.

He didn't know I was just telling the truth.

What other pictures never got taken, that might help me find my missing brother?

These pictures, to prove how much I loved him, how we once depended on each other, shared everything: late at night, just before

we went to sleep, the two of us literally reaching out to squeeze one another's hands, say, "I love you, goodnight," from the twin beds we had on opposite sides of the room, all the way through high school. The two of us, even as teenagers, lying flat on the roof of our family car, looking straight up at the stars and planning our futures, away from McKinney, like teenage girlfriends would plan their weddings. Even more embarrassingly, the two of us in the bathroom together, one on the commode, the other sitting on the side of the tub, or on the tile floor, telling each other about our days as if there were nothing at all out of the ordinary about two boys doing that, like a husband and wife at the dinner table.

If I told that to Sean and Dave, would they look harder for Tim, or run from me, recoiling in disgust and horror?

Or what if I had a picture of this, in a darker shade: Tim and me playing our favorite made-up game, "Baggy Pants and the Electricity Lady." One of us—and we would switch roles back and forth— would put on a pair of our father's baggy pajamas and be the victim, Baggy Pants; the other would put on one of our mother's night-gowns and become the Electricity Lady, who threatened to electro-cute Baggy Pants with the long, thick electrical cord that hooked up the air conditioner in our bedroom. The cord only reached so far, but Baggy Pants naively, stupidly stayed within its perimeter, as the Electricity Lady feinted and jabbed at him. Baggy Pants hopped around, futilely trying to evade the cord, but the end was always the same: he died, the second she touched him.

Where did two little boys get that, the idea of a woman always trying to kill a man, and the man not putting up any fight to save his life, two people whose very touch was lethal to each other? No wonder I willed myself into going blind; I didn't want to see what was going on between my parents.

Or maybe this picture, never taken with a camera but seared into my mind: our whole family, watching *The Wizard of Oz* on a big-screen color TV set at the downtown furniture/appliance store where our father worked. Dorothy and her friends are fighting off sleep as they cross the field of poppies, when Tim wanders off and finds a box of rat poison buried along a baseboard. He's a smart boy—at six, he already knows that if he eats it, it will make him sick, or even kill him—but he wants to try it anyway. He thinks he's invincible, that nothing will happen to him. He picks up the box and starts to empty the powder into his palm, just as our father walks by, looking for him.

Years later, in telling me that story, Tim said he wanted to see if he could survive it.

That's a photo I'm glad I'm not in, a picture of one of the twins, finally, by himself: a little boy about to lick rat poison off his palm, to prove he could survive death.

⌒⌒

I gave up on the photos, both real and imagined, and was about to slam the file cabinet shut when I saw the crumbling pages of Tim's letters to me over the years. More than any pictures, I wondered if they told where he was, held clues I might have missed, images that never needed to be clues before.

I started looking through them—the paper of some so brittle it broke off at my touch—for one in particular, from the summer just before Tim's breakdown, the summer before he "went swimming." It was after our junior year in college, 1978, when Tim spent the summer in Texas at a theater called Mo Ranch our college was just starting, and I worked at a bigwig professional theater in Williamstown,

Massachusetts. I wanted to be an actor; Tim didn't. For him, it was just something to do. It would change his entire life.

We were twenty years old, and it was the first time we'd ever spent longer than two weeks apart.

Vilhelm—

Dar air is very thin, here on Der Magic Mountain. An hour ago I arrived vith my valise packed in abundance vith mutton sandwich and borscht. The feeling comes—vhere does it arrive from or vence?—that I may live here through a Vorld Var and write a mastervork in my crabbed yet inimitable, dialectical style. There are not many of us left. As you vell know, ve are a dying class, my pale-cheeked bushkin. Herr Doktor Narramore showed me my accommodations—very adequate and sanitary. Yet I am disturbed by der thought of der many tuberculors who have died here. The crowd—flotsam and jetsam of der Europe ve once knew—is interesting: a fading actress who vas directed by Chekhov; her young protégée, a ninny of a girl doting on her every word; an adventurer or two; the usual opportunists; and the like. Vell, I must retire now. I have been here but an hour and yet it seems like an eternity. My cough has returned. Vhat can that mean? The air is so thin.

Well, brother, it is both good and eighth-grade-paranoia bad today in the natural splendor of San Antonio's Hill Country. Our classmate/leading lady Cindy M is pretending to be Margo Channing and but moments ago was lounging bathrobed with a cigarette hung carelessly from her luscious lower lip. My darling Carrie plays Eve Harrington and follows after Cindy with an ashtray. I . . . I just play.

This morning we began cleaning out the barn and chomping cactus out of the hard Hill Country earth: hey, kids, let's put on a show! We can use my dad's barn! (Literally—that's what it is. A former cow barn.) There's nothing like nature to scare the hell out of you. This morning the aforementioned

Dr. Narramore, our leader/cruise director, killed an incredibly hulkish taran-
tula while I looked on in terror. He arched his brow and said: "Don't tell
the others. It's hard enough to get people to stay here as it is." Sleep was
fitful. Bugs, critters, creatures—and that was in my bed alone! I screamed
several times during the night and thought a great deal about existence itself.
I may spend all of my days off in a motel somewhere. Or in an institution
for people suffering my sort of affliction. Should I be careful? Do people in
my situation have breakdowns? Is life really a frowsy business? Can I ever
fall in love?

At one point this week, a small black child attending camp here came up
to me. His name was Brent, and he had the boyish good looks of a young
Poitier.

He asked, "Does you have any bruvahs or sistahs?"

I, whose boyish good looks have long since disappeared, answered, "I have
a brother named Kim. This is a letter I'm writing to him."

Brent, no doubt dazzled by the thought of long distance, asked, "Is he in
de army?

My answer was immediate, "No. He is an actor."

At times, you seem so far away that I, too, am dazzled by thoughts of
your long distance. Oh, Kim. I am so glad you are my brother. At the first
of the summer, you called me a "vicious monster." I realize now that that is
partially true. I've been far too self-indulgent over the past two years and am
responsible for most of my unhappiness, and possibly some of yours. As are
we all, I think, in the long run. Forgive me. I will not blame society or civ-
ilization; it is not going to be that simple. Sometimes I wish for a complete
breakdown. It would be nice to fall completely apart and have someone else
put me back together. But luxuries like that don't come easily, and probably
many more problems would result.

I think these letters will be important in the long run. We decided upon
some sort of battle years ago. Today, I feel we reach discerning years. I think

Margaret Hamilton spoke for us all when she looked up from her puddle of
black wax and said, "What a world! What a world!"
   I loves you, bruvah. Is you in de army?

                                                                    Tim

The scariest thing about that letter? Not the fact that we used to
love each other so much, my heart wants to break. Not the fact that
he wished for a nervous breakdown, and then had one. No. The
scariest thing is that I didn't have the slightest memory (this from a
boy who remembers everything) of calling him a "vicious monster."
After he moved to New York, and was drunk more often than not,
those words would always be at the tip of my tongue, ready to come
darting out. But then, in college? It must have been worse than I
remember.

"These letters will be important in the long run," he wrote. "We
decided upon some sort of battle years ago. Today, I feel we reach discerning years." Tim stated our battle as a fact for the first time that
summer before the breakdown, but he could only do it through the
anonymity of long-distance pen and paper, not face-to-face. I couldn't
do it either way, but I knew it was there. And I didn't know why.

That was the biggest, saddest mystery of all, one I didn't know if
I was already too late to solve.

In a house where so little was acknowledged or said, we'd always
depended on family letters to find out the truth about things, beginning with Porky's letters from our mother. When we were little, and
he was away at college—we were just starting grade school when he

was starting his freshman year—we would sneak into his room to look at his things, secreted away in a brown accordion file folder at the back of his closet, the better to keep our grubby little twin paws off them. He must have known we rooted through his room, because at some point he installed a chain lock high up on his door. But clever things that we were, we soon learned to drag a chair over, tiptoe up on it, and unlock the chain; nothing could stay a secret in our house for very long. Maybe Porky knew this, that we'd figure out a way into his room; maybe he just wanted to challenge us a little and see if we were up to the test, keep the letters out of sight, but not quite hidden, as a kind of lesson about our family. The things he couldn't tell us in person but wanted us to know. After our mother died, and our father shortly remarried, we read those letters as a sort of unspoken bid at stability, a bridge between mothers; we used them to hold on to a past we barely knew.

Whether it was Porky's room and the reminder of security it gave us, or the connection to our mother through the letters, I don't know, but Porky's bedroom became our safe place. We existed as we had in the womb when we were there, unconscious of our elbows and shoulders colliding into each other as we rolled into the middle of the sagging bed. I found there what Tim later found in the water: my own private world, a world suspended, a world of no cares or worries, of happier times. We never dared leave the sanctuary of Porky's room with his letters for fear we'd be found out; we wouldn't even talk in there, afraid our whispers would alert the house to our trespasses. Nothing could give us away, but nothing could keep us from coming back, to try and keep our mother alive, at least in our memories. We called her "Mama" as children, but after her death, we switched to calling her "Mother," as if it were more respectful. "Mother" became the sainthood name, "Our Mother" who art in heaven.

In that room, in an often-stuck, water-warped drawer, Porky kept mementos from "Mother's" life: a gold watch-pendant on a chain; a ruby-encrusted bracelet; a necklace—clear glass beads that turned yellow or turquoise or pink depending on how you held them to the light—the most memorable pieces retrieved from her cornucopia of costume jewelry. The day after she died, I walked around the neighborhood, clutching a big fat purse filled with her jewelry. I showed it to the neighbor ladies and said, "These could be yours if you play your cards right." Where I picked up that phrase, or dared to use it, at seven years old, I don't know; I was Dill, the little Truman Capote of Woodleigh Drive.

In that same drawer, Porky also kept our mother's last grade book from school, the school year not yet finished when she died; scattered classroom pictures, our mother sporting a different hairstyle in each one; and lying uncertainly on top, like an afterthought, the register of guests from her funeral. Things purloined for remembrance from a lifetime of artifacts, left there for safekeeping, or as a lure to keep us coming back.

One night, our mother had some sort of spell and was laid out in Porky's room, not able to make it to her own. Laid out there, or sought it herself, like an animal seeking its final resting place before it dies, knowing its time has come? The family doctor, Jim Wilson, was sitting at the bedside, taking her pulse and asking her to count backward from ten, to name the day, the current president. Porky and our father were there, as Tim and I cowered in the hallway, the adults too caught up in the emergency at hand to block our way.

It was never explained to us what had happened.

Our mother was crazy. One time, I saw her scream the "Divine Apostle Paul" was telling her to beat my father with a frying pan, which she did, as he raised his spindly arms over his head in defense.

When she acted like that, she terrified me, but Tim and Porky, her first-born, worshipped her. Mother, Porky, the twins: we were an odd quartet, a sort of Mother Courage and her children, with Porky serving as a surrogate father in place of the real, missing-in-action one.

One of the final weeks before she died, Porky took us on a weekend vacation, an escape from the betrayals and drunkenness of our father, to the fantastic sounding Aquamarina Springs near San Antonio. In our hotel room, we watched the Tony Curtis movie *Houdini* (and I took in more about escape and death, and mothers and sons) and saw make-believe mermaids underwater as we rode in a glass-bottom boat. On our way back home, we ate in an A-frame-shaped restaurant called Shangri-la, a concept of Utopia Porky patiently explained to us, and made us think could be ours, as we stirred sugar into our iced tea with long, swirl-handled silver spoons.

With Porky and our mother, we saw *Mary Poppins* on New Year's Eve and emerged after midnight from a Dallas movie theater into a fog as thick and mysterious as that on the streets of London we had just seen, not knowing it would be the last movie we would ever see with her.

Soon after that, she whisked us away to the nearby town of Plano to look at an apartment near her sister's giant, rambling farmhouse. Tim and I bounced on a giant bed in a bedroom that had a beautiful glass sculpture of grapes on a mirrored bureau. We wanted to live there, just because the grapes were so pretty. Out of earshot of the real estate agent, we were told never to tell our father about the trip, that we might soon be living someplace else, without our father.

We didn't, and a week after that, our mother was dead.

I don't think Tim ever recovered.

Enough already. Enough with the past. Enough with the dead mother. Your brother is missing—now. *Do* something. Words on paper, airy-fairy memories of sad childhoods—who the fuck didn't have one?—aren't going to help. A poster; that's gonna help. More calls, those'll help too.

Do something.

But there was nothing left to do, except try to figure out what had brought us to this place.

That meant thinking.

That meant remembering.

And what I remembered—what I had tried to make myself forget all day long, with my beautiful, poignant, feel-sorry-for-me memories—was that this was all my fault.

"Why," you ask?

"I'll tell you," says the twin who tells everything.

Just a few weeks ago, I had gone out for drinks with a friend and come back to find Tim in the apartment. Jess was out of town; Tim had let himself in with his own key. He was drunk and delirious as he struggled to sit up on the couch, mumbling the phrase, "Oh yes, I have adapted all my life" over and over again.

From nowhere, he kept saying that phrase.

One of our rusty kitchen knives shook in his hands; I wrenched it away so he couldn't finish the job he had so recently attempted, cutting myself in the process when I grabbed the blade. When the knife fell to the floor, he grabbed one of the beer bottles he had brought with him and tried to smash it, so he could use the jagged edge on his wrist, or maybe on me. As I tried to save his life, or mine,

with—God believe me, God help me—every bit of strength I had or will ever have, as I held a friend's plastic rosary over Tim's squirming body and begged God for help, Tim turned to me with the face of Lucifer, knowing he would never fly back to heaven, never see his Father again, and said, with absolute resignation, "Oh, yes, I have adapted all my life." Tears streamed down his face, and mine.

I have never been so sad, so ready to die.

"Our mother, our mother . . . she left us . . ." He screamed about that mysterious night neither one of us could forget, when she was laid out in Porky's room, and a doctor tried to revive her, and we never found out what was going on.

"I have tried to put pen to paper about that night, pen to paper, but the words won't come . . . the ink dries up . . . my blood dries up. . . ."

He screamed and cursed and ranted for half an hour, until, drunk and exhausted, he finally fell asleep on his own. I sat up against the hard wall in the living room to keep watch, to keep him from trying to kill himself again, but I, too, finally dozed off, no better in a pinch than the disciples who fell asleep when they were supposed to be guarding Christ after the Last Supper.

In the morning, Tim left for work, but there was no sense that the crisis had been averted or that he had slept it off; if anything, it seemed even worse. Surviving the night had not saved him, it had just brought him to another day to try all over again. I couldn't hold him back, as much as I tried; he pulled away and smiled at me, saying he still wanted to die, instead of saying good-bye.

When is a good-bye not really a good-bye, but a curse? When it's your twin brother saying he'll probably be dead before you see him again, and then smiling in your face and closing a heavy metal door behind him.

That door clanged shut, and I called a friend who had seen shrinks all his life, who had a laundry list of them to recommend, to see what steps I needed to take to have Tim committed.

But I didn't follow through on any of them.

Instead, later that day, I called Tim and told him that if he didn't change, didn't quit drinking, didn't pull it together, I was prepared to "cast him out of my life"—ah, now the language really gets Biblical, locusts and pestilence and threats, oh my.

Prepared, I said, but could I have really done it?

It doesn't matter; the choice has been made for me. A choice I forced Tim into. I told him I would leave him; he saved me the bother and left me instead.

His life, or death, my fault.

So you see, there really was nothing left to do, except go to bed and pray, once again, that Tim didn't feel any pain when he died.

BOOK TWO

SATURDAY

CHAPTER THREE

The night was filled with dreams of cutting and blood, of swimming and flying and escape.

In one of them, Tim had seen his boss Frank, the has-been movie director, murder someone. Frank knew Tim had seen him, so he had to kill him. But in the dream's logic, and maybe the world's, that meant Frank had to kill me as well; after all, everybody thought we were one and the same. But Frank could only do his killing in front of witnesses, who carried vases embedded with razor blades, knives and spears, even scythes. As Frank began cutting, Tim crawled away to a rushing stream, blood trailing behind him, to escape. Brave brother that I was, I flew away, not even trying to save Tim, *my* blood flowing through the air like exhaust from a plane on takeoff. Tim swam, I flew. Fish and fowl.

The dream continued or switched; I couldn't tell. I flew as high as the tops of light poles on either side of an isolated country road, while other bleeding hands and fingers clawed at the air to get me, just inches below my feet. It took all my strength, my arms literally flapping like wings, to stay aloft, out of harm's way. Who, or what, was trying to grab me, I didn't know; that's probably a blessing.

The dream was so real I was surprised there wasn't blood on the sheets when I woke up, startled out of sleep by the phone ringing. It was early, seven or so. I snatched it up—quick, breathless, desperate, like a scene from some movie I couldn't remember, but knew I was supposed to play out—as if it might be Tim, even though I knew it wasn't.

I was right. It was Peter, wondering if I had heard anything from Tim, no doubt to expiate his guilt—or at least that's what I wanted him to feel. Guilt, just like me. I may have told Tim I was going to cast him out of my life, but Peter is the one who did it: cast him out, drunk, into the night. He thought Tim might have stopped off at Uncle Charlie's, a gay bar near his apartment. I decided I'd go there and see if Tim had stopped by, if anybody remembered him.

I took a quick shower, then selected a picture—Tim in a pink Izod T-shirt, his face smiling, snaggle-toothed—to take with me; I'd go back to the police with it after Uncle Charlie's.

I stuck the photo in my shoulder bag and took a quick look around the living room to make sure I hadn't forgotten anything before I left. My eyes landed on the small, antique drop-leaf table we ate at, next to the kitchen. *There* was something I couldn't forget, no matter how much I wanted to: the site of Tim telling me, just weeks ago, right before his suicidal, drunken night on our couch, the "real" story of how our mother died.

For whatever reason, Tim had kept that bottled up until then, even though he had learned it years ago.

No wonder he went crazy.

No wonder he went running into the night.

No wonder I'd had to wrench a rusty knife out of his shaking, desperate, needy hands.

Wherever he was now, whatever had happened to him, it had something to do with that story coming back into his life, as if it had ever left.

⌒

It was a Saturday afternoon, and Tim swatted the drop leaves of the table back and forth, as if he were working up courage, coming to a decision. He nervously smiled that rueful, head-shaking smile of his, and said I should know the real story of our mother's death.

Silly me.

I thought I did know.

Our mother had died, he finally said, not of the random, bad-luck brain aneurysm we'd always been told, but of an aneurysm caused by a prescription drug overdose. Whether it was accidental or she had taken her own life, he didn't know. (That phrase—"taken her own life." Taken it where?) He'd somehow found this out during his time away from school, after his breakdown, when our family doctor Jim Wilson had tried to patch him up.

My first thought was guilt, not grief. It was our fault: she got hooked to stop the pain of having two children so late in life. An aneurysm caused by a drug overdose caused by an addiction caused by the pain we caused. Of all the things I know, this one thing I know for sure: Tim felt no malice toward me, only love, when he

told me how our mother died; as much as he's said to wound me in the past, I know that much is true. For all the things he hasn't told me over the years, he at least shared that one truth. And the truth of how your mother died, however painful it may be, equals so many other little truths.

For once, he became the big brother, and I the baby—or drama queen, take your pick—literally crawling into the kitchen to escape the news, writhing on the floor. Tim, on his knees, held me, called my name and tried to stop my keening, as I had tried to stop his on so many other occasions. (On the kitchen floor, where I have always imagined our father found our mother when he came home for lunch that April Fool's Day, the silly day she picked to die. I have never seen my father cry and wonder if he did, even then.)

I kept saying, "This is going to kill me," over and over, but I can't tell you how I felt. Maybe because I couldn't *feel* anything; my body had gone numb, and I was floating above it, looking down at myself. I can tell you what I *saw*: the linoleum against my skin, the little gold capillaries of its design indented into the creamy white base color, the legs of the metal counter in the kitchen that Jess and I had covered with shelf paper and painted fire engine red. I can even describe the toast crumbs on the floor, that pressed into my cheek, but I can't tell you how I *felt*, other than I felt "this is going to kill me."

That's my problem, my shrink says: I can tell the story, but I can't feel the emotion behind it; I can only use words to describe it. Maybe that's because I don't feel anything, I say; I'm dead inside. You *have* to feel something, he says, you're too smart not to. No, I'm just smart enough to use the right words, but not know what they mean. If I were dumber, I'd be a better patient. He wants me to yell at him, yell at somebody, but I can't; he doesn't understand that I've already used up my lifetime's allocation of yelling at Tim.

As Tim held me on that kitchen floor, he said his breakdown had its roots in that, our mother's death: he hated her for leaving him. It was the most he'd ever said about his breakdown; whenever I'd asked before, he'd just smile, a smile on the verge of a story, but not the story itself.

So that was the first domino in the line-up of them that had set off a chain reaction in these past few weeks. Just a few days after telling me the "true story" of our mother's death, Tim would hole up on our couch, drunk, with a rusty kitchen knife in one hand and a broken beer bottle in the other, and cry, "I have adapted all my life."

Just a few days after that, he would find another knife, or broken bottle, or something else very, very sharp, and almost finish the job.

And now, he would completely disappear—and maybe finish the job for good?

Oh, yes, this is going to kill me.

Ready to head off to Uncle Charlie's and the police, I grabbed the big crumbling envelope of Tim's letters and stuck it in my backpack, along with Tim's picture. Talk about following breadcrumbs: did I really think there might be telltale clues in the letters about where he was, a sheet of instructions, in some secret code only I could interpret, about how to find him? If I did, then I'd gone as crazy as he had. I always took something to read on the long subway ride into Manhattan; why not take the letters, the letters that told, between the lines, of that certain summer at a makeshift theatre in Texas, when he began to fall in love with our classmate Carrie, but couldn't tell her; when he began to fall in love with boys, but couldn't tell himself; when he began to fall apart, and disappear.

Oh, yes, I thought, as I left our apartment and closed that heavy metal gate on what would become the longest weekend of my life, this is going to kill me.

⌒⌒

Starchild,

At least for now, we have not heard all about Eve.

I have decided there is something basically sordid about summer theater, no matter where you do it, in a cow barn in Texas or on a fancy college campus in the Northeast, where you are. It's seedy to take off make-up after the show and not be able to go home. I get depressed watching myself in an orange bathrobe with yellow skin paint and silver eye shadow.

"Mr. Powers, you're on."

"But I don't want to go on."

"Mr. Powers, are you alright? You seem a bit delirious. What are those dark circles under your eyes? Stein's? Max Factor? Or something much deeper? Oh."

"No, no, I'm O.K."

"Gleetings, Exarted Audience, you are most wercome . . . TO GO FUCK YOURSELVES!"

OH MY GOD! HAS IT COME TO THIS? FUCK THE CHINESE! AND THAT GOES FOR YOUR RITTLE DOG, TOO!!!!

Yes, it has come to this. The above is a sample of what almost happened at a recent performance of Land of the Dragons, *our very dericate (diarect, you understand) version of* Cinderella, *à la Wong dynasty. I almost lost it in*

my role as the Honorable Chinese Stage Manager. That night, before the show, we had been laughing about the possibility of ending the play five minutes after it started. Four scenes into the first act, we almost did. Something snapped. After banging my gong five or six times instead of the customary once, I time-warped the entire cast and our captive Presbyterian audience into the last act. Dub, as the Property Man, shuffled over to my bench and whispered to get the hell back to the first act. He thought it was funny. I'm sure Moliere dreaded the same thing from time to time.

But that was nothing compared to the trials of opening Summer and Smoke. We had ten days to go at the Barn—ten days that could possibly shake the world, or at least the world as far down Highway 27 as Kerrville. In the past week, Carrie and I have escaped every night to the Circle K grocery store there, hot on the trail of Doritos and bean dip. Carrie's Malibu knows the way. Friday night, we escaped as our set for Smoke was being struck by Dub "The Incredible Hulk" Narramore. And the play had not even opened.

Around dinner that night, Dub started mumbling and glaring the way he does before he kicks and throws chairs. Later that night, after a sloppy dress rehearsal, he finished the process and started screaming full voice. I paid no attention to him, planted my feet firmly in the dirt, and said, "I don't even have to take this." I went upstairs, leisurely changed my clothes, and had a wonderful time deciding what I would wear to my first all-night tech party.

In the meantime, Dub threw a 150-year-old table across the stage, came close to ripping one of the flats, and permanently alienated most of the troupe. Carrie and I drove like bats out of hell and reached Kerrville at three A.M. We stopped at the Circle K and bought apples, Doritos, and the newest Time magazine, to learn what has been going on in the world while we have been away. (Answer: not much.) We have learned that two people can finish a bag of Doritos in the time it takes to drive across town to the other Circle K.

Summer and Schmuck *(aren't theater people just about God's gift to* *everything?) is a solid production. Cindy, as Miss Alma, and I, as Dr.* *Johnny, bring tears to the house every night and an unmistakable melancholy* *to Mr. Williams's little piece of lopsided symbolism. (Dr. Johnny, you'll* *remember, drawls and leans a lot. I bring blond hair and a nice tan to his ice* *cream suit; my new exercise, swimming, is responsible for both.) One sees* *many things here: a mouse drowned himself in Miss Alma's cut-glass* *lemonade pitcher and bats swoop in and out of Dr. Johnny's exam room.*

I will leave Mo Ranch with the sadness that comes with survival. Carrie *has been a beautiful friend to me this summer. On a recent night off, we* *drove to nearby San Antonio and Happy Hour at Bwana Dik's. We laughed* *over a Watusi Witch and a Tequila Tiger while watching the prostitutes come* *in from a hard day on the River Walk. We had forgotten how to deal with* *the real world. We coped as best we could.*

Yes, I coped as best I could, but it just might not be enough.

Tim

⌒

Outside Uncle Charlie's, the famous West Village gay bar I had never been to, and likely never would have if it hadn't been for my brother's disappearance, I thrust my hands into the pockets of a fleece-lined jacket; a crisp chill had blown in hard in the past few days. Soon, all the leaves would be gone, but for now, they were making a brave last stand.

Charlie's, as those in the know called it, had little tissue-paper ghosts hanging in its windows, alternating with orange accordion-pleated pumpkins. Ghost/pumpkin, ghost/pumpkin. Those god-damn pumpkins again. There was no escaping them.

I thrust my hands deeper in my pockets, for courage, telling myself just to do what I had to do, and went inside.

Disco music blared, even though the place had emptied out just a few hours earlier this Saturday morning. The stench overwhelmed me. How could you pick up somebody—how could you even *breathe?*— in here: a triad of piss, beer, and a million desperate cigarettes. It was the smell of last dance, last chance for love. This was the place businessmen in nice suits came after work. Now I knew what those suits smelled like in the wee hours of the morning, when those businessmen staggered home with or without the kindness of strangers.

One guy was cleaning up; another was restocking behind the bar. I went to him, without a badge to flash, just a picture of my missing brother. I know what I had been hoping for, but I hadn't actually expected it to happen: he was one of the bartenders on duty the night before last, the last time anyone had seen Tim.

"Boy, was he wasted."

Not exactly what I wanted to hear, although I don't know why I had expected anything different. But at least he had seen him. At least he remembered. At least the sort of magical coincidence, or grace, that always seemed to pop up at our most desperate moments, had come through yet again, with maybe the first piece of tangible news of the past twenty-four hours.

But instead of thanking God for grace, or thanking this bartender for a clear memory, I blurted out my anger, my blame: "Why did you let him drink so much?"

"Easy, cowboy. He was wasted before he got here. If your friend. . . ."

"He's my brother, my fucking twin brother. Watch it."

"Whatever. Sorry." But he couldn't resist a rejoinder. "If he's the one with the drinking problem, he's the one should be watching it, not me."

I tried to calm myself down.

"You remember if he went home with anyone?"

"I'm not their goddamn babysitter. I don't know . . . most of the time, he was sitting by himself. At the bar."

And they say the twins' popularity speaks for itself, as Tim's first-grade teacher had written on his report card.

I wanted to cry.

Then, an afterthought from the bartender: "Gave me a good tip, though. Said he'd just cashed a paycheck, bought a plane ticket with it. Said he was going swimming."

"What?" I pounced.

"That's what I thought. 'Swimming'? It's October, but maybe he means he's gonna clear his head. Maybe he just means a shower. I'm used to hearin' all sorts of crazy things. That's when he gave me a ten and left."

I was halfway out the door when the bartender called out, "Hey, sorry about your brother. I've got one too. I know what it's like."

I stood outside Uncle Charlie's, already thinking the impossible, the ridiculous, bouncing the pros and cons back in my head as if I were having a conversation with myself.

Swimming. It's like his breakdown. What he wrote in his calendar. Swimming. Austin College. Where the breakdown happened. That's where he's gotta be.

But he could barely scrape together enough money for the subway, let alone get to Texas.

And he was drunk.

Because he was drunk. That's the only way he *could* have done it, without thinking. He'd just hop on a plane and go.

No.

Not even Tim was that crazy.

Only Tim was that crazy.

The only sounds—besides those crazy, warring voices in my head—came from the foot traffic on Greenwich Avenue, and those cases of beer sliding into the basement of Charlie's, where drunks and those who loved them would be assembling later this Saturday night, the loneliest night of the week.

With that cheery thought, I took off past St. Vincent's Hospital—wondering if I should stop in to look for a body without a toe tag on it—on my way to the subway, the police, my brother's crummy apartment, and possibly his body.

           ⌣

My brave and driven brother,

Medvendenko: Why do you always wear black?
Masha: I am in mourning for my life. I am unhappy.
                    —*Anton Chekhov,* The Seagull

I picked up The Seagull *this morning, read those two lines, and laughed for the rest of the day. Hell, I'd wear black if I had any.*

Everything would be fine if you were here, my ruddy-cheeked Pante-leyavitch. Everything goes on. We are 21 years old now, brother. And I take it we've learned some of the same lessons this summer, yours at Williamstown and mine at Mo Ranch. We can survive. And we have. And we will prob-ably survive for days and hours to come. That is probably the most fright-ening lesson we will ever have to learn. I can't think of another that would be scarier.

My days since July twenty-third, the blessed occasion of our birth, when Creola and Lloyd did at least one good thing, have been a search for that

moral or spiritual glue that holds it all together. I'm not depressed. I think I am what the Romantics call "dejected." But I do laugh a great deal and find a certain happiness in knowing that you are reading this letter. You are reading this letter, aren't you?

Carrie, who has helped me survive the summer, and I had a nice birthday together in Dallas. I wore the pants from my Summer and Smoke *costume and drank gin to excess. We went to the Stoneleigh P and played Cleo Laine. We smoked a packet of Benson & Hedges, the long ones in the green and gold package. We then went to the Bagatelle Lounge, listened to Nancy Paris sing of blighted love, and drank Manhattans. It was shallow. That's why I liked it.*

Several drinks beyond reason, I took Carrie to Strictly Tabu. Some loud jazz band was playing. When we told our waitress we just wanted a drink, she mumbled something in one of the Slavic Romance languages and withered us with her eyes. Fortunes were made and we played whist.

Yes, I have been wistful these past few days; most of this summer has a distinct air of unreality surrounding it. It is much hotter here at home than at Mo Ranch. When I first heard the reports of people dropping in the Dallas streets, I thought of them as weak. I had been to Mo Ranch. I had built risers and pulled cactus. But after a few days back, I reconciled my vanity to our room and my new best friend, the air conditioner.

I have missed the river most of all. For the first time since our early childhood, I enjoyed swimming. For a few weeks, I did better than just stay afloat. I swam and basked (yes, BASKED!) in the sun. The water in the Guadalupe is green and very clear. With a small leap of the imagination, it was all very primitive. Water is a therapeutic medium, I now believe; one day very soon, I may go live in the water. You can come along, my friend, and join me with your inner tube. Would you like that, Precious Baby?

I am wiser for my summer in Hunt, Texas, and look forward to senior stoicism in the months ahead. When we are not holding court or acting

lavish, we can huddle in a corner and worry about our futures. I think we can make even that exciting. We will both remain highly serious about our academic work—you will conquer Advanced Psychology and experiment on live human beings. None of those piddly rats for my brother. No, ma'am. I will tackle Advanced Biology. Together, we will make test-tube babies and have many friends, and it will be said that the twins' popularity spoke for itself. Iced tea will flow, brother, and I will have no roommates except those I choose. For as they say, many are called, but few are chosen.

You are one of the chosen, my fellow twin, who also remembers once upon a time, when we swam in the sun.

Tim

On the subway to the Upper East Side, back to Tim's apartment and the police station, I looked at Tim's picture, shielding it so snooping strangers looking over my shoulder wouldn't think he was my lover, this boy who looked so much like me, who had such a poetic soul. Under my breath, I practiced my story, already worried I'd have to repeat it for a new set of cops, already worried I'd have to pay for a locksmith, already worried I'd have to face the same super from the day before. I worried about the police finding Tim's porno, and judging me for it, even though I probably had the same kind. I worried what they would think of me, and my family who had let things get so bad.

I worried about everything except actually finding my brother.

I walked into the police station, my lone picture of Tim clutched in my hand. Fortunately, both Sean, my Irish leprechaun, and Dave, my hunky Italian, were on duty; I didn't have to repeat my story.

They were free to go back to Tim's, although I didn't know what we were going to do differently from what we had done yesterday. Maybe break the super's kneecaps. I soon got my answer, as we crossed the courtyard, bypassing the super.

"Shouldn't we check in with the super?" I asked Sean, even though it was the last thing I wanted to do.

"Why? He'll just say no."

"But he can't. You're the police."

Dave chimed in, with a goombah accent that was used to getting its own way. "Evah hear of a search warrant?"

Tim's door was as impenetrable as it had been the day before, but we knocked again. No answer, again. We pulled it. We rattled it. Nothing.

Now something.

Dave looked around to make sure we were alone, then pulled a gigantic set of keys from his belt. He looked at the lower lock on the door and found a number on it, then pinched his fingers directly around the one key in a million that matched the number. He put the key in the lock; the fit was immediate. I heard the bolt slide open from inside.

"One down," he said. "You better be who you say; this ain't exactly by the book."

He looked at the top lock with more discernment, found another number on it, but this one took a few more tries before it clicked open.

Without thinking, I put my hand on the door to open it.

Sean pulled me back.

"Slow down. Let us go in first." Then, "You *sure* you're ready?"

"No."

Sean sniffed. "There's no smell," he said and immediately knew it

was the wrong thing to say. But it *wasn't* the wrong thing; it was a good thing, a hopeful thing. It meant there was no body. But on the other hand, how much stink could a rotting corpse make in just a day or two, especially in cool autumn weather?

He twisted the handle, and it was done.

The door was open.

There *was* no overpowering rush of smell, just an overpowering rush of mess. The apartment was in even worse shape than the last and only time I had visited. We could immediately see Tim wasn't in the big front room. That left only three places for him: his bedroom, Liz's room, or the bathroom. All those doors were closed; it would be like the Lady or the Tiger opening them. I went to Tim's bedroom door and sniffed; it didn't smell clean—dirty clothes and leftover food, no doubt—but it didn't smell dead. But I had never smelled that before, so what did I know?

I turned to Sean; after all my hurry, he now saw in my eyes that I couldn't be the first one to open the door. I turned away from it as he swung it open slowly, but I couldn't not look, either. I turned back around, keeping my eyes straight ahead, as if I expected to see Tim's feet dangling in my line of sight. But there were no feet, as I should have known. If he was going to go on his own, he would do it by cutting.

Sean went in.

"He's not here."

I followed, and it was the same mess as before—green trash bags and a mattress with dirty sheets on the floor.

"What about the closet?"

Sean opened it cautiously to find about a million pairs of khakis, crammed two and three to a hanger. That was Tim; if he needed a clean pair of pants, he'd just buy one, instead of washing the ones he had.

Dave had been opening the other doors—Liz's room and the bathroom—and called out, "Nobody here neither."

Even without a body, I looked around for a suicide note, but there was barely a single clean space where he could have left one, if he wanted somebody to find it.

It was early morning, about nine, but the apartment was still dark; there were only one or two windows, both looking out onto gray brick walls. But a blinking red light from the answering machine relieved the darkness. I looked at Sean, as if to ask could I listen, and he shrugged yes. I used a corner of my shirt to press the play button—why I was suddenly consumed with not leaving finger-prints, I don't know—and Sean laughed. The first laugh of the day. I hit the button; the tape rewound, and messages started spitting out: Peter from Thursday night, saying what a great time he had had and hoping Tim had gotten home all right. Yeah, thanks, Peter. A mes-sage from Dan M from Friday morning, asking about their drink date that night. Several messages from Joyce, another from Frank, all translating to "Where the fuck are you?"

A message from someone at a car service, telling "Mr. Powers" his car was waiting for him downstairs; they had been buzzing and buzzing but no one had answered. He was going to miss his plane.

A car service.

A plane.

He had gone back to Austin College.

My brain stuck on that as my own voice, frantic at first, then more and more deflated, started spitting back at me from the machine, three and four and five times.

I turned to the police with my mouth open, then snapped it shut and left the apartment. I didn't stop until I got to the outside side-walk, where I had placed the 911 call the day before.

"He's gone back to Texas. To our old school. That's what it means. That's where he is. Austin College," I said, talking more to myself than to them, trying to convince myself. Austin College, where I had decided to go to college at the last minute, in the waning days of our senior year in high school, after one too many people had told me I would never fit in with the rich fraternity boys of SMU, where I had already been accepted. When I told Tim I was going to the same college he had decided on, he didn't speak to me for days.

With barely a wave good-bye to the police, I stepped off the curb to flag down a cab that was racing by.

Sean thrust some papers in my hand, as I opened the cab door. "Here's a missing person's report, fill it out if you want to, but sounds like he's—"

I closed the door and didn't hear anything else.

CHAPTER FOUR

It was the craziest thing I'd ever done, and believe me, I've done crazy.

Standing at an airport ticket counter, racing to make a mid-morning flight to Dallas, no suitcase, no nothing in hand except my brother's letters and some acting lessons left over from college.

I argued with the counter attendant that their ticket prices were too high, that I was just trying to get home for my twin brother's funeral.

I jumped ahead, and said he was dead.

And then my heart stopped for saying it aloud and making it more of a possibility.

The counter person said they could give me a cheaper ticket if I were traveling to a funeral, but they'd have to get a letter from the funeral home to prove it.

I amped it up to screaming then: he wasn't even in the ground yet.

They were burying him this afternoon.

I didn't have time to get a fucking letter.

I should have stayed with acting, instead of giving it up after two weeks in New York.

They gave me a cheaper ticket.

My dream from the night before was coming true, in reverse: instead of flying away from Tim, I was flying to him.

I hoped.

I didn't know.

I didn't know anything anymore, except that I both hated and loved my brother, beyond words, beyond dreams. *Odi et amo* . . . I hate and I love . . . . . . the only three words I remember from four torturous years of high school Latin. What other dork takes four years of a dead language and remembers just one phrase, two words?

Hate.

Love.

The two words carved into the fingers of each hand, with a little pinky left over for punctuation—like an exclamation point!—on each.

Love, more than life itself.

Hate, when he was drinking, which was most of the time now.

Love, except when I had to save him, which was also most of the time.

Hate, because I knew I couldn't save him.

Hate, how he depended on me.

Hate, knowing my arms weren't strong enough to catch him when he fell.

Hate, how he's wasted his talent.

Hate, not knowing how to fill out the missing person's report Sean and Dave had given me.

It practically screamed in my pocket, above the drone of the airplane engine, the rattle of flight attendants and beverage carts and cutlery wrapped in plastic.

"What was the person last seen wearing?"

That was the loudest question of all, and I didn't know the answer. I'm his fucking twin brother and I don't know what he was "last seen wearing."

I do know one thing he wore: a yellow Oxford cloth shirt and just-shined shoes.

Actually, that's two things, what he was wearing when he tried to kill himself, just weeks ago. Sean and Dave should have asked me then, I would've known. Tim staggered in my front door, his yellow Oxford cloth shirt covered with blood that had missed his "just-shined shoes." That's what he kept mumbling, "I just shined my shoes, I just shined my shoes." He had; I could tell. I could've seen my face in them, my horrified face, if I had been able to look there, instead of at his hacked-up wrist. He should have said, "I just cut my wrist, I just cut my wrist," because who could look at his shoes?

But that was then, this is now. He had to throw that shirt out, it was so covered with blood, so what would he be wearing now?

I don't know.

I was shaking uncontrollably and trying to forget Tim, covered with blood, when the plane landed.

A flight attendant asked if I was okay.

It was another answer I didn't know.

Dear Brother Porky,

It is late October, the twins' favorite time of year. I have just been to the Homecoming carnival and have sensed why some people are so frightened of ghosts. The carnival reminded me of the one you took Kim and me to our senior year in high school, when our going to Austin College was not yet a reality. I had delivered medicine to the McKinney East Apartments, in the poor part of town, that evening and wore a pullover sweater and ill-fitting pants to the carnival. We saw the Sig Tau Follies, and a drunk sorority girl fell on Kim while we were laughing at jokes we did not yet understand. You knew everyone that weekend, and I could not help but be impressed by your social skills and alumnus charm. Almost three and a half years later, after Medea, Elaine Ringer—a Jesus freak turned doper in the spring of our freshman year—the Sig Tau Tire Roll, skiing with the guys in Breckinridge, a trip to Wyoming with one of the freest spirits in the world, a funny summer with small Negro children in McKinney, Martin Luther, William Shake-speare, and William Blake, I feel a little tired and would like nothing more than a glass of iced tea at Aunt Bessie's. The living are funny that way.

Last year, after a homecoming daiquiri party with the frat boys, I staggered home and wrote a letter to Don Jacobs, my dumb but loyal jock friend from high school, about the people we knew and what they would be doing twenty years from then. Pat Murray would have become a small-town minister of Baptist Youth music—why the Baptists sing, I could never decide—and would have made some shady investments in a gospel music corporation. Jennifer Wilson would have married well and retired to a Country Estates station wagon in ritzy Highland Park. The one I cared most about, Ellen Truett, would have been married several times—and divorced the same number. She would have wandered about the party asking friends if they had heard from me—the probable reason for all those marriages and divorces. As fate and humorous God would have it, Ellen did get married last Christmas. A week

before the wedding, she sent me a letter saying she needed to talk to me very much. We never talked. She got married. Life is—how they say—interesting.

I have been wise tonight concerning the Homecoming carnival and am not letting the red and gold balloons bother me as they have for the past two years. Sometimes it surprises me that I get an urge to talk to you, but yes— as I'm sure it might surprise you, too—I do. Memory is sometimes the only clear picture I have of you. The times I think of you are always wrapped in a need for family and the very strong emotions of security that you have given me in the very distant past. One of my strongest memories of you is from my fifth or sixth year. I was very sick and Kim and I still slept in the bunk beds that had been a part of Daddy's furniture-making period—God knows, he's had so many different periods while we've known him. Fever and vomiting were parts of my affliction and in the middle of the night, you came in and gave me a very large and cold apple. I think the fever went away, but whether or not it really did, I went to sleep and woke up well. When you would visit from college, I always slept better knowing you were there. Daddy scared me to death when he drove fast, but you did not. These are the things that I can never tell you in person and the reasons that I always cry on our visits. I am not, by nature, a cry-oriented person.

I think Kim and I are especially sensitive about our family. We try so hard to know you, because our memories of our family are very, very hazy. You always seem to get mad when I try to be close to you. In such situations, I cry or become quiet. On our last telephone call, I got very defensive about the London trip that I borrowed money for and I hope I did not hurt your feelings. But the truth of the matter is that I wanted you to get mad for all the times you have made me mad. This is honest, brother. I am working very hard this year. All of my courses are challenging me and teaching me to think on my own, something one of the blue-haired widows from North Baptist Church warned me against when she said: "Now, don't you go away to college and come back 'de-arranged.'"

I pray for it nightly.

I have really enjoyed visiting with you in this letter, Porky, and hope that it has made you happy. That is its purpose. School has its depressing moments, but I am working on the bizarre assumption that the real world will have its share of the same. If you have the time, write, but if not, a cold, very large apple will do.

Love,

Tim

In a rental car from the airport, I drove to Austin College and Sherman, an hour and a half north of Dallas. There had been no time to think all morning, just do; actually taking the time to think would have stopped me in my tracks. By now, it was about two in the afternoon—an hour earlier in Texas than New York—and I was operating on nothing but adrenaline, a bad airplane lunch, and even worse coffee, and an insane sort of hope. I'd checked in for messages and tried calling Tim again from the airport, and there was nothing, so maybe this wasn't so insane.

Or maybe I'd lost all ability to reason, and I was running away from something, as much as he was.

On that route to Sherman—a stretch of highway unbroken by anything except Dairy Queens and an occasional industrial plant—it was impossible not to drift back to my earliest memories of that same route, when our parents took us to visit Porky at Austin College.

In those years long before Tim and I would make that journey as students ourselves, when we were seven, eight, nine, and ten, we would fill the time in the backseat, counting down the small towns we passed and turning them into a competition our father at the wheel joined in, about the order of our births:

"Anna or Melissa? Which town comes first?"

"Anna."

"Me or Tim, who came first?"

"You, by five minutes. You know that."

"I win! I win!"

In the backseat, we made up another game called "Baby on the Hill." One of us would climb into the sloping little crawlspace under the back window, threatening to "fall off the hill" if our mother didn't get the doctor to come quickly enough.

"Doctor! Doctor! My baby's falling off the hill! Come quick!" she'd scream into a pretend phone.

Depending on our mood, the baby—we'd take turns playing that role, the far more desirable one—would fall off the hill.

Or not.

Until this very minute, I've never realized it was the baby who called the shots: he was the one who decided whether or not to fall, and when; he held all the power, not the mother or doctor. Sometimes the doctor would arrive just seconds too late; sometimes the mother wouldn't call quickly enough, but it was the baby who decided what the rest of their lives would be, if they'd be wracked with guilt for what they did, or didn't do, on time, or just seconds too late.

A baby who held the power of life or death over his mother, threatening to fall off a hill if she did something he didn't like; a woman who wore nightgowns and shocked—literally—a man in baggy pajamas to death. Forget Kick the Can or Hide and Seek; this was our arsenal of childhood games, created from seeing a mother who wandered around in a stupor, and a slip; a father who drank away his spare hours at home; created from hearing that our older brother could die at any minute.

Just as Tim would many years later, Porky had spent some unexpected and interrupting "time at home" during his college years. From his teenage years on, he had been plagued by a life-threatening ulcerated colon, a term I would recite by rote as a child, without knowing what it meant—except that it hurt his stomach. My father would always warn me that if I didn't relax, the same thing would happen to me. While Porky was home from college, about to go into the hospital to have it treated, I heard my mother cry out late one night, "Porky's going to die. He can't make it. *I* can't make it. He's going to die. . . ."

I froze in the top half of our bunk bed that was part of our father's furniture-building period, just feet away from our parents' bedroom; froze the same way I did when the call came that Tim was missing from work. (It's not an explosion of thought, but the immediate absence of it, as if everything is power-sucked out of your mind, all at once, taking your last breath with it.) I carried that secret terror with me for years, that Porky could die at any minute; until now, I've never told it to anyone.

Tim slept in the bottom bunk, but I never dared ask him if he heard those same damning words as well.

Porky got better and went back to college; we continued to play Baby on the Hill on our visits to him, and we never talked about the fact that he could have died.

On those visits to Porky with our parents, Tim and I would race inside Baker Hall, Porky's dorm, and the boy working behind the desk would play along with us, making us sign in with our careful, grade-school penmanship before he'd allow us entry. We'd shove each other out of the way to be the first to push the elevator button to the fourth floor, where Porky lived, and where I would live so many years later. We'd always go to the same fancy restaurant in

town—the only one in town—where an organist swathed in a tulle
wrap performed standards of the day. Daddy would give us change
to put in her tip jar. By the time Tim and I got to Austin College as
students, the restaurant, and the pretty lady in tulle, and our own
mother, were long gone.

Even while he was away at college, Porky helped to save us after
our mother died, coming home on weekends to take us to movies
and musicals in Dallas. We saw *Mame* with Celeste Holm, about little
Patrick coming to live with his eccentric Auntie Mame; meeting her
years later, and telling her about that, she told me I was beautiful. We
saw *Peter Pan* with Sandy Duncan, about lost boys going to live in a
make-believe forest, with a changeling child who tried to be both
mother and father to them. We couldn't escape our missing parents
wherever we went, even in the guise of entertainment. Driving
home with Porky from those late nights, Tim and I would crawl
over the front seat, where we had begged to sit, into the back to fall
asleep, lulled into a world of absolute assurance and safety.

Porky introduced us to our first Chinese food—egg rolls, egg drop
soup, and sweet and sour chicken—and our first cheesecake, with
blueberry topping. I once picked through an entire bag of fortune
cookies Porky had brought home, breaking them open one by one,
then throwing them away, as I looked for the one fortune that would
predict happiness for our family. Porky taught us manners. He once
set our dining room table with a twice-a-year tablecloth and poured
salad dressing from bottles into small bowls, telling us that is how it
would be served in nice restaurants. He showed us off to his friends
in college, and bought us the Nehru jackets we begged for, and sent
us souvenirs from his trips around the world, and told us the definition of poetry was "a mirror on a lonely road."

He saved us after our mother died, but we were afraid of him. We

tried to be adults with him, thinking that's what he wanted, but we were never anything but scared little kids around him.

Once, in the fourth or fifth grade, we flew to visit him in Austin, where he was going to grad school. As we taxied in, I thought I saw him from my window seat, looking out onto the landing strip. We shared a look—I will never know for sure if it was him—that said so much, a look of sad panic for which we were both too young. I hadn't yet put on my face for him, nor he for me; we hadn't revved up to our too-excited smiles and high-pitched, hyper hellos. What did his anxious, not-ready look mean? That he couldn't stand the burden of having to raise us, that he wished it had all been different? That, despite the novelty of having twins as little brothers, twins we were told he loved to show off to his friends, we reminded him too much of the mother we had all lost? That he was afraid that he wouldn't be able to take care of us, to give us what we needed, as I am so afraid right now that I will not be able to save Tim this time?

ᴄᴄ

All these thoughts, two generations of brothers' worth, by the time I got to Austin College, a little before four, and pulled into the parking lot by Baker Hall, my old dorm. I wondered if I should check in somewhere before I started looking, but check in where? There was no protocol for this. They didn't give you a set of rules for "Life 101," tucked inside your diploma, when you graduated—what to do *in case* your brother disappears and you decide to go back to your old school to look for him. They didn't list anything in the freshman handbook for what to do if you saw a strange-looking boy/man prowling around campus, asking questions, showing a picture of someone who looked just like him.

I thought back to what I knew of the breakdown, to the little Tim had told me: that it was about our mother, his anger at her for leaving us by dying. (*Him.* Anger at her for leaving *him.* Sorry; I can't even let him have his own anger, his own *pronoun,* I have to share it.) He'd first written about our mother's death in an autobiography we had to write for a class assignment our sophomore year; we'd met in the school cafeteria early one morning to read them to each other.

Was *that* where he might be then, the cafeteria, guzzling the iced tea that I was craving?

I had to start somewhere; I could get a drink if nothing else.

No guards stopped me as I walked into the Student Union Building, or SUB, where Slater's Dining Hall was. I still looked young enough to pass, if you didn't look too carefully at the silver hairs that were already overtaking my head; at a certain angle, they could pass for something sun-bleached. It was long after lunch, but a few stragglers were still sitting at the long tables. I stood at the top of a short sweep of steps that led in and scanned the cavernous room for Tim, the same way I used to look for friends in the crowd, needing a destination before I waded in.

He wasn't there, not on first glance, at least, but with a little jiggle of memory, I was back in that same cafeteria our sophomore year, and he *was* there.

~~

The bios were assignments for a series of courses under the epic title "Heritage of Western Man." Tim and I had made plans to meet early that morning to read them to each other, as if we needed each other's approval before we shared them with our teachers, needed each *other's* approval for the separate lives we had fashioned from the same materials.

Over the cups of coffee we were just learning to drink, we proudly, nervously, slid the assignments across the table to each other, like ransom money being exchanged. Even in the center of that hangar-like room, with a few early risers and minimum-wage workers in their mustard-yellow uniforms, it was as if we were all alone, able to block out the intruding world around us. We were the little twins once again, having snuck into our brother's room to read his letters and lay claim to a family we didn't know.

I went first, as I had in the womb, and began reading what Tim had written about our lives up until that point:

Lloyd Powers met Creola Perkins in a train station somewhere at the beginning of the Great War. She came from a long line of fierce pioneer women; he came from a long line of drunk Yankees and had a funny way of pronouncing certain words. Under contract, they produced my brother Edwin, later called "Porky" because of his baby fat, and twelve years later, twin boys, henceforth known as Tim and Kim, or "the Powers twins." In my sophomore year of high school, when I discovered the specifics of procreation, I determined that we—a pronoun I instinctively use—were conceived around Thanksgiving. My parents were forty. My brother and I were displayed in a twin carriage for quite some time. This summer a neighbor told me: "I remember your mother used to be so proud, pushing you two around in that stroller. Don't you forget her." A teacher, my mother would take us to school on in-service days and we would perform for her friends. I felt we lived a charmed existence. Applause at an early age allowed me to be nice to everyone. It was my place.

In the third grade, I defended a black girl, Bonita, who had been accused of stealing paper dolls from a white girl. With confidence, I told the class they were judging her because she was black. People were moved. Later, I discovered Bonita had stolen something from everyone in the class. Not only paper dolls, but a lightly-held security.

On April Fool's Day of that year, my mother did not go to school to teach. My father took Kim and me to breakfast at the Townhouse restaurant that morning and picked us up that afternoon at school. He took us into the backyard and told us Mother was gone. We were taken into the house through the front door, already wreathed, and set in the den on a couch in front of the TV. We never watched cartoons, but that day, Someone Who Thought They Knew Better turned on the television. Teachers filed past the Powers twins as we cried, looking straight ahead, far beyond the "Peter-Potomous" cartoon that was playing.

That night I ran outside and played basketball for the first time with neighbors across the street. At first they would not let me play. I did though, jamming my finger in order to make a basket, the first in a fruitless athletic career. I ran home as quickly as I had come and into the kitchen. For a minute, I looked for my mother to show her the finger, more proud of the basket I had made than hurt by the pain. The kitchen was filled with awkward old women and Scotch-taped casserole dishes. I realized I would be doing many things from that moment on that my mother would never see. Show and Tell would be played for quite a while for people who really did not matter.

The following year saw us through a series of babysitters who did not care. Good intentions could go to hell, and we looked for replacements for our loss. I was stoic, still very much the defender of those less fortunate. Noble deeds were still performed, but this time, for the memory of past performances. As the final lines of such acts, I often found the self-accusation: "Who do you think you're fooling?" I told one babysitter "I love you" as often as I could. She returned the sentiment, in lip-service only. Kim became a bully for a while, ganging up with a different young babysitter against me. I felt very alone and cried a great deal.

Lloyd remarried; this time to Reta, whom I love very much. Last Christmas, I saw him for the first time for all the sacrifices he has made for

me. He is a man capable of charming high school lunch companions and growing beautiful front yards.

High school no longer seems important, but I developed a great deal there. A renaissance found me my junior year; I became a writer of sorts, and a performer, on and off many stages. "Introduction to the Humanities," a pretentious class for the likes of McKinney High School, gave me a friend for whom my Show and Tell periods were appreciated. Being certain of that friendship made me certain of my own capabilities, and from time to time, a charmed existence returned. I fought many wars against human cruelty and realized the importance of shooting baskets for those who are still here.

An hour ago, my brother came to my dorm room and shared a part of his autobiography with me. I cried, thought about ghosts, kissed my brother goodnight and understood even more of my life. He is a major force in me and his influence is immeasurable. I have thought about those I love now and have wondered what late-night opportunities lay before me in revelation. My friend Travis once told me: "Never think you have anyone figured out. They change too quickly and you would miss so much if you stopped at just one definition." Adaptation has been a key value in my life, and it is that motivation that leads me to marvel at others.

I excelled in French this morning and have made many people laugh during the day. These things have been a part of my life and damn continuity. They will become symbols very shortly. Some hours from now, I will remember them again, impose some order on them, and go on from there.

"Adaptation has been a key value in my life, and it is that motivation that leads me to marvel at others."

"Oh yes, I have adapted all my life."

The very words he had told me, over and over, the night I tried to wrestle a knife from his hand.

If this is how I had to find Tim, reliving the past, following that path

of bloody breadcrumbs, I couldn't do it. Remembering how much he loved me then, the "immeasurable influence" I was on his life, remembering how much *I* had loved *him* then . . . I couldn't do it.

But I couldn't not remember what else happened that morning years ago, as he began to push my Heritage bio back toward me, across the table.

"Did you read it?" I asked.

"You read it to me last night."

"I added some new stuff."

We stared at each other, the way we would later, just before his breakdown, the way I imagine we did in the womb, daring the other to go first.

I caved and spoke first, as always. "You're right. You saw most of it last night. I just changed a few things. No big deal."

"No, I'm sorry. You're right. You read mine; I'll read yours."

"No, really. If you don't want to, it's okay."

"No, I'm sorry. I want to read it."

And so he did, whether he wanted to or not, read the paper that was virtually identical to his, as if our mother's death were the only significant thing that had ever happened to us:

"Our mother died on April Fool's Day when we were seven years old. She was a fourth-grade teacher; Tim and I were in the third grade of the school in which she taught. I used to think she died then so she wouldn't have to choose which one of us to teach, in our elementary school that had just two teachers for every grade. She was sick that morning—nausea, headache, stupor—and stayed home from school; even so, I begged her to let me wear my patched-up "hobo" pants from a Cub Scout skit as an April Fool's prank. She said I couldn't, but I wore them anyway. I think Tim wore his regular school clothes; I have never

thought, until this very minute, about what he wore that day, as if it made a difference.

It did; I was the one who killed her, because I disobeyed her and wore what I wanted."

"Oh Kim,"—that fucking "Oh, Kim" again—"you don't think just 'cause you wore those stupid . . ."

"It is what I think and maybe I'll get over it one day but until then, just . . . I do, so keep reading."

"But that's ridic—"

"Just keep reading. Please."

"Our father came to pick us up after school that afternoon—unusual by itself, even more unusual because one of the men he worked with, who would later have a heart attack and die on the job, was driving. I don't remember if it was our car or the other man's.

When we got home, our father took Tim and me to the backyard, crouched us down in the little alcove behind the house where our dog Penny's house would later go, and told us our mother—"your Mumma," he said, with his hybrid Southern/Yankee accent—was gone. Tim asked where. I don't think Daddy was prepared for that; we were smart kids, and he thought we'd automatically know what he was talking about. He had to say the words then. "Well, she passed away. She's dead."

Neither of us asked how.

He might have said she's in heaven now, but I don't remember.

Not crying—I didn't cry about my mother's death until many years later—I said I wanted to go to Carla's, my little girlfriend down the street. Daddy said he would walk me there but I said I wanted to go alone. I was already embarrassed (by death, by difference?); I didn't want to be seen by staring neighbors on the sidewalk. Without warning—I didn't even know I

was going to do it myself—I hauled myself over our fence and climbed over seven or eight more backyard fences—metal, wooden, spiked, smooth—to get to Carla's.

From her bedroom window, we watched for a hearse—we called it "the morgue" by mistake—to come down the street, not realizing an ambulance had long since come and gone.

I later heard that the principal at our grade school had announced our mother's death over the loudspeaker at the end of that school day, when only the teachers were left and all the students had gone home. That is, all but one, Kathie Green. What do you get for being a bad girl and having to stay after school for detention? You get to hear that somebody's mother has died before anyone else does, even her own children.

Porky was called home from college; he greeted my mother's fellow teachers, who started coming by that night like a Delphic procession: Mrs. Sweeney, in her expensive clothes; Mrs. Fry, the giantess; Mrs. Bradford, the art teacher whose first name was Jo, after Little Women; *Mrs. Moore, with her beautiful, long white hair and ruby ring, a teacher we had both at school and church, teaching us the alphabet and the Golden Rule. They said, "Oh, Ed," and collapsed into his arms, knowing he was old enough to understand. They hugged me and Tim in silence, just giving us "sugar" on the neck. Our father wandered around in his undershirt and made coffee.*

I didn't really understand what was going on and was more overwhelmed by the choices of food that neighbors had brought than by grief. Fried chicken or ham? A cupcake decorated with jellybean Easter eggs or a piece of chess pie? I thought, even then, how macabre it had been for someone—Mrs. Marshall, who lived behind us?—to decorate those cupcakes as if they were going to the school Easter party rather than to the family of a dead person.

The next day, we were taken to the funeral home to see our mother, laid out in one of her fancy school suits. "Don't you want to say good-bye to your Mumma?" our father had asked, as I kicked and screamed in the garage that

I didn't want to go. "This will be your last chance." Dressed up and taken to something I didn't quite understand but knew I wouldn't like.

It was Porky's decision that Tim and I shouldn't go to her funeral. I can still hear him say, "The boys aren't old enough to understand." I'm not sure I would have understood, but even now, I still get mad at him for taking that choice away from me.

We did not go to her funeral.

I have still never been to a funeral, and I am almost twenty years old.

After the funeral was over, at our aunt Bessie's house I overheard Porky say, "They didn't do a very good job getting the ink off her hands." Her hands were always covered with red ink from correcting papers and marking her grade book. Now, I see those red marks, rubbed into a beautiful, rich pink, as part of the texture of her skin, so ingrained it's become part of her.

That is my final image of my mother: in her coffin, her arms crossed over her chest, her hands a beautiful, glowing, rosy pink.

Tim pushed the paper back to me. "I never knew you climbed over all those fences," he said, vamping for time to pull himself together.

"I've got this scar from Mr. Henry's to prove it." I pointed to a red mark on my right palm. "I'm surprised I didn't get gangrene. I never knew you tried to play basketball that night. Over at Mike Willis's?"

"Yeah. They didn't want me to. They were right."

"Was Jim Poston there?"

"He was always there."

"They were there when I broke my arm, too, jumping at the end of the block."

He gave me a wan smile and started to say something but then stopped and shook his head no, leave that for another time. He shrugged his shoulders and left, moving on to the class where he

would have to turn the bio in, leaving me to wonder what he had
been about to say.

I tried to shake myself back into reality, not quite sure where I was:
back home, seven years old, kicking and screaming in the garage; at
my Aunt Bessie's house, comforted by the syrupy iced tea she brewed
and served after the funeral; watching Tim leave the dining hall years
ago; or now, in the present, looking for him.

I was in the past and present both as I watched him leave, in my
mind, and wanted to hold on to him and never let him go, because
I knew what he did not: that years into the future, he would disappear, and I would grieve, because I didn't know if I wanted him
found or not.

I walked outside to escape the cafeteria and that memory.

A breeze came up.

Golden leaves fell off a tree.

A chill ran through me.

I took a minute to soak it all in: the autumn leaves, the coolness,
sweaters pulled out of mothballs, Halloween coming on, Homecoming. I could literally smell it, feel the tingle in my gut. This was
my favorite time of year, with or without my brother. All those
leaves around me . . . they were a clue. I've said, "Twins know," and
somehow, this is something I knew, that Tim was somewhere around
leaves. Gold and ocher and blood red and orange, I saw them lit-
tering his feet. I closed my eyes, closed my mind, and that's what was
left . . . leaves.

Tim.

I stuffed my hands in my pockets for warmth, the same way Tim had in a picture in one of our yearbooks. It's an autumn night, he's at the Homecoming carnival with his friend Leslie, who feeds him something—a chili dog, maybe?—bought for seventy-five cents at one of the sorority booths. Tim and Leslie look happy and carefree.

It was a good picture.

I looked up from that memory to see another picture from that same annual coming to life, a distance in front of me.

Now.

Not just another memory.

It was Gerald Hinkle, the philosophy professor who had been Tim's mentor. That wasn't just an honorific, or some coy Greek reference, but a quite literal part of the Austin College experience: you selected a "mentor" to guide you through your four years, advising you on class selection, approving the "I.D." reports you'd write—for "Individual Development"—six different areas guaranteed to turn out the perfect, liberally educated human being. "Hink" couldn't have been any more wonderfully stereotypical for a college professor: he smoked a pipe, always wore a tweed or corduroy jacket with leather patches on the elbows. His hair was grayer, the wrinkles on his face more pronounced, but it was him, barreling down the walkway, his stooped back the propelling motor that pushed him forward.

This was my first test:

Before he saw me, I still had time to veer off that sidewalk, hide behind one of the peeling birch trees that lined it, and not let him or anyone know I had lost my mind in the last twenty-four hours.

Or I could start doing what I had come to do: play detective and try to find my twin brother. What did a detective do? Ask questions.

Here was someone I knew.

Here was someone who knew Tim.

Here was someone I could ask questions, who was about as close to the events at Austin College as I could get: he was the first person who called me the morning after Tim went crazy, to tell me Tim was gone.

He thought I already knew.

I acted before I thought and stepped out onto the path in front of him.

"Dr. Hinkle?"

He stopped.

"Yes?"

His hair was silvery gray; his eyes were, too. Clouded over. Not seeing.

"It's . . . I don't know if you remember me . . . Kim Powers."

Hink moved closer to look at me, pulling the bottoms of his glasses with Coke-bottle lenses closer to his eyes, coughing the words out with his pipe smoker's rasp. "Powers. My villain. Tim's brother."

"That's right," I acknowledged, in my nervous, aren't-we-clever-laugh, but both descriptors were accurate. In my one and only experience with "Hink" other than being Tim's brother, I played the villainous landlord in something called *The 24th of February.* It was the sole surviving example of a form of German drama called a "fate tragedy," popular for about five minutes in the 1840s. Hink had directed his own adaptation of it, goading the actress who played the lead with tales of his own mother's botched abortions and manic depression. After the play was over, he told her he had made it all up to get a better performance out of her. In a yearbook photo that summed it all up, I'm threatening the comely lass who ran what looked like a gay Bavarian B&B with a hunk of Styrofoam cheese, speared on the end of a prop knife.

"You've got to forgive me. I can't see so well anymore. It'll all be gone in a few years."

"I guess you've read too many papers over the years," I said lamely, not knowing what else to say.

"No, just genetics. Bum luck."

He started walking again, so fast it seemed like powerwalking. "Follow me. I'm late for a meeting. This your first time back?"

"Yeah. I mean . . . yeah. More or less."

I had graduated in 1979 and had never gone back while school was in session, only during quick trips home for Christmas, when I'd drive around the dark, deserted campus and remember the last place I felt truly safe, remember the glories I'd achieved on campus that I hadn't yet achieved in New York. Now, at twenty-eight, I started to explain all that to Hinkle but ended up just saying, "I haven't come back, but I . . . I do think about it a lot."

"Don't know how healthy that is."

"I know what you mean."

"Tim called the other day. Is that why you're here?"

It was the most straightforward thing I had ever heard.

I stopped.

He did, too.

"You haven't seen him, have you? Is he here?"

Maybe I wasn't so crazy after all.

"Who knows if I could've seen him even if he was here? But no, he just called. My office. First time I'd heard from him since he graduated. Sounded like he'd been drinking."

How much more straightforward could this guy be?

He started walking again, even faster.

"Sorry, I don't mean to tell you anything you don't already know. . . ."

"I know."

"You get used to it. A lot of students call up, with the courage of the bottle. Old times and all."

"Was he okay?"

"Depends on your version of 'okay.' He wanted some of his I.D. reports, wondered if I still had 'em. I didn't. I know that sounds bad, but I've read a lot of I.D. reports over the years. Some are good; some aren't. His were good—I remember that much. Different, but good." He paused, as if trying to remember them, see with his mind's eye what he could no longer see with his real eyes. "I know we're supposed to remember all the special ones, the special people, but . . . is something going on?"

"He's, uh . . . he's kind of missing. I . . . I had this crazy idea he might have come back here."

There was silence, which he finally broke.

"He seemed disappointed too, that I hadn't kept them. Just like you. Like I said, I can't see very well these days, but I'm getting better at seeing silence. How's that for a line I should write down? 'Seeing silence.' Maybe I'll take up poetry."

He must have "seen" it again, because that was my response.

More silence.

"You all think we're gods. I'm sorry. We're not. We're just teachers."

"No, no . . . I mean . . . it's okay."

"You're not a student anymore. You don't have to be polite."

"I wasn't trying to be polite."

But I was. I *was* trying to be polite. Some things you shouldn't get rid of, like Hink had gotten rid of Tim's I.D. reports, the papers that might have traced the path to his breakdown. How many of Hink's "mentees" had that happened to? How many times had Hink had to break the news, that a student had practically been carted off to the

booby hatch? Didn't that count for something? Shouldn't he remember that, want to solve the mystery of why it happened as much as I did?

"I just . . . I don't have the room. Anywhere."

He shrugged and tapped his noggin.

Buy a fucking extra file cabinet, I thought.

"Is he really missing? Is there something I can do?"

"No, he's done it before. Don't worry. He'll show up. Please don't say anything to anybody. I'm sure he'll be fine."

Liar. He hadn't done it before, not like this. And who knew *how* he would be. *If* he would be.

"Listen, I need to run. It's been good to see you," I lied.

"That's the second time you've sounded disappointed."

"Sorry, it's just . . . I've gotta find him."

I couldn't take being there another second.

I walked away from that path as fast as Gerry Hinkle did.

Only he had somewhere to go, a meeting that was waiting for him.

I had nowhere.

CHAPTER FIVE

W alking away from Gerry Hinkle, I felt like a ghost. On campus when I shouldn't be, roaming there until I was set free, my past resolved. Except it was Tim's past I was trying to resolve, his past I was trying to make give up its secrets. But maybe I was getting close; Tim had called his old professor. Another breadcrumb on the trail, I thought, as I was almost bowled over by a giant tractor tire— then another, and another—being rolled across my path.

A giant breadcrumb.

The giant tires of the Sig Tau Tire Roll.

I remember Porky talking about that rite of passage, the thing that separated the Sig Tau men—Porky's fraternity, then Tim's—from the rest of us, long before we started school there. Each frat had its own activity; the Betas did something with bricks, another group did

something with paddles. The Sig Taus rolled gargantuan tractor tires for miles and miles into the woods and then drank—and probably did other things men isolated with men do. I wasn't part of those activities—I derided them—but secretly wanted to be. I wanted that connection to Porky that Tim had; the same secret handshake and rituals, the same male bonding and do-or-die promises for life. They both knew what parties with kegs of beer and boys were like; I didn't but wanted to.

My friends and I laughed at them, although we reverently moved to the fringes to let the festivities pass us by.

We made fun but still moved aside to let them pass us by.

Tim's Tire Roll was one of the strongest memories I have, even though I wasn't there to witness it.

Can you have memories of things you didn't see?

I do.

This is what I saw, in my mind, from Tim's Tire Roll:

As the tires (six, seven feet in diameter, at least) were rolled by the pledge class deep into a forest, senior members of the frat egged on the pledges and jeered at their lack of strength and stamina. Girl-friends dotted the route with water and wet towels. Somebody started a chorus of "Ninety-nine Bottles of Beer on the Wall." Harvey Wallbangers, the "theme drink" Tim's pledge year, were mixed and passed out in the hot sun.

It was all in fun, all that sweaty, dear love of comrades. Except that laughing and joking and sweating and swearing and drinking turned to silence and pain, at least for Tim. The boys—for they *were* boys, not men, no matter what anyone said, or what they themselves wanted to believe—crossed a bridge, the final one of many on their journey. (And I'm not just being metaphoric: they crossed a bridge, a real one, made of brick and stone and concrete.) To celebrate, the

pledges wanted to splash in the water below and cool off, retrieve the tires the nasty, punishing older classmen—the "actives"—had thrown overboard.

Rob, a swimmer, and one of the actives mixing drinks, also wanted to splash in the water. (Rob: handsome, chlorine-blond, watery-eyed, even when he was away from the pool.) He wanted to prove to someone—Tim?—what a stud he was. He dove off the bridge, not seeing that the water wasn't deep enough for a graceful entrance, or exit. He didn't *see,* period.

They thought his back and neck were broken.

I wondered how he kept from drowning, if he felt pain, what final thoughts flashed through his mind. Did he think he was going to drown, this man/boy who had spent most of his life in the water? And what thoughts came to the other frat boys: should they call an emergency meeting to decide what story to tell the authorities, each boy wrestling with his conscience about how to tell it? Was there just one story to tell, or many? Mark Schumann always recorded the Tire Roll; did he have film of the accident, like the Zapruder film? Was it like *A Separate Peace,* was there a Gene to shake his unspoken love Phineas off a tree limb and headfirst into the shallow water? Would a tribunal be called? Would the boys go off to war and come back shell-shocked, only then ready to tell the real story?

Would someone die at the end of the book?

No, none of those things would or did happen. This wasn't *A Separate Peace,* but something far more real and disappointing; more bad luck around water and the Powers twins. A boy, clowning around for attention, clowning around to attract a loved one, jumped off a bridge.

Rob was lucky. In reality, he just broke his ankle and compressed two lower vertebrae. After time in a hospital and at home, he was

back on campus. Tim switched rooms with him so he wouldn't have to climb the stairs to his third-floor room.

I remember Tim saying, with the concern you only hear in a lover's voice, that Rob was going to hurt himself because he had come back too early.

I remember seeing them from afar: Tim teaching Rob to walk again, supporting his back as Rob inched forward on a cane. I saw them from the expanse of lawn in front of Luckett Hall, the yellow stucco monolith Tim lived in his first two years at school. I stood back and kept quiet; I somehow knew this was a special meeting, a first, or maybe last time, for them to talk and explore, and me not to intrude.

How quickly they moved, for two people who were learning to walk anew.

Not long ago, I had my own late-night, drunken phone call with Rob, out of the blue, to finally ask that same question that had obsessed me all those years ago: Did you fuck my brother? (Too many drinks, too many memories, too much sadness, and directory assistance—a lethal combination, if you haven't figured that out by now.) I asked it a little more politely than that, but that was the bottom line, after some warm-up that was equally weird.

"Uh . . . I'm trying to reach Rob."

"This is he."

Now what? Did you fuck my brother and leave town? Is that what made him go nuts?

"Rob, I don't know if you remember me," I began but stopped. How many conversations would I start this way before I found my brother?

"It's Kim Powers, from AC. Tim's brother."

"Jesus. Wow. Uh . . . how are you?" His tone switched from excited to guarded, as if it had suddenly hit him why would he be getting a call from someone he had last seen nearly ten years earlier, and barely knew then.

"This is gonna sound weird, I know, but . . . could you have made the Olympics?"

"What?"

"That's what Tim always thought, if you hadn't hurt your back. That's what he was so proud of, that he knew someone who might have made the Olympics." What I didn't say, what broke my heart: that he wasn't proud of himself, and had to take pride in other people.

"God. I don't know . . . I mean, sure, it was my fantasy, it's every-body's fantasy, I probably lied and said I could, but . . . I knew I couldn't. I wasn't fast enough."

Now he was lost to the past, as I was most of the time; I could hear it in his voice.

He was swimming again.

"I didn't want it enough. I was too lazy. I don't know what I wanted." I could almost hear him shake his head to knock the memory away, knock the water out of his ears. "I'm on a swim team here, a gay swim team."

"Is your back okay?"

"It's fine, but that's not what kept me from the Olympics. I never could have gotten there, with or without jumping off a bridge."

"When you fell. . . ."

"I jumped. Period. I was drunk. I was showing off. Water and drinking, it doesn't mix. Take my word for it."

"Were you showing off for Tim?"

"Tim? No . . . Lee Ridge. Remember him? That diver? He was always saying divers were better than swimmers."

I heard him move the phone away, talk to someone else.

"I'm married. To a man. Charley. Did I tell you that?"

"Oh, God, no. I mean, congratulations."

"Everybody's flipping out. Two guys don't get married in Michigan every day. Two *schoolteachers.*"

"My mom was a schoolteacher." Where did that come from? It was the only thing I could think to say.

Until this, my A-bomb:

"Are you in touch with Tim?"

"I haven't even talked to him since school. I wrote him once or twice, but he never. . . ."

"Did you ever have sex with him?"

Jesus, Kim.

"Jesus." That's what Rob said, too.

"I'm sorry, I can't believe I just said that."

He should've hung up on me—*I* would've hung up on me—but he answered anyway. "We sort of rubbed each other's crotches. I came. I don't know if he did. We never talked about it." There was a pause. "Now *I'm* the one who can't believe I said that."

We talked about it, we talked about other Sig Tau men who were gay, or at least had sex with other Sig Tau men.

I got angry that they were all doing each other, and I was the only stupid fag on campus who was bearing the cross of actually *saying* I did it.

What was I supposed to do now?

Call everybody Tim had ever known?

Ask all of them if they had had sex with Tim, if that's what made him go nuts?

Only to find out he was nothing special to all of them, just like he had been nothing special to Gerry Hinkle, who hadn't kept his papers, or Rob, who hadn't even been showing off for Tim, but someone else?

Maybe I should call Rob again.

"Hey, is my brother there? Starting what he never finished?"

Another giant tire almost ran me down, shaking me out of my reverie. A quick "Sorry" from one of the Sig Tau boys and a giggle—old guy, get out of the way—and they were gone.

They were gone, and so was my brother, and so was I, lost to the past as I stood on the sidewalk like a bump on a log, trying to figure out what to do next.

I might as well climb to the top of the Student Union Building (the SUB) and yell "Olly olly oxen free" through a bullhorn at the top of my lungs, see if that smoked Tim out.

My phone calls weren't working.

My talking to old teachers wasn't working.

The top of the building. . . .

That might work.

That's where the Sig Tau "archives" was, one of a row of closets all the Greek societies had on the second floor, for storing their archives.

Archives.

More like beer cans.

Kegs.

Maybe Tim was there, hiding out, reliving the past, like I was.

I went up two flights of stairs, past the row of doors with their

unfamiliar Greek symbols. I was smart but not that smart; four years of high school Latin didn't translate to Greek.

Thank God for decals.

I saw one of an armadillo on one of the doors and knew I had found the right place.

The armadillo, the unofficial Sig Tau mascot, the icon of Texas roadkill.

The door wasn't even locked.

It was a closet full of rickety metal shelves crammed with black binders and boxes, poster board cutouts and felt banners, like something from Vacation Bible School.

Those binders, the minutes of their meetings over the years. Tim had been corresponding secretary for the frat, the keeper of their weekly newsletter. I fingered my way across a helter-skelter row of black binders to the one that had his year labeled on the outside and opened it, to be engulfed by his trademark doodles, the odd little caricatures he began drawing in high school for special friends, the familiar bluish/purple ink on sheets of Ditto paper he wrote on in longhand, never typed.

Those papers, my madeleine.

It was like I could smell him.

He had been here, in a way.

I flipped through the newsletters, familiar names going in and out of sight. . . .

"Sir?"

I whirled around.

A security guard.

"*Sir?*"

He couldn't be talking to me; I was only twenty-eight years old.

"Sir?"

He *was* talking to me.

"Can I see your I.D.?"

"Uh, oh . . . I used to be a student here . . . in Sig Tau. . . . I was just looking at some old stuff. . . ."

I wasn't a Sig Tau, but he didn't have to know that.

"I'm sorry. Campus security and all. We've had some break-ins."

"Sorry . . . the door was open. You know . . . old times."

I should have asked him if he had seen another stranger wandering around, someone who looked almost just like me, but I didn't.

He ushered me out of the room and closed the door, barring it in case I changed my mind. I walked away and made it outside, where I sat on a stone bench that circled an old tree.

Make a plan.

Keep from going more crazy.

Find Tim.

That was a plan.

What had made Tim go crazy, when he was here, at this very same place? The frat, all those guys piled in together; that was part of what made him go crazy, the Homecoming carnival and its ghosts, its red and gold balloons.

The frat made him go crazy, the Big Boys on Campus with whom he was probably falling in love, but not admitting it, under the guise of hazings and keg parties and cookouts on the beach.

Maybe Tim couldn't face that, not yet.

When Tim finally did quit the frat—"commit Greek suicide," as he jokingly called it—he signed off the final set of minutes he wrote as recording secretary with the name The Ghost of Young Tim.

Our junior year, that's what he had started becoming to me, as he began disappearing bit by bit: the Ghost of Young Tim.

As I sat on that stone bench outside the SUB, I forced myself to stay focused on our junior year, after he quit the frat; the year when everything changed, when the events, good and bad, that primed the breakdown were to take place. It was a year that could be traced from love to love, threat to threat, despair to despair.

That year, a girl fell in love with Tim, and another boy tried to kill himself because of it.

Another boy fell in love with me and then tried to kill me when I said I didn't love him back.

Our best friend was raped.

And Tim and I would separate yet again, without him even knowing it.

I was lost to the spell of it, then and now . . . autumn, this place, Tim's spirit. I *felt* it. I felt *him*. He was *here*. Things were taking on their own momentum, and my body raced forward, as much as my mind. The smallest twitch of thought . . . where is he? where would he go next? . . . and my feet followed, taking me from the flagstone bench where I sat to the large auditorium of Ida Green, the theater building, where we had spent so much of our time.

I flung open the door to the theatre. . . .

. . . it banged into the wall behind it . . .

. . . and a high-pitched voice exploded on stage, at exactly the same time.

"We've had this date from the beginning!"

Stanley and Blanche were going at it.

Stanley—all 118 pounds of him in Stanley's requisite red silk pajamas, with the hint of a milk mustache left over from lunch—was shaking a Valkyrie Blanche, six feet tall if she was an inch. And strangely unmoving. Literally. She was stiff as a board, unbending, as he shook her, and then I saw she *was* a board, or almost. A mannequin.

He was using a dressmaker's mannequin from the costume shop as his scene partner.

"Oh, God . . . sorry . . . I was just . . . I didn't mean to interrupt."

"Please. Interrupt," said the Stanley. "I was just practicing. In acting class they say I have to work on 'owning the stage.'"

"They used to say that to me, too."

I smiled at him.

He smiled back.

It was our secret.

"But between us, I don't think anything's gonna make this scene work. Maybe I need a real girl. I guess that's what Tennessee Williams meant."

"I'm not so sure."

We smiled again. This kid was smarter than I had been back then.

I made my way down the black linoleum steps of the auditorium, past the orange seats to the stage, where I had spent so many lonely, obsessed Saturday afternoons myself, practicing when the rest of the campus was off watching a football game. How desperate I had been to be in *A Streetcar Named Desire* my sophomore year, thinking me as Stanley was the perfect way to deconstruct that old chestnut. You want hunky Marlon Brando in a tight T-shirt? Try a skinny geek instead, who can't see without his glasses, and see the play anew. Fortunately, no one agreed with me. I ran the light board instead, a likely fate for my new friend Stanley, on stage now. He could have been me, almost a decade earlier: skinny, geeky, glasses-wearing, desperate to impress any older alumni who might come wandering through. Desperate for sex, if only someone would make the offer, or take him up on it.

Maybe I was just thinking about me.

I might not have starred in *Streetcar* all those years ago, but I finally

made it into a leading role on that Ida Green stage, in Tom Stoppard's *Rosencrantz and Guildenstern Are Dead*, my junior year. The play began with me flipping pennies into the air and catching them; how much time I'd spent practicing those tosses. Chance, they were meant to convey; heads or tails, who can ever know what will happen next?

I used to think I did.

⌐⌐

I played Rosencrantz, on stage for nearly the whole play; Tim played Osric, who came on only in the last few minutes, to clean up the mess. ("That's what makes this one a tragedy," he would later write.) Until then, Tim held court in the greenroom a flight below the stage, dabbling in theater but never really serious about it, making the best friends of his life. The friends who would soon make him go crazy. Carrie, whom he nicknamed Toujours, an *homage* to the French classes we struggled through, was Ophelia, lounging in a padded vinyl chair, her heavy black Elizabethan gown incongruous against her flirtations and cigarettes. Roy Simmons, Tim's new best friend now that Rob was at home, recuperating from his jump off the bridge, was a spear carrier and shared Carrie with Tim; they were the *Jules et Jim* of Elsinore.

Tim fell in love with Carrie, as she would later, I think, with him.

Selmore Haines, my black boyfriend, was the Player King; Kent Johnson, the department's star, was a brilliant Hamlet (angry that he didn't get a lead, but the only actor haunting enough to pull off the relatively small part of Hamlet).

Michael Ditmore, a fat, bearded English major, played Polonius and also fell in love with Carrie.

He wrote a much-publicized poem about her betrayal of him

with my brother, and his attempt to kill himself because of it. Maybe it was true, maybe it wasn't. I don't know.

Peyton Place, while I was acting my guts out a floor above, completely unaware, and having the best time of my life.

In my gold velvet costume, just like the golden leaves outside.

Michael Ditmore's poem, "The History of Suicide," told the exact time and place at which he tried to buy a gun to kill himself, only to be saved by the "much talked about Kent Johnson." Yes, ma'am, real names and everything. (Same thing for me. It happened; fuck 'em, let 'em come after me. I've got the truth, and a missing brother, on my side. What do they have, besides some adolescent hurt feelings?) Michael wrote of Carrie and Tim, "But she has no idea yet that he is homosexual. . . . I would say her name out loud but for libel laws."

The show continued; few of us knew of the suicide attempt until the poem came out in the campus literary magazine that spring. Carrie's friends refused to let her read it, as if protecting her from a bad review. Ironically, a prose piece Tim wrote about first love was in that same issue, as well as a poem from the boy whose offer of love I refused. God, we were a literary bunch; if we couldn't kill ourselves or someone else, we'd just write about it.

After the play's Friday night opening, I laid my head on a long makeup table, too exhausted to move. I had literally given all I had to give, as clichéd and college-melodramatic as that sounds; my autumn-gold costume was soaked through with sweat, the velvet wet to the touch. I radiated heat. I had to focus myself like a drunk, like I had seen my father do on so many occasions, close my eyes between each thought, each breath, just to get to the next one. "Okay. Come on now. You can do it. Atta boy."

I finally pulled myself together and went to the cast party at Dub's house, a crumbling old Victorian just off-campus. Selmore and I

drank and danced to Bette Midler, while Kent Johnson raced to find Michael Ditmore, shaking the chained-up door of a pawn shop and screaming because he was too late to buy a gun.

Later that night, still unaware of Michael Ditmore's dark night of the soul, Selmore and I, Tim, Roy, and Gil, who would later become Tim's first lover, left the party and wound our way to our dorms. In my mind, we were like the celebrants in *The Seventh Seal*, led by a hooded man carrying a sickle. Only he wasn't a symbol of Death, but of Triumphant Youth. We were a silhouette, a tableau, moving across the lawn, our tennis shoes damp with buttons of early-morning dew.

We passed a small stucco building—the old YMCA, turned into a teacher-training lab—that was surrounded by a fence. Electrical poles carried heavy wires to antennas on top of the building; looped coils of barbed wire topped the fence. I fantasized that it was some sort of control center for the college, a power plant whose constant electrical hum was the white noise behind our studies.

My hair bristled as I walked near it.

In my imagination, a guard was stationed inside, watching monitors where he could zero in on suspicious activity. That night, he zeroed in on the five of us: frozen on his screen in a reverse image, our background dark, our expressions time-exposure silver. Tim and Roy would photograph the most vibrantly, with their high spirits and blond hair; their auras would center the photograph emotionally. The guard was impressed with the silvery beauty of that image and wished there had been moments like that for him when he was a young man, before he put on weight and had a wife, and three kids in diapers.

But the beauty turned ugly. The guard blew the picture up a thousand times and saw something almost imperceptible to the human

eye. At the peak of the merrymaking, Tim pulled in one direction, drunkenly trying to get us to sing the Pointer Sisters' "We Are Family" and hold hands "like European men" as he kept saying, and I pulled in the other, unwilling to share the party with him.

Tim wanted to be able to recall dew on his feet, to never have them dry; he wanted that night to last forever.

I wanted it to end, pissed off that he was drunk like our father, pissed off that he was so clearly gay but wouldn't come out like I had—and suffered because of it—pissed off that my feet were wet.

He loved me so much, and I treated him like shit.

He wasn't the only one.

Several months after *Rosencrantz and Guildenstern,* a boy named Brian fell in love with me. He'd seen my performance, had seen me in my gold tights, and he still fell in love with me. I didn't return his love, so he wrote a poem about it, cursing me, as Michael Ditmore had cursed Tim.

Brian came to my fourth-floor room in Baker Hall, the first time I had ever seen him break away from his Dean Hall premed crowd. He was a big guy; stocky, a little straight-laced, a little bumbling. He haltingly told me he was gay; I was the big fag on campus; I was the first stop everybody made, when they finally figured it out about themselves. Brian hung around me the next week or so, and one night nervously asked me to meet him up in his lab, high above the Moody Science Building pine trees. I went, perhaps suspecting what was going to be said, but almost more excited about my first trip into those hallowed halls. Just as the subterranean world of the theater was mysterious to so many others, this world of test tubes and lab coats was *terra nova* to me.

As far as I knew, they were cloning humans in there.

After showing me some of his work, clumsily rushing through the

end of a project, Brian told me he was in love with me. At first, I pretended I didn't understand, played like he meant some kind of general love for his gay brothers, natural when he was first coming out. He knew I was lying. I knew he knew I was lying. As much as I have craved love, I couldn't love him, either emotionally or physically.

He is the only person in my life whose gift of love I did not return.

He began rattling one of the animal cages, knocking the rat inside to a corner. The rat's eyes widened; he was as scared as I was. For a split second, I thought Brian was going to kill the rat, or me—stab me with one of his medical instruments, make me drink poison, push me off the fourth-floor balcony outside, and claim it was an accident.

But he did none of those.

He just wrote a poem about it, without using my name, but telling the entire campus of the exact time and place at which his world blew apart, and how he would always hate the person who caused it.

Me.

If I knew differently, if I thought Brian might be reading these pages today, I would beg his forgiveness. I would say I was just as mean to my beloved brother, so he shouldn't feel alone. But forgiveness isn't possible; Brian is dead, an early casualty of AIDS.

I beg his forgiveness anyway.

⌒

Had I actually said any of that aloud?

Silence from the Stanley, staring at me in shock.

That must mean I had.

He spoke first, this stranger who didn't know me from Adam, who made me feel like I was looking back at myself.

"Are you okay?"

"Not really. My brother's missing. I thought he might be here. A lot of stuff happened to him here." I took a breath and plunked myself down on the lip of the stage, the whole day finally catching up with me. "Maybe I'm just hungry. I haven't eaten much today."

"You wanna . . . should I get the nurse's office or security or something? Are you *okay*?"

He didn't know what to do.

Neither did I, except to look embarrassed.

"Come on, I think you should eat a little bit. I'll take you to Slater's, get some food. Some iced tea with lots of sugar," the Stanley said. "That always makes me feel better."

"Me, too."

He took his red pajama top off from over his regular school clothes and draped it over the mannequin's torso, then led the way out, like the doctor carting Blanche off at the end of the play. I whispered under my breath, not sure I even meant for him to hear, her famous last line, "I have always depended on the kindness of strangers."

He did hear it.

"I can't believe you just said that. I love that line. It's so true. You think anybody'd notice if I switched it to Stanley instead of Blanche?"

⌒

It was about six P.M. by now; Slater's, the cafeteria where I had started off my search at AC, was in full swing. The Stanley stuck two

gold plastic glasses against the ice machine, then moved them to the iced tea dispenser.

"I love crushed ice, don't you? It's so much better for my teeth than regular ice cubes. I've always gotta be chewing on something, and the crushed ice is mushier."

He handed me my iced tea, then popped the top off a bottle of baby aspirin he pulled out of his pocket.

"Hope you like orange. They're a little chalky, but I prefer 'em . . . you can take up to six at a time without dying. I know. I've tried," he said, rolling his eyes. "You just get a little . . . sleepy. Sometimes you don't really need aspirin, just . . . the *idea* of aspirin. That's why I take the baby ones."

I had fallen down the Rabbit Hole.

"Now we need food. You shouldn't take aspirin on an empty stomach. Even baby ones." He continued his running commentary, as he walked me through the cafeteria line that was still so familiar, from seven, eight, nine, ten years ago. "It's Saturday night. That means steak or shrimp, but you can't get both, or seconds, when they serve nice food like that. Well, most people can't. I can. The cafeteria ladies like me."

With that, he winked at one of them.

She winked back.

Food tray in hand, he led the way to the glass-enclosed patio called the Loggia, off the main part of the cafeteria. I could have predicted it: it was where I had eaten so many meals, the automatic beeline my artsy, outsider friends and I always made to get away from the din of the jocks and the frat boys in the main part of the cafeteria.

Moving, cutting up his food, eating, he never stopped chattering away. Whether he was just naturally talkative or nervous—I would

have been, talking to an alumnus, even a crazy one, as I was probably coming off—I don't know, but I was happy for him to take the lead for now. I had told him a little bit more about my glory days in the theater department, about the pros and cons of trying to make it in New York, but now I needed time for food to kick-start my brain, while I decided what to do next. Whether that was to keep looking here, or to chalk it up to an expensive, wild goose chase and head back home to New York, I didn't know. Since it was Saturday and there were no classes, none of our old teachers (except Hinkle) had been on campus; I'd have to call them up at home if I really wanted to see if Tim had made it back here, and I wasn't up to looking that ridiculous, or needy, in front of anybody but this kid I'd met an hour ago, and would never see again.

"Whatcha think about my Stanley? Don't answer, I know . . . I shoulda done Blanche."

Oz.

"That was a joke."

He put on a pair of glasses, which magnified his eyes about a million times.

"I didn't think Stanley wears glasses . . . the script doesn't say, it just says the red pj's . . . so I couldn't see when I was doing the scene. Could you tell?"

Never-Never Land.

"Would you mind doing something, even if it sounds kinda weird?"

"Weird hasn't really been a problem for me today."

"Could you call me Stanley? I wanna see if it helps me find my character. I need all the help I can get."

"Let's make it Stan. You just need a little help."

⌒

"I love Saturday nights. There's so much . . . magic to do. You know that song? From *Pippin*? I auditioned with it once. I shoulda sung the grandma's song instead. I was flat the whole time. Dub had me do props instead. I'm big on props."

Stan shoveled down a steak, covered with A-1 sauce; I had the fried shrimp. That, or the baby aspirin with an iced-tea chaser had helped; I was feeling better, even if I was no closer to finding Tim. It had been about eighteen hours since I'd first gotten the call yesterday morning that he was missing, eight hours or so today since I'd flown from New York to Texas. Since I'd been here, I'd called home at least half a dozen times to check for messages from Tim; there were none. I'd called his apartment just as often, holding my breath for a pickup, but none came.

Finally, I had called Jess, still out of town, and confessed my insane notion that Tim might be at Austin College and oh, by the way, so was I. Jess hung up, more furious at me than scared for Tim.

At least a hang-up was better than nothing at all.

I stared at Stan, lost in his youth, his innocence, his need to impress, even with silliness. He was better looking than I'd thought at first; his face was fuller, set off by a red flush on his cheeks that hadn't diminished. At first, I'd thought it was adrenaline from the *Streetcar* scene; it wasn't, just the adrenaline of being twenty years old. Don't grow up, I wanted to warn him; there are only hang-ups on the phone and pissed-off boyfriends and missing people in the "real world," on the other side of college. Saturday nights, yeah, they're great, "magic to do" and all . . . but there's always the Sunday morning after. The morning after. . . .

"What?" he asked.

"Nothing."

"No, what? You're thinking how weird this is, right, you just meet this kid and now you're eating with him. It's okay, you can leave, I didn't mean to . . ."

"No, I was thinking how this is the exact same table I was sitting at when I found out my best friend was raped. Back when we were all your age."

Now he was the one who stared.

"Tim being gone . . . going nuts . . . I think it has something to do with that. She was in plays, too."

On that particular Sunday morning, our friend Sarah came to brunch late. She bypassed our usual table in the Loggia to sit with a group of girls from her dorm. Not the fun girls, as she was, but the tough ones, the ones who abided by the rules and told on people, the ones we suspected were lesbians. It was as if they were her honor guard, preceding her in a V-shaped motorcade, protecting her.

She set her tray down, then came over to Tim.

"I need to talk to you after lunch. *Real bad.*" (Not "really bad," not "really badly," but "real bad." How I will never forget those words, never forget the searching in her large, liquid eyes as she said them, as long as I live.) Tim asked if something was wrong. She just repeated, with eyes that were already round and now got rounder, "I just *really* need to talk to you."

Several girls, in the past, have asked Tim to save them, to be with them. He could barely save himself, but they didn't know that: he was sensitive, he was certainly more fun than most of the redneck boys they dated, and he wasn't a threat, sexually, even though I think

they did want to sleep with him. One girl, a kindergarten sweetheart of Tim's, once said, when her own marriage was on the rocks, "I should have married Tim." The girlfriend she told that to reminded her that: 1) Tim never asked her, and 2) he was gay. It didn't matter. Girls loved Tim, were drawn to him, in the same way little puppy dogs like Stan were drawn to me (and I to them). The girls never asked Tim for anything directly, but between the lines of letters, or in an oblique phone call, or a particular turn of phrase. But the letters always got lost in the mail, or the phone calls didn't get returned, and the girls were forced to go ahead without Tim's help, sometimes saving themselves, sometimes not.

This time, it was too late for Tim to save Sarah.

The call never even came.

That Sunday morning, in the cafeteria, she said she was going to one of the music rooms to play piano and sing with Casey. I was included in the glance, but not the invitation.

Sarah, who'd spent that first, inaugural summer with Tim at Mo Ranch, was short. She had an oval face framed by a fashionable, short haircut, freckles, and expressive, bottomless eyes. She introduced us to so many things: Reuben sandwiches, homeopathy, decency. Early on, when our nosy friend David kept bugging her about what her parents "did," she yelled at him, "My father died when I was two. He doesn't *do* anything. He *isn't*." She told us about her mother and aunt, who lived in the same town but hadn't spoken in years. I once spent a Saturday night in the student lounge rubbing her forearm, as she told me how much she enjoyed *feeling*, what a tactile person she was. When the curly-headed David went through his trauma about my gayness and we "divided up the property" of our shared dorm room, she came over for a date with him but seemed more interested in helping me and Selmore settle into a quiet Saturday night.

I loved her.

So did Tim.

After brunch, he went off to find her, and I went off into my day, this Sunday "morning after" that I somehow knew was shaky around the edges.

That night at dinner, our little band gathered again in the glass-enclosed Loggia, the second table in from the door. The Loggia held about twenty tables and was implicitly reserved for the fringe, the artists and outsiders of the school, like us. From it—although this isn't why we sat there—you could view a particular Austin College tradition: frat boys being pulled out, through an adjoining glass hallway, and thrown into an outdoor fountain on their birthdays.

Happy birthday—wet, like you came into the world.

I was always afraid the stunt would get out of hand, that one of them would cut himself to shreds, falling into a plateglass door, or wall of glass.

I was always afraid of how much blood I might have to witness, sitting there.

On this particular Sunday, a frat boy had a birthday. He was chased through the Loggia, whose narrow passageway was already jammed with books and backpacks. Games of chase don't get more sophisticated as you get older, they get simpler: just run and catch. But the running becomes clumsier, for even the most athletic twenty-year-old is no match for that same child, ethereal and weightless, at seven.

The running got clumsy that night.

After tolerating several of the frat boys running through the Loggia, I picked up my tray and slammed it back down on the table. The moment was unpremeditated; the tray became an extension of the nerve synapses that clicked my arms into action, the arm that had been broken and mended in the fourth grade, that I was always afraid

of breaking again. I yelled at Paul Bunnell, with his pink, acne-scrubbed skin and yellow swimming-pool hair, to live up to his responsibility as the just-elected student body president, and get rid of the troublemakers. Cynthia Manley, the new French teacher, with a scar on her throat, looked on. In my imagination, violence had caused that scar; I took her look as a stand against vigilantes. I started talking to myself and ran out of the room. Everyone, Cynthia Manley included, thought I was standing up for the rights of decent, well-mannered students.

They were wrong.

I was standing up to run away from a secret.

Tim had released it, as the Sphinx did before crumbling, just moments before I threw my fit.

He had just told us, "Sarah was raped last night."

Tim's best friend had been destroyed.

That was the moment of his breakdown; only the need to see the look in my eyes when he told us, to pass some sort of challenge on to me, kept him from going home right then and there, instead of months later.

I couldn't accept what I had just been told. I could only yell at everyone, and know, as they did, that they were the wrong people to yell at, that the right person to yell at would never be caught, that the only release was hysteria and running away.

I ran into the Music and Art Building, home to the muses, across the promenade from the Loggia.

Maybe I ran there because I remembered Sarah saying she was going to play piano and sing with Casey. Maybe I needed man's impulse toward something higher, like art, at that moment. Maybe I needed to be alone, away from frat boys, away from the possibility of broken glass, away from rapists. I needed the solitude of that

building; I needed Sarah; I needed music; I needed it not to have happened.

Tom Luck was on the first floor, getting a drink from a water fountain. He was the leader of the flock, the spiritual guide to Tim's fraternity. He wanted to become a priest, as they all did, but was the only one of those guilt-motivated Presbyterians and Episcopalians who actually did it. He succored me, even then.

I said, "Something horrible has happened."

He said, "I know."

I must have said the words "Sarah" and "rape," but I don't remember. Tom took over, and I let go. I told him everything through my salty tears: I cried for the anguish I knew Tim felt, and I cried for Sarah and the very specific terror she must have felt (a terror I have never come close to feeling, even now).

Shelly Tappa, ethereal hippie daughter of Dick Tappa, campus music teacher and band leader (an'-a-one-an'-a-two) came out of the bathroom by the water fountain; she knew about music, and pain. She might not have known what happened—she didn't know me—but she hugged me anyway, brushing the hair off my face and soothing my brow. We never did introduce ourselves, although we shared embarrassed smiles after that. (Days later, I dreamed that I married her on a wonderful old train going through the Swiss Alps. I was strong and manly; we were embarking on a wonderful life together, blessed by her father, who led the band at our wedding, in love with our youth. I swore to her every fidelity, every hope.) She and Tom gave me the courage to go on, as I exhausted my tears and went up to Sarah.

She and Casey had been playing piano and singing upstairs; I must have heard them. I have often wondered, in the years since, if they heard me downstairs; they didn't seem surprised when I came in.

Casey was without his usual bravado; Sarah, who had belted out the leads in musicals, looked up sheepishly, with tears in her eyes. It was one of my simplest times with her. I approached her cautiously, already nervous about touching her, for fear it would trigger some horrible memory.

We were all very quiet.

Somewhere, maybe then, maybe later, I heard the few details: a black man had come in through her unlocked door and told her he would kill her if she made any noise. She wasn't wearing her contacts and couldn't see him. He left behind a footprint in the flower bed outside her window.

Sarah recovered, although she's never returned to campus in the many years since she graduated. I have wondered, at times, if her husband holds her with the thought that nothing will ever hurt her again; I hope he holds her with all the love he can, as I did that Sunday evening.

Whenever I started missing the "old" Sarah, I realized it was really Tim, the Tim who had always been safe, whose friends didn't get raped, that I missed most of all. I cry for his pain and do everything I can to keep from running back to the Music and Art Building, even though it wouldn't do any good. Art and music, I believe, are gifts of the gods, but the gods are gone right now. Their songs and their paintings are creations I cannot understand, while my brother is still missing.

⌒

Jesus wept.

So did I.

Could you blame us?

"You need some more aspirin. Maybe the real stuff this time. And some more iced tea. That'll do the trick."

My new, old friend Stan to the rescue yet again, making me laugh with his blunt simplicity. With his belief that problems could be fixed, with something as simple as a beverage, when I knew they couldn't.

"If I have anymore I'll float away."

"Then let's go for a swim. That's what I do to clear my head. C'mon."

"Right after you eat? Is that safe?"

"Hasn't hurt me yet. I do it all the time. Plus if I stay here, I'll keep eating. I'm getting fat. Don't think *that'll* work for Stanley. Get me *away* from the desserts."

He weighed 118 pounds, soaking wet.

With shoes on.

Heavy shoes.

I shoveled a last fried shrimp into my mouth and let myself be led away, once again.

Being led away was easier than thinking. I was tired of thinking, of doing, of remembering. I wanted somebody else to take over, and right now, the Stanley was the only candidate. ("Are ye able?" said the Master. "Yes," said Stan, at the same time I said "No.")

Outside, it was already dark, about seven o'clock on a cool fall night. We approached the '60s-looking "nautatorium," where Stan took me toward the locker rooms, the smell of chlorine guiding our way.

We were getting closer to swimming.

Maybe we were getting closer to Tim.

In the days that followed Sarah's rape, Tim and I, unbeknownst to each other, both went to John Ruff, head of campus security, to express our outrage. Tim blamed "them" for the rape, asked if they had even thought of calling Sarah's mother, to offer a lame apology or some sort of restitution. They jumped on his suggestion as if it would erase everything that had happened. I just yelled; John Ruff defended and explained. The only officer on duty that night had been a fat, goofy kid, a Keystone Kop; he couldn't have done anything, anyway.

I was, once again, a missile without a target.

Tim made an appointment to see Howard Starr, the dean of students—a weasly man, I thought, capable of tapping phones, despite his well-cut suits and gold bracelets. In my fevered brain, he was the secret police. Years later, Tim told me about his meeting with Howard; I forgot whatever he told me, preferring my own version of the scene, although I don't think I was far off. In front of Howard's massive, marbled desk, polished daily to a high gloss sheen by his slavish secretary, Tim sits in a high-backed green leather chair, its worn leather tacked down by brass studs that are imprinted with whorls of black gold. Tim nervously picks at the studs and gets a chewed-off, bloody fingernail underneath one of them, one that another troublemaker had already managed to pry up. Tim joins that legacy of troublemakers, of rabble-rousers.

It's fun to imagine that Tim told Howard Starr to go fuck himself, but I think it's just that, imagination. I think, instead, Tim was put in the place Howard wanted him in, shaking and bleeding in a leather chair. It was but a short walk from there to his second-floor dorm room, a floor down from mine in Baker Hall, from which Tim looked out and saw the school for what it was, and started screaming for our father to come rescue him.

⌒

Stan tossed a baggy pair of blue checked swim trunks at me.

"Here. Wear these. They were my dad's."

At his locker, Stan had pulled out two bathing suits: a little red Speedo, still damp from other swims, and a baggier pair of trunks.

"Sometimes I wear 'em. It connects me, ya know? You need connection. I think maybe if I swim a mile in his trunks, it'll help me like him more."

Maybe all fathers wore the same pair, because they were remarkably like the baggy swim trunks my own father had worn, that I had absconded with on a trip back home, in my "shabby chic" period. I had gone through a period in college of taking a bunch of his old clothes, from the '40s camel's hair coat he had, to a pale orange jumpsuit he wore when he went hunting. I didn't think the clothes would help me like him more; I just thought they would make me look more "bohemian."

Stan discreetly stepped behind a locker to shimmy out of his clothes and into his Speedo. I had the feeling he stepped behind the locker even when he was by himself, to shield his own eyes from his naked body.

I stuck the knapsack of Tim's letters that I had been carrying around in his locker and got rid of the bathing suit as well. How could I tell Stan I had barely been swimming since the first grade, that summer of swimming lessons that ended in a car wreck? That I was afraid all swimming would end in a car wreck, or a broken arm, or a broken leg? How could I tell him a grown man was afraid of the water, because of what happened to him as a kid? Maybe I could pretend a dip in the pool was the shower I hadn't taken this morning, and that would pave the way out of my fear. I wasn't afraid

of the shower, after all; I could pretend the pool was just a really big bathtub. Of all the nutty things I had already said, that would sound the nuttiest: a twenty-eight-year-old man afraid of the water.

Stan stepped out from his changing space and reached in his locker for a snorkeling mask, the kind that stuck a few inches out from your face. "Gotta wear these over my glasses, or I'll knock myself out on the walls. I did once. They had to fish me out. Six Eyes," he said, rolling just two of them at himself. "You're not dressed."

He said it like a question.

"You take the first lap. I'll . . . uh, do it in a minute."

He shrugged and headed to the pool; I followed, remembering how the soles of my feet used to prune up as I tiptoed over tiny damp tiles that formed a red-and-gold kangaroo, the school's mascot.

Stan dipped his mask in the pool, swished the water around, then dove, perfectly, into the pool. The water pulled down his Speedo, just an inch or two. A flash of surprisingly shapely ass, of tight white skin. He sliced through the water with incredible ease and power, for someone so frail.

He was so skinny, he looked like an old man.

But he looked like a kid, too.

He looked like Oscar the Ghost, who was said to haunt the old YMCA building on campus, that had been turned into a theater-in-the-round. From the first time I heard the legend, I created a story around it, that Oscar was a swimmer who could have been a little boy or an old man. I imagined that a wood platform of a stage had literally been built over the pool, trapping the live person who was swimming there. The underwater lights were on, and Oscar was too hypnotized by the beauty of his underwater world to realize what was going on in the real world above him. Maybe he was happier

there. By the time I was a student actor at AC, and plays were performed elsewhere, I still imagined a little boy—surely a skeleton by
now—swimming away underneath me, negotiating for a few more
minutes in the water, happy to go home tomorrow. I dedicated all of
my performances to him.

Now, it was Stan, not Oscar, who pulled up to the tiled edge of
the pool, and raised his mask to the top of his head. His glasses
underneath were all steamed up, dotted with drops of water.

"Whatcha waitin' for? Get dressed and come on in."

"Uh . . . I haven't really been swimming in a long time. I'm sorta
rusty. 'Sides, I can't see without my glasses."

I wasn't about to tell someone who weighed 118 pounds—119,
now that he was wet—that I was afraid of the water.

"Wear my mask. It'll come back in no time. C'mon . . . it feels
great . . . just what you need. . . ."

He reached his skinny little hand out and touched my skin. "See,
the water's warm. Heated. It feels good."

He looked like a skeleton trying to pull me in.

"You can just float. I'll start ya easy. What are you waiting for?
Come on."

It's exactly what I had said to Tim, begging him to follow me out
of the womb.

"*NO.*"

I yelled it and pulled back, plopping onto the hard wet tiles.

Stan finally stopped trying. "Sorry. You okay?"

"Yeah. Fine."

Fine, except for the fact that I had just freaked out when a friendly
kid tried to get me to go for a swim.

Fine, except for the fact that this kid, a complete stranger, seemed
to have a crystal ball back to my birth.

I wasn't mad at him; I was mad at Tim, for not coming out first, as planned.

I was mad at Tim for disappearing and leaving me alone.

I stomped back to the locker room, slipping just a little bit on the tiles. I heard skinny little Stan pull himself up after me; I could visualize his wet footprints, like footprints from the Invisible Man, left behind him.

"What? What did I do? I was just trying to—"

"Nothing. I . . . it's not you . . . it's just . . . this is bullshit. What am I doing swimming with a kid in a red Speedo when my brother's missing? Trying to play like I'm eighteen again? I'm hanging out in a pool and he's somewhere probably bleeding to death. This is insane."

Nuts.

This whole fucking thing was nuts.

"I'm sorry. I just thought . . . maybe you need a little R&R, a break from whatever—"

"Maybe you just need to shut up . . . and I need to get back home. What am I doing here?"

"You're looking for your brother. It makes sense, from everything you've said. I'll help."

"'Help,' right. A complete stranger. Guess that shows how many people really wanna help."

No, Kim, it shows how many people you'll *let* help. Or won't. You're pissing and moaning, but you won't let anybody else in. You never have.

I yanked my knapsack of letters out of the locker.

"Here. Ya wanna help?" I tossed the knapsack at Stan. "'I present them to you with a box of aspirin tablets.'" Those were Blanche's words, tossed at the brute Stanley as she turned over her papers on

the lost Belle Reve mansion to him. My little helper should know them, if he wanted to be Stanley.

These were my papers, on the lost Tim Powers.

"Read 'em and weep. Better yet, read 'em, take two *baby* aspirin, since you're so big on it, and call me in the morning."

He stood there, speechless, shivering in his Speedo, clutching my knapsack, looking on in shock at this ogre who had turned on him for no apparent reason.

And like so many fights with Tim, I wouldn't let myself be the first to say I'm sorry. I wouldn't be the first to say it wasn't Tim, or Stan, that I was yelling at—I was yelling at myself, for being such an idiot. For letting life become such a mess. For getting on a plane to Texas, when I should have stayed home. For not knowing what else to do.

Now we were *both* missing.

"You wanna find him? Be my guest. Have at 'em."

I waved at the letters Stan now held and left.

I would not look back.

But I couldn't look anywhere else, except back to the day Tim had his breakdown, seven years earlier, in the fall of our senior year in college, when he'd gone swimming for the last time.

I'd avoided it long enough; there was nowhere else to turn.

Oh, yes, as Stanley would say, we've had this date from the beginning.

CHAPTER SIX

The buzzer in my dorm room always made me jump, especially this early in the morning. I opened one eye, looked around as I got my just-out-of-sleep bearings: on one wall, a giant James Dean, from a French movie poster of *East of Eden*; on another, Raul Julia, in *The Threepenny Opera*. The sights and smells of a (gay) college senior: a dirty towel on top of a pile of even dirtier clothes on the room's lone, vinyl chair, the baggy jeans and red-and-white shirt I wore for days on end, the smelly clothes that said I was too busy for piddly little details like hygiene, that said I was an artist.

Artist or not, the buzzer kept buzzing, announcing a phone call, like a fly that wouldn't go away no matter how many times you swatted it. I hit the white button on the wall, throwing in a few extra jabs—Morse code for "fuck you" to the work-study

student at the front desk who kept buzzing—and went into the hallway to pick up the phone. But even at seven-thirty in the morning, it was in use, so I flew down the cold stairwell to the third floor, barefoot and in an antique bathrobe I had stolen from the costume department.

Inside the wooden phone booth, I traced my fingers over names and numbers that were carved into the wood. Dr. Hinkle, Tim's mentor, was on the line. His first tumble of words, before hello: "Did I wake you? Have you talked to Tim yet? I just came in and got the message from Charlott."

"What message?"

There was a long pause when he realized I hadn't yet been told that my brother had been taken home, babbling like an idiot, the night before.

Can you hear silence?

I could.

In that silence, I heard that my twin brother had just had a nervous breakdown.

I was barefoot; the linoleum floor was cold. People conducted their waking-up business around me: showers turned on, urinals flushed, doors opened and closed.

Nothing stopped because of my bad news.

I thanked Hink for filling me in—never let it be said I forgot my manners—and called home.

Our stepmother, Reta, answered, as if she had been standing by, expecting my call.

I asked my questions in a very small voice. Reta answered the same way, as if Tim were asleep and she didn't want to wake him. She was confused by what had happened but was doing what she did best: nurture, offer simple hope and love that everything would be

set right. She knew that softness and quiet were the right kind of medicine for now; she always knew the right kind of medicine.

Rather than ask to speak to Tim, I asked if it would be *wise* for me to speak to him, worried that my voice, my questions, might set him off even more. That's another thing I'll remember for the rest of my life: asking if it would be *wise* to speak to my twin brother, the person who had been by my side from the moment of conception onward. Not if I could speak to him, but if it would be wise.

Why I asked that I'll never know, but Reta and I decided that, for now, it was best—it was *wise*—that I not speak to him. Something shifted then; before, I could demand anything of, or from, my brother. Now, the rules were different. We were no longer the same person. Something had happened to him that had not happened to me; the egg that divided when we were conceived had divided once again.

As Reta told me about my father's bringing Tim home the night before, I visualized the bedroom Tim and I had shared from the fourth grade on, when new green carpet and black-and-white checked bedspreads turned what had been a den into our bedroom, and signaled that a new mother had come into our lives, that our family had begun again after our mother's death, whether we wanted it to or not. I imagined that same bedroom now draped with thinning white gauze, as if it were a malaria ward in the jungle, and Reta was its Lady of Mercy. She would have swathed Tim's head in bandages if that had been called for; his head is what hurt.

I remembered even further back, when Tim's head had been swathed for the very first time, at my hands.

It happened early one Sunday morning, when Tim and I were in the first grade. We were alone in the den, the room that would later become our bedroom, when Reta came into our lives. We had watched an old rerun of Lawrence Welk on TV the night before and were imitating the dance moves of Bobby Burgess and his dancing partner, Sissy something. Strange I can remember Bobby's last name, but Sissy was only that. I was Sissy, in more ways than one, wearing one of our mother's long, filmy nightgowns, in imitation of the real Sissy's elegant ballgown, and Tim was twirling me around.

The music changed and I decided to twirl *him* but swung him into a sharp corner of the couch instead. Not sharp because it was supposed to be, a part of the design, but sharp because the upholstery had worn away, leaving an exposed wooden edge. Worn away, exposed, and unfixed, like so much in our family. There was a three-inch gash across Tim's skull, on the right side.

Blood gushed everywhere, but before I could help him, I had to get out of the nightgown, which would get me into far more trouble than splitting my little brother's head open. I hid the nightgown somewhere, then let loose with a blood-curdling scream.

My little brother, waiting for me to hide my stolen finery, before I could save his life.

As usual with emergencies in our house, our father wasn't there. Sunday morning, the day of rest, and he was taking "inventory" at work—the excuse he'd trot out whenever he'd been up drinking all night, or whoring with some waitress.

As I held Tim's head in my lap in the front seat of the car and pressed a towel to it, our mother drove us to the emergency room at the hospital.

The same hospital whose basement we were supposed to go to in the event of a nuclear attack, a makeshift fallout shelter.

The same hospital she had driven us to after our car wreck at summer swimming lessons.

The same hospital she had taken me to when I broke my arm jumping across the ditch at the end of our block.

We knew that route well.

At the hospital, outside the emergency room, I barricaded myself inside a phone booth and screamed that I had killed my brother.

I looked directly into the operating room and saw his little body covered completely over by a white sheet, except for a single hole that had been cut out, to let them sew up his head.

Covered with a sheet, like a dead person.

I wouldn't let anyone open the phone booth door to get me, as I continued screaming that he was dead, and that I had killed him.

Tim had to wear a white skull covering on his head for weeks; friends signed it, as they would a cast covering a broken limb. I signed it first, as he had signed the cast on my broken arm.

His head, covered by a jumble of words, trying to escape; me, barricaded in a phone booth.

∼

Somebody banged on the booth from the outside, gave me the finger, and only then did I release my grip on the phone and leave, realizing I was twenty-one years old, with a twin brother who had just had a nervous breakdown.

I went to Tim's room, just down the hall. It was unlocked; I let myself in. I was so used to the mess inside that my eyes could immediately zero in on anything new.

And there was something new: a sheaf of pages from a yellow legal pad, ripped from their binding and stuck between the pages of a book.

I went closer: the book was *Two Years Before the Mast,* the novel he'd been reading for Jim Gray's Literature of the Sea course.

I went closer still and opened the book to the pages stuck inside, almost afraid of what I would find.

I was right to be afraid.

On the top was written, "The History of Swimming, Part Two: The Kingdom of Fish."

This is what covered those pages, Tim's familiar handwriting, grown loopy with the race to get it all down before it was too late:

It didn't matter whether he went to bed with the girl or not. What mattered was the beauty of the possibility. Physical attractions had never come easily to him. He wasn't particularly afraid of them, nor did he seek to avoid them. They just didn't happen to him very often. But that day, on the rock in the heat, the attraction was strong, though lazy and leisurely, like he felt after a morning of swimming in a clear, cool current. The leisure was the best part of knowing Carrie. She was often the first person he saw in the morning at the barn. There was something pleasing in the pace of those early-morning meetings. Sometimes in the middle of a good-morning kiss, she would fall gently back to sleep on his shoulders. It was that slow, easy intimacy that made him love her as he did.

On those mornings, they shared with each other what they had dreamed the night before. She told him once, in the middle of the summer, that she had dreamed of having a baby. Furthermore, she told him that girls often had this singular dream in the early days of knowing and beginning to love a new boy. Tim had never heard this and felt proud to be shown a glimpse of this strange, new kingdom.

He closed his eyes and stretched back out across the rock. The heat felt good to him and the backs of his legs burned from his best days on the river. Heat fell like sleep and there was nothing to do but remember.

The summer had given him back a simpler mind and he rarely thought of the world of books.

He turned, instead, to the kingdom of fish, and a game he used to play after rehearsal, when he got in the water and spread his arms and legs out until he could see his own shadow, floating alongside him. When he dived deep into a cool place, the shadow flickered like a school of fish along the moss beds at the bottom. Sometimes, he'd stay so quiet, minnows swam right up next to him.

It was easy there.

Carrie sighed, as if she had just had the same, silent memory, and spoke first. "I dread going back to school. We'll get crazed and forget we ever sat on this rock. Ever swam in a river."

They smiled, with just the smallest feeling that could be called the beginning of regret, then walked down the hill toward the barn. At the door, they smiled again, half sadly, exiles from the kingdom.

She turned away from him and began tracing pictures in the dust: cactus, rocks, trees. On top of the rocks, she drew a boy and a girl and a huge bottle of wine.

"White or red?" he asked.

"White. I think we'll have fish for dinner." With that, she drew a fish swimming out of the mouth of the bottle.

The wind lifted and eddied old leaves into the sky. At last, the clouds broke in the west. In a moment, before the first rain, they finished the wine by erasing the etching in the dust.

"It will be cooler now."

"Your hands are brown."

"We look like we've been somewhere, Powers. And through something."

The first rains did fall, washing the face of the barn. For the first time, they saw a great stone heart, carved in the 1930s, that had been covered by dust the whole time they had been there.

They marveled at it, then Tim's hand met Carrie's and rested in the etching of a tree.

"Is there any left?"

It was a question about the wine, but it summed up the whole summer. Is there any left?

Is there any left?

There was no question that Carrie and Tim were back, and it was probably on that evening that their real sense of loss began.

Tim never knew where to focus his eyes when Carrie was with Neal. He liked Neal far too much to ignore him, or, even worse, patronize him. But Tim felt funny about getting to know him for Carrie's sake alone.

Carrie squeezed Neal's hand so tightly that his knuckles turned white. "What was that for?" he asked, taking his hand back.

"I just wanted to be sure of something. Can we leave now?"

"Sure. I'll get our coats." When Neal went upstairs to find the coats, Carrie went into the kitchen, where she found Tim drinking wine by the sink.

"I hoped you'd be here tonight," he said.

"You didn't think I'd forget, did you?"

"I wasn't sure," he answered, realizing after he said it that he had sounded mean, though he had not intended to. "No," he said, hoping to amend his awkwardness. "I take that back. I never had any doubts you'd be here. I've been looking forward all day to seeing you."

"I'm glad. What have you been doing in here all night?"

"Leaning a lot. Pretending I was a young man of letters again," he said, trying to be as easy with her as he had been during the summer.

"I like the patches on your jacket. They're nice."

By now both wondered which one of them would ask the next question. She knew, without him telling her, that the time back at school had worn away some of his confidence. He knew that she didn't know what to say about Neal.

And he didn't know what to say about Gil.

Without speaking, each conjured in the eyes of the other an image from that last day on the rock. Each traced, as Carrie had done in the sand that day, a tree, a river, or a fish, in the other's face.

Half sad, half in love with the pictures he saw, Tim spoke first. "Have you been trying out for plays?"

"Yeah. And I still don't get parts."

"Do you bitch a lot?"

"More than people are willing to hear," she said, smiling with the knowledge that neither of them had anything to lose. "Do you still talk Keats at lunch?"

"To anyone who'll listen. 'Pass the salt, please, and by the way, are Truth and Beauty REALLY all you need to know on Earth?' Someday they're going to lock me up with a bunch of crazy old women who think they're the Brontë sisters."

"Well, Powers, I don't know who set the traps, but we sure as hell fell for them."

Reaching for his glass and pouring another for Carrie, Tim proposed a toast: "To inmates."

"To inmates," she echoed, clinking her glass to the edge of his.

The next thing Tim said, coming out of the blue, like a fish out of the mouth of a wine bottle, surprised them both. "I like Neal."

"Good. Maybe you can play baseball together, or better yet, we could fix you up with a really nice girl and double date for the senior prom. That would be keen, Old Bean," she laughed, beating him at his own game. "Silly boy."

"And I like Gil," she added, too fast.

"No, you don't. But that's okay. Nobody does. Except me."

He felt the need to defend why he liked someone no one else did.

"Have you ever seen him smoke?"

"Uh . . . I don't think so," she said, wondering where this was going.

"That's why I came in here, at first. To see him smoke. He was here. He smokes better than anyone I know. I know I shouldn't like that, but . . . he does it so well. Ask any of those people out there what they remember about tonight, and they'll say 'Gil, smoking.' The cloud of haze around him. It's like a halo. And when the smoke clears, he's smiling . . . like he's just seen a miracle."

Carrie started to say something—such a recital demanded a response— but at that moment, the record in the next room skipped.

The conversants were too drunk to notice.

A tall, attractive girl by the record player worried out loud about her future. "But I don't want graduate school yet," she said, wondering what mystical experience could possibly take its place.

A blond boy in one corner told sad stories about his family.

In the opposite corner, a young boy who had had too much to drink began telling the details of a homosexual affair he had during the summer. "It was soooooooo painful, I can just now begin to talk about it," he said, waving his cigarette back and forth like Bette Davis.

"Oh, God," yelled someone across the room, "I've seen this movie before."

Is there any left?

Is there any left?

Is there any left?

That one was underlined, three times.

The paper had been torn through, he had done it so hard.

Clearly, the answer was no.

There was nothing left.

It was the story of Tim's summer, and the fall that had just come crashing down after it.

It was the story with which Tim went "swimming every night for a new adventure in space."

I took the pages—it would be obscene to leave them there, like leaving a dead body uncovered—and made my way out of his room, slightly east of Eden.

⌇

"Did you fuck him?"

Carrie was in her dorm room, just waking up. She grabbed for her cigarettes as well as her cat's-eye glasses, which she wore to be able to see to put her contacts in.

"Good morning to you, too. Excuse me?"

"Tim. Did you fuck him last summer? Is that why he went crazy last night?"

"What?"

It would have been funny if it hadn't been so awful: a girl with sleep in her eyes, cat's-eye glasses, a cig hanging from her mouth, and me, hopped up with my questions and my panic.

"My *brother*. He had a nervous breakdown last night. I think it's because he couldn't decide whether or not to fuck you last summer."

She opened her mouth; nothing came out but smoke. She choked on it.

"Tim's gone."

Carrie found her voice. "What happened?"

"I don't know. Last night. While we were at rehearsal. He freaked out and went home. Charlott called my dad to come get him."

Carrie stubbed out her cigarette.

"Come to the bathroom with me."

She grabbed her robe, a tawdry silk kimono she had snagged from a production of *Cabaret*—we were big on stealing our costumes—

and left. She opened the bathroom door down the hall and yelled, "Man alert."

Hardly, but that was beside the point.

One or two girls scurried out; we had the place to ourselves.

She went to the window ledge and grabbed the bathroom kit she kept there, digging through it for her contacts, and started sticking them in, a harder task than usual.

There was no preamble.

"We didn't fuck last summer. I think he wanted to—I did—but he was afraid. I don't know. We loved each other, I know that much. But the only time he'd say he loved me was when he was drunk. I think he was in love with Gil, too. I don't know what happened with them. He came to visit a few times; Tim'd always get depressed after that. Is Tim gay? I don't know. That's as much as I can tell you."

"Jesus, what happened last summer?" I asked, then answered, my own question, at least in my head. His heart split in two, that's what happened. He couldn't save Sarah from rape, so he moved on to Carrie. He couldn't save her from falling in love with a gay boy, as Michael Ditmore had already known. And he couldn't save himself, from being hurt by Gil.

Carrie's second contact was now in. She could see. "Forget last summer. What happened last night?"

"He couldn't stop crying. He went to Charlott's room and had her call our dad to come get him. Hink called me this morning; he thought I already knew. I tried to call him, call Tim, but Reta said he didn't want to talk to me. Why didn't he tell me? Why didn't he try to find me? Tell me. . . ." I stopped, knowing Carrie couldn't answer my questions. I don't even know if they were questions; they were just white noise, stuck in my head.

"You poor baby." Carrie hugged me, but she couldn't forget last

summer, not yet. "He changed last summer. The river . . . it changed things. It made him happy."

"Tell me about it."

"Last summer?"

"The river."

"Talking about some silly river's not gonna do much good when he's home and hallucinating."

"Please. I need to see it."

She closed her eyes; the river had cast a spell on her, too. "It's all these colors at once, blue and silver and green, and when he swam there, his hair was gold. I used to hide in the grass just to watch him. I've never seen anything more beautiful."

⌇

I decided to go eat to calm myself down.

Amazingly, one of the first people I saw in the dining hall, as if I had willed her into being there, was Charlott, the last person who had seen my brother. I made a beeline and reached out to her, no words, just as those teachers pouring into our house had reached out to Porky, no words, after our mother's death.

Charlott was the strong one. She wouldn't cry.

Or maybe she already had.

"What happened?"

"What's your truth?" she asked, instead of answering. It was as if she'd been expecting me, just like Reta.

"What?"

"What's your truth? What's the one thing you know is true?"

It was a typical Charlott question: indirect, enigmatic, like "How many pieces of bubble gum can I chew?"

Charlott: indirect, enigmatic, mercurial. She once bought me a beautiful washcloth, just because she loved its emerald green color. She introduced us to caviar, because it was "sophisticated," even though we all hated the taste of it but pretended not to. In New York, where she now lives, she bought me an antique enameled pink teacup, to celebrate my new job. Tim loved her without loving her, the way he did Carrie or Sarah. That's why he could ask her to save him, and call our father.

"What's your truth? Tell me."

I knew what she wanted. I knew this was her way of telling me what had happened to Tim.

"Tim," I said.

It didn't take me a second to say it, or know it.

"That's right. Tim."

She didn't say "He's going to be alright"; she didn't say "He loves you" or "You were the last person he asked about," even though that's the thing I most wanted her to say.

She just said he was my truth and held out a scrap of paper. On it Tim had scrawled our phone number in McKinney, the number that brought our father to Tim's rescue. She'd called him, then waited with Tim at his dorm for our dad to pick him up.

"Did he at least ask where I was? Say he wanted to find me?"

We had started with the truth, and she couldn't start lying to me now.

"No."

CHAPTER SEVEN

N^{o.}
    No.

Nononononon. . . .

"Your brother. . . ."

"JESUS. . . ."

". . . writes a damn good. . . ."

". . . you scared me. . . ."

". . . letter. Wish he'd send *me* one. I never get letters."

I jumped, jolted back into the present by my skinny friend Stan. He'd materialized out of the darkness, my backpack in hand like a peace offering.

"Jesus. How'd you know I was here?"

"I looked everywhere else. I had to give you back your letters. Plus I come here all the time. Thought you might, too."

"Here" was somewhere I used to go when I was a student: the bleachers out by the football field. Ironic that I'd barely ever gone to a football game there, but I loved the mystery after the game, the trampled grass and the crisp air, the darkness that high up, the fantasy of meeting up with a lonely, sensitive football jock looking for love. (It never happened. I guess that's why they call it a fantasy.) From the top row of seats, you had a 360-degree view of the entire campus, of Sherman, of the world. Tim had told me he used to come here as well, but he wasn't here now, and he hadn't been anywhere in Baker Hall, the closest dorm, where Tim and I had both lived, in separate rooms.

I'd gone there after my swimming pool fight with Stan. The main doors had combination locks on them, but a student held one open for me. It was surprisingly easy to get into; it continually amazed me how easy it was to get into *any* building on campus. No wonder they had break-ins.

No wonder people got raped.

I'd wandered up to Tim's second-floor dorm room, the one he had thrown an alarm clock out of, just to hear the sound of glass breaking, when he had his breakdown. But it was one of the few things that *was* locked; I couldn't get in, to look for my brother there. After I took a little tour of duty—past the three different dorm rooms I'd had, past the phone booth where I got the news of Tim's breakdown—I headed out to the stadium for a final good-bye. It was near the parking lot where I'd stowed my rental car, close enough for a quick getaway. Since it looked as if no fantasy jock was going to show up to offer me his bed for the night, I'd grab a cheap motel room and head back early in the morning, to the reality of my

brother being missing, the reality that no matter what I'd called my trip to Sherman, I'd run away from looking for him. It was like closing my eyes whenever I had a near-miss accident driving on the highway; I thought if I couldn't see it, it wouldn't happen.

If I didn't *see* Tim missing, he *wasn't* missing.

And all I'd given up was one day, one crazy, jam-packed day when I'd begun to experience life as a "twinless twin," as if twenty-eight years of history had never even existed.

No brother, no fantasy jock, just little bobble-headed Stan, reminding me I was breathing; and I was sitting there, and my heart was still pumping in the present, not just the past, and life was really going on, on a cool October night.

For once, I would apologize first.

"Listen, I'm sorry I snapped—"

"Don't worry, I understand."

"How could you? Some stranger goes off on you for no reason."

"And sometimes I wake up mean. I get it. No big whoop."

All was forgiven, so easily.

Oh Youth and Beauty. . . .

"The letters. . . ." Crunched down next to me, he opened the backpack and took out a handful, then paused, lost in his own memories of a stranger's letters.

"I've never read anything more beautiful. They should teach a class here on 'em."

"Yeah, 'Warning Signs of Going Nuts 101.' Mandatory, like P.E."

"I was never very good at P.E., were you?"

"Disaster."

"My legs were so skinny in those shorts. Dodgeball. Ugh. And taking showers with everybody. . . ."

We both paused, lost in another set of memories. The night

sky—the blackest of black canopies, stars so bright they seemed like ice crystals—did that to you.

We could see our breath.

"Thanks for bringing them back. I didn't really mean to throw them at you. They might be all I have left of him. That sounded melodramatic, didn't it? I'd've tracked you down somehow, gotten them before I left. Thanks for bringing them back," I said, standing up, looking out over the campus.

"This is what he saw, the night he went crazy. I think it must be close to that anniversary, when it happened. Somewhere around now, 'round Halloween. Seven years ago. He started yelling and crying and went crazy. Or maybe he'd already gone. He was just making the announcement."

A figure just like me, same shape, same soft Texas accent, opening his dorm room window and yelling out, except we were too nervous. He didn't yell; I knew that much. He wanted to, he tried, but it just came out a whisper. I knew that much without having been there. People talked about it in the days afterward; everyone had heard by then, but no one actually *heard*, heard him make noise, heard the things he had said.

Just as I thought, it was a whimper, not a bang.

"I really did think he might have come back here, you know? Get some crazy idea in his head, come back to the past. Me, too. Go a little crazy, run away from the present, come back to the past. But it was stupid. He's not here, or he'd show himself. What's the point of hiding if nobody finds you? What's the point of cutting your wrist if there's nobody to get back at and let them *know* you're getting back at them?"

This kid, the night air, was bringing out all the truth in me, that I didn't have anybody else to tell, now that Tim was gone.

"Maybe I just wanted to run away from really looking for him, delay finding out for sure that . . . if . . ."

That he was dead?

I don't know.

"Ugh," I said, shaking it all away, "I've gotta get back home, look for him there. He's not here."

"That's what I came to tell you. I know where he is."

"What?"

Stan, who'd been quiet for so long, was now almost busting with pride at his discovery. "Mo Ranch. The Guadalupe River. That's where he is. I figured it out from the letters. It's six hours, we take turns driving, we get there before sun up. Road Trip! We'll stop for snacks."

I laughed, even though it wasn't funny.

"You've gone as crazy as I have."

"I'm serious. I think that's where he is. It's all he talks about in the letters. It's like they're clues, they're all there. I know clues. I read every Nancy Drew there was. Twice." He looked at me, almost begging. "You sleep. I'll drive. We'll stop at Dairy Queens and get iced tea."

No.

The insanity had to stop somewhere.

After everything else I'd done today, I was not about to get in a car with some kid who wanted to be Stanley Kowalski and drive all night long. One wild-goose trip per lifetime was enough.

It's like he read my mind.

"Please. Just . . . you can't get back to New York tonight. What else are ya gonna do? Sleep? Wait around? I've got this weird feeling about this. It's where *I'd* go, if I was him."

Was it really that crazy? Mo Ranch is probably where I should

have gone in the first place. It's where he'd fallen in love with both a girl and a boy and didn't know what to do about it. It's where he'd really had the nervous breakdown; the few months back at Austin College were just for show, the time it took for the "disease" to spread through his system.

Okay, I could rationalize that part of it, a trip to Mo Ranch. I'd always wanted to see it; now I could, with or without my brother. It would be the road trip I'd never taken in college, that my friends and I had always weenied out on at the last minute, after the initial rush to hop in a car and go to New Orleans for Mardi Gras. It would be like reliving my past, only fixing it, making it better.

But none of those would-be trips involved a twenty-year-old kid I had just met, that I'd so easily let in on the mysteries and intimacies of twins, of breakdowns, of best friends who got hurt. Where did Stan fit into this: what did *he* want? Earlier, at dinner, it was perfectly innocent: he'd said he really needed help figuring out what to do when he graduated. Should he go to grad school, or straight to New York? Could he really make it as an actor? How hard was it to find an apartment there? What kinds of jobs could you get? How much did it cost to live, if his parents would even let him go there. All the practical, how-to stuff I wish somebody had answered for me when I first moved there.

All well and good, if more appropriate for dinner conversation, or a college seminar with a bunch of other students, than suitable for an all-night drive, alone, in the dark.

Maybe he didn't know what he really wanted from me any more than I knew what I wanted from him. Was he really just somebody to drive, to talk to, to keep me awake? An aspiring actor, a captive, willing audience for six hours? Or was there something else I was unwilling, or too uncomfortable, to admit? Something like this had

been my fantasy in college: an older man to seduce, or be seduced by. He had to be gay, even though he hadn't said, and I hadn't asked. He *was* cute. I'd followed him into a swimming pool to see him in a bathing suit.

I closed my eyes, so I wouldn't see it.

If I didn't see it, it wasn't there.

I'm not even sure what "it" was.

"You win. What do we do now?"

"We go to the river."

CHAPTER EIGHT

This is so much fun! I've never gone on a Road Trip before!"
There's nothing like an excited child, bouncing up and down
in a car, to get your adrenaline going, especially on a dark stretch of
highway, near midnight on a Saturday. An excited child, but a sad,
lonely one, I thought: what else was he doing with a stranger on an
all-night "road trip"? Didn't he have friends, to do other things with
on a Saturday night? I did, when I was in college. For all my thoughts
about how much he was like me, or like what I had been in college,
we were different in that respect: I always had plenty of friends to do
things with, no matter how alienated I pretended to be. I didn't want
to think about how lonely he seemed; right now, I didn't have the
extra emotion to spare, to get wrapped up in the sadness of a sensitive kid, almost throwing himself at a stranger. What did he want

from me? Just the trip? A set of wheels, back to the place he'd spent the summer as part of the Austin College Acting Troupe at Mo Ranch?

I was too confused about myself right now to try to figure out what was going on in his head.

But would I have hopped in a car with a stranger, even with the "safe" credentials of an alum, for this weird sort of joyride?

I'd had sex with strangers; how could this be any more risky?

Yes, if I'd been Stanley, a curious little college actor, and he me, a successful alumni, I probably would have gotten in the car, too.

"Tell me when you get hungry. I'll pull into a Mickey D's for food. And iced tea," the Stanley said. "I promised."

We were already about an hour away from Sherman, driving past McKinney, where I was born. We could see it off to the side, in the distance, a sprinkle of lights from the homes of the eighteen thousand or so small-town people who lived there.

Home.

We would drive past it all those years ago at just about this same time, making our Saturday night mad dash from Sherman to the gay bars in Dallas, to go dancing. My boyfriend Selmore and I were out, but the rest of the drama group, shoehorned into one of our cars, were just along for the ride, "just to dance." There was something almost illicit about passing so close to our house on our way to the bars, our home just a few blocks over from the giant water tower and highway, in one of the developments that had been built on the outskirts of the town, ringed by woods and wilderness and long stretches of flat Texas highways and the brand-name restaurants that came closest to a "nice place to eat" in town.

My parents would have gone to sleep hours ago, but there was no thought of stopping there and waking them up. That's the one thing

I knew—that Tim would never have gone back there. Just as "Tim" was the one truth I had been able to cough up for Charlott, "not gone home" was the only other truth I knew right now. He wouldn't be there. He hated being there when he left school, even though he hated school then, too, and he hated being there after he graduated. He wouldn't be there.

Twins just know.

We drove past McKinney, as I remembered driving there three days after Tim's breakdown . . . the soonest Reta had deemed it was "wise."

Tim was in the bedroom we had shared as children, the bedroom we still shared on vacations home from college. I was the by-invitation-only guest; a guest, in the very room where we had shared so many excited, scared, middle-of-the-night talks, back when I innocently told him (and he admonished me) of my grade-school love for any number of boys: Bobby Talkington, who played John to my Michael in a community theater production of *Peter Pan;* Lynn Raines, who stuck mirrors on the tips of his shoes to look up girls' dresses; Rocky Bailey, whose father hit him so hard one day that he came to school with the imprint of a hand on his cheek.

But on that first postbreakdown visit, we didn't talk about boys, or love—or maybe we *were* talking about those things, just under a different name—but about what had happened.

And, as he would do for years to come, he just smiled, that smile of other places and other rooms that couldn't, or wouldn't, be shared, but he didn't give me any answers.

"What happened?"

He just smiled.

A smile that said you aren't smart enough to understand.

He only wanted to know what our friends thought about his absence; he certainly wanted them to know he was gone, that he'd had a "nervous breakdown." It was an odd kind of curiosity, tinged with arrogance. For some reason, the tag to a Bible verse or church song I couldn't quite place came to mind: "They are weak, but I am strong."

Yes, Jesus loves me.

Yes, that was it.

The Bible tells me so.

With no answers forthcoming, only silence—silence delivered with a smile—my eyes darted around the room I used to know so well, the brother I used to know so well, and landed on the souvenirs of childhood Tim had tucked away in a cubbyhole on his bed stand: *The Gospel According to Peanuts,* a ceramic bust of Beethoven won in a choir contest, a plastic photo cube stuffed with pictures of our mother (that was a new addition), an atomizer from a childhood bout of asthma, a bottle of Valium.

That was new, too, prescribed by Dr. Wilson, our family doctor who'd been having unofficial visits with Tim, not really "therapy." (Dr. Wilson had been a twin, his handsome brother killed in a car accident; he knew.) But Tim didn't want to take the Valium, because it made him too "out of control."

Tim went to the bathroom, and I put the atomizer in my mouth and squirted, just as I had done as a child, wanting to share his illness. That gush of cold air, the fresh metallic taste; I wondered if this was medicine that had been trapped inside for fifteen years, or newly prescribed, along with the Valium. What else had been trapped inside for fifteen years?

The atomizer made me think back to one of the first times I had been cast in the role of Tim's savior, during his quick and mysterious bout of asthma that had gone as quickly as it had come. I remembered playing at the end of our prefab block, the opposite end from the ravine in which I had broken my arm. He began having an asthma attack, gasping and wheezing for breath, and I pushed him down into our little red wagon to race him home, to his atomizer. I pulled the wagon with all my eight-year-old might, yelling into the wind against me to "just hold on" as he coughed and coughed in the wagon. "Just hold on," I said, but he's going to die, I thought. Porky would die, Tim would die, our mother had already died. It was a life-or-death mission, but one bizarre thought came to me as I ran half a block: that somewhere in these two rows of houses on opposite sides of the street was another house just like ours. The block was made up of exactly seven ground plans, each house repeating every seventh. If I could just take the time to count them down as I flew like the wind to our own house, maybe there would also be an atomizer in the house that was the duplicate of ours.

But I finally got Tim home, so out of breath myself that I took a whiff of the atomizer, and he could breathe again, and so could I.

And soon, the asthma was gone.

But this time, along with a whiff from the old atomizer, I took some of the Valium. If one Powers twin couldn't get any use out of it, the other one could.

Waste not, want not.

When Tim came back from the bathroom, I said I had to go.

I just wanted to get away, so I could take the drug and forget my brother, who wouldn't answer any of my questions.

Tim came outside with me, where David and Selmore were nervously waiting in David's car, on our way to Saturday night dancing

in Dallas. (Was nothing sacred? Going dancing while my brother was going crazy?) Tim bid us good-bye, have fun, as I had done so often in high school when he went off without me.

Before we left, he whispered to me he didn't know when he'd be coming back to school and stuck a handful of pages in my hands.

For the first time, there was an answer of sorts in his eyes, almost an apology, as our hands touched for that brief second.

I read the pages to myself in the backseat, street lamps flashing by on either side of the car my only illumination, as we escaped my crazy twin brother for a gay bar in Dallas. The pages held Tim's answer about what had happened, only they were addressed to someone else, not me. He'd written the letter to his best friend Roy, in the class behind us, whom we'd first met during that calamitous *Rosencrantz and Guildenstern Are Dead.*

Once again, I'd been denied.

Once again, if we couldn't kill ourselves, or someone else, we'd just write about it.

Dear Roy,

It came as a surprise to some (but probably not all) when Tim Powers, Austin College Senior, climbed to the top of the chapel and began to denounce the college in the manner of an Old Testament prophet. Girding his loins, Powers began:

"Where is the true spirit of liberal arts?

"Is this school here only for the purpose of cloning little Berry Spears, the model frat boy, to take over the graduate schools of the world?

"Why does George Sipper, head of college dining services, grow fat and contented, while the masses are starved and unhappy? Why are the ugly turned away from second helpings while the attractive and muscled take all they want?

"Why does Tom Miller, campus minister, turn the Word of God into an Abbott and Costello routine?"

At the end of his oracle, after screaming from the top of the building, Powers walked sadly to Clyce Hall to find his friend Charlott. "Please, Charlott, call my father and tell him to come get me. Here's the number. Tell them all I've gone swimming. Again."

Before leaving, Powers threw his alarm clock out his dorm window and collected his dirty clothes in a trash bag. Powers's father, a gentle man from Vermont, found Tim, called Precious by his friends, crumpled on the steps of Baker Hall, by his bag of dirty clothes.

"Take me home," said Tim.

Oh, Precious Baby, at least part of that story is true. (Which parts, I'm not even sure.) I have been home for just a few days now, but already I feel alive and rested. Yes, Precious, the two can exist together. And home is beautiful: remember the see-through shelf paper on the windows that looks like Chartres Cathedral?

I think I am taking what they call a "leave of absence." You can call it a leave of absence, or you can call it a "fried egg." Either way, I need one badly.

The days before I left were very intense. All of a sudden, though none of these things happen by accident, I grew tired of dull and listless classes. I started telling the truth as I saw it. My Prophets class was wonderful; everyone started contributing and we were getting a very vivid picture of Amos and his situation.

I wanted to be a prophet.

I loved Literature of the Sea, but then, you know I've always loved things about the sea. Jim Gray is wonderful. He has a way of looking very gently at someone and they begin to tell the truth. He reminded me of me in twenty years, if only I can be that lucky. He's one of the most responsible professors I've ever had.

I started asking silly questions in biology to deflate a bully who monopolized Dr. McCarley's time.

Well, to make a long story a little shorter, everything was going well with academics. I started reading books about children's development in my spare time; did I have any spare time, I now ask? I read about children like we were, like I used to be, and was very happy.

The morning you left for England, I stayed up all night to work on a paper on Two Years Before the Mast, the story of a boy who left Harvard in 1830 to find himself at sea. (I'm not sure I wrote exactly what Jim Gray was looking for, but I wrote what I needed to. And isn't that what's most important about a liberal arts education?) I wrote until around seven-thirty that morning, then looked out my dorm room window at the rising sun of a beautiful morning and said a prayer for you. A very real prayer.

I had not slept in several nights, too much on my mind. That morning, I dressed for the fun of it: a pretty blue shirt with a cellular print (like something you'd seen in a petri dish, or under a microscope), my khaki pants, and a nice brown vest. My friends said I looked like Huckleberry Finn.

"Where ya' goin', Huck?" asked Mark Thompson.

"You'll know when I do," I answered.

That afternoon, I began to think about injustice and started crying in the library. When I calmed down, I went to work at the post office ten minutes early. The day was windy, and my hair, not to blame the wind, looked as it usually does. Mrs. Shurley, the postmistress, screamed at me to comb my hair before I stepped into the post office. Imagine my working there for two years and not realizing it was holy ground! What's an idiot to do?

Instead of screaming back at her and stuffing aerograms in her mouth, I walked to my room and combed my hair.

You have seen broken men, I am sure.

When I returned and began to work, she rose to the already pleasant occasion to tell me: "I don't know what's wrong with you, but you act like you belong in a trash can. Don't you have any pride in yourself?"

That was a tense moment.

I answered with a small but firm voice: "I do not belong in a trash can, and I have a great deal of pride in myself. In fact, Mrs. Shurley, if more people dressed comfortably, our lives would be happier. Now, I'll begin my campus route."

One of the first people to see me was dear Dr. Hinkle, the Man Who Would Be King. He pulled me aside, emptied his pipe (barely missing my shoes), and said, "Well, you know, Powers, you're up for Phi Beta Kappa, the Society for Sacred Sheep and Goats." (My description, not his.) "But we have this matter of an F in your directed study on the House Un-American Activities Committee with the Martins last spring."

"Well, Dr. Hinkle, I'm sure that is a mistake in the Records Office. Cheryl told me she would send a grade and I'm sure it wasn't an F." Like an idiot salivating for a bone, I went to the Records office and checked the grade. It was an A and I was so happy that I could be in Phi Beta Kappa, with all the other smart boys and girls.

At the end of the day, I had an incredible headache that would not go away.

"I'll go to Slater's and eat. That will calm me down."

Stupid thinking, if I've ever heard it. And I've heard plenty.

I stood in line behind Pierre Filardi. Pierre is cool: a swimmer, a long-distance runner, blue eyes. He asked for a fresh plate of spaghetti.

"No," screamed the angry cafeteria worker. "They ain't no fresh spaghetti!"

Pierre, still swimming, repeated, "Please, may I have some more, ma'am?"

She screamed back, "NO," and told him, "You ain't gettin' any now!"

She then made the mistake of handing some fresh spaghetti to me. I said, "He's the one who asked for it. Why don't you give it to him? He'll be happy. You'll be happy. And all those people standing in line behind us will be happy."

It was not her day to make anybody happy. I got some salad (forgoing the

spaghetti I had so craved before this unfortunate incident) and went back to the Loggia. As unhappy fate would have it, it was Pierre's birthday. I have never seen anyone struggle so hard against being thrown in the fountain. I have never been more afraid of watching a boy fall through plate glass. Before they took him outside, Pierre looked directly into my eyes and screamed: "THIS IS WHAT HAPPENS WHEN THERE IS NO FRESH SPAGHETTI!"

I started crying, yelled for a while (although I don't think anyone heard me), then went to Charlott. You know the rest, as, I'm sure, does the rest of the campus. (Did the whispers reach you all the way in England?)

I am very happy now. I will probably not go back until January. There's nothing wrong now but anger. McKinney is really beautiful in the fall, my favorite time of year. I am confused now but think the rest will do me good. The "Theme from Valley of the Dolls," if you get my drift.

I'll be looking at the moon, but I'll be seeing you.

The Ghost of Young Tim

"You have seen broken men, I am sure," he had written.

I would never forget the line, because I had just seen one—a broken man.

I had just become one, reading that letter about the biggest event of Tim's life, sent to someone else.

In the weeks while Tim was gone, I continued rehearsing for *The Faust Project*. When I, as Faust, had to look into the gaping jaws of hell—a stupid wooden box with glowing tin-can red eyes and fake fog—I tried, instead, to imagine what Tim had seen the night he went home.

One night in rehearsal, I tried to cut my wrist with a prop knife, to draw the blood that Faust uses to seal his pact with the Devil. (I

would make a pact with whoever answered first, God or the Devil, to make my brother well.) The director ran onstage and snatched the knife out of my hands; I just smiled and said I wanted to see what it felt like.

We finished rehearsal early that night.

On opening night, Sarah came to me in the cool, dark space of the theater as I did my warm-up exercises and gave me the tiniest little Bible that she had sewn into a black velvet drawstring pouch. I pinned it to the underside of my costume, where only I would know it was there. She told me it was to keep me safe as I was forced to flirt with necromancy and the black arts. I looked in her big round eyes, and we both knew we were thinking the same thing: that she wished she had had a little toy Bible sewn into a drawstring pouch on that fateful night, to keep her safe.

Tim came from home to see the opening. He gave me a postcard with a painting of medieval monks on it and wrote on the back, "You have prepared the way for us, Strong Brother." Way to where, he didn't say; I don't think I had done anything for us, except maybe cause his breakdown, by not being there when he needed me. I wanted to make it up to him, make him proud of my masculinity, my ability to swing myself upside down on a rope swing that was part of the set. I held myself there an extra minute for him that night; the cast wondered if I was stuck, if I was about to hurt myself again. I wanted to stay there until my muscles ached and bled for him.

After the performance, Tim told me he was chilled by that scene, that I looked as if I had truly glimpsed Hell.

No, just you, I wanted to say, not unkindly.

As he said good-bye to me that night, still not sure when he would return to school, he rolled down the window of the car he had borrowed from our father and said, "Bye, Faustus," just as Donna

Jean Moore had said at the end of the play, when I was lowered into the flame.

'Bye, Faustus.

'Bye, Tim.

My pact was answered, by the Devil, I think; Tim did come back to school, just before Christmas break. That same week, a girl in the graduate teachers' program went crazy, as if she were trading places with him, a hostage exchange. She ran around campus with her hands painted white, stamping them on sidewalks and trees. I had long worried about plain, lonely girls with an interest in science or education, worried if they would ever find companionship. She was one of them, with pale skin, wire-rimmed glasses, and blouses with tall collars she kept buttoned all the way up to her chin. She had one of those reserved, polite, "good girl" laughs that always seemed on the verge of hysteria, and now she let it tip over, no longer on the verge. With her laugh finally unleashed, she was reported to have laughed her head off as she skipped up and down the main prome-nade of the campus, imprinting the sidewalk with her glistening white hands, a record that she had been there.

Tim cried when he heard what had happened, and he didn't even know her.

She was now his sister.

He seemed to hate everybody who hadn't gone crazy like they had, who hadn't seen the other side.

He came to hate me even more when I wrote an article calling for a "gay lib consciousness-raising" group on campus; he told me I had no right to have done such a thing without his approval. He had been judged guilty by association; someone had written "fag" next to his name on the message board in his dorm lobby.

Tim acted like he hated me; he acted like he hated everybody.

The day we graduated, I swallowed the last Valium from the supply I had stolen from Tim, then went off it cold turkey. I looked, and acted, like a drug addict that semester; trying to get used to hard contact lenses, I went around in a perpetual stoner's daze, my eyes red and glazed over. My mind was the same.

Leaving the campus that afternoon—for the summer, for the rest of our lives—Tim locked the keys in the trunk of the car that would take us away.

I yelled at him, high on the drug that was supposed to have taken away all his pain.

I broke the silence of that reverie.

"I can't believe we're doing this. Going all the way to Mo Ranch, I mean . . . couldn't we just call the police there? Have *them* go out and look for him?"

"And have them think we're crazy?" Stan blurted out, then realized his faux pas. "Sorry," he said.

"No, crazy? That would be my brother."

Tell the truth, Kim: that would be you as well. On the road all day, planes, trains, automobiles, searching high and low for something you know is going to end up. . . .

"He's there, you'll see." Stan said, trying to convince me, trying to convince himself, since he'd initiated this last leg of the journey. "We'll find him . . . it's the only place that's left. Where he went nuts. Where he fell in love."

"Where he learned to swim again," I added, so quietly I wasn't sure he heard me. Had those things happened there to Stan as well, when he'd been part of the Mo Ranch acting troupe last summer?

Is that why he was so eager to go back, to recapture something from his past, same as me?

Stan got me back on track. "C'mon, tell me the whole story. Start to finish. He comes back to AC after the breakdown, you graduate, what happens next, that summer?"

That summer after college, the summer that completely changed the direction of our lives.

"All you need to know is . . ." What? What did he need to know? Everything, and nothing. "I went back to that summer theater in Massachusetts; I fell in love, I moved to New York. Tim stayed home and worked in a nursery."

"He went nuts and they let him work with kids?"

"A *plant* nursery."

"It was a joke. You gotta get a sense of humor."

"Yeah, well, you get my brother, I'll get a sense of humor."

⌒

Well, my Gypsy feet,

Around this time last summer, I had begun my hot dog regimen with more iced tea and D. H. Lawrence than a boy was ever meant to stand. Perhaps a little later in the summer, I stayed awake all night, watched TV and saw my summer float away. I wished I could float away with it. When I returned to school soon afterward, I tried to, but I'm not sure I floated far enough away.

Before the rains, it had been the heat-wave summer. More than a month's worth of days had passed 100 degrees and I felt somewhat brave that I had survived them all. At Mo Ranch, I sat on rocks a lot and watched the earth crack open as it's wont to do in that part of the country. We helped with a

forest fire that almost burned the place down in late July. Everything was dry. The sun looked orange for a week, and shadows and colors took on a different quality because of the fire down the road from us. I was quieter and more still than I have ever been in my life, except as a small child, when we would sneak into Porky's room and read his letters from Mother.

On one of our last days at Mo Ranch, the rains started. Carrie and I discovered there was a great stone heart, carved sometime in the 1930s, over the door of the barn where we lived and worked. The dust of centuries had covered it. The rain washed the dirt away and we saw it for the first time, just days before we left. On the trip back home, Carrie dreamed about Chekhov—something about waiting and loss—and woke up crying.

In the days after we got home, I sat in front of a television set and watched my summer wash away. The rains did not stop. Houses in the Hill Country washed away, two or three people died, hills changed shape under water. The worst flood of several decades began on a single, lovely Sunday afternoon, with a small rain that washed the dust from an old stone heart.

Those are some of the true things about the way a river changed the land around it and a boy who swam there.

At this point, my biggest fear is that I will turn into a fat black woman named BIG VICKI and water ferns for the rest of my life at the nursery (where, for a white male college graduate, I do a pretty convincing imitation of common laborer). During particularly trying times at work, I catch glimpses of Vicki stuffing cookies in her bra. Her immediate supervisor would probably be a svelte young thing, named "Little Debbie," or little debbie, in obvious contrast to the mammoth proportions of the sad, BIG VICKI. But BIG VICKI, even though she is so fat and unpleasant, can see through little debbie's facade:

"Uh, Vicki? Why are all these ferns dead?"

"What ferns?"

"Vicki, take off those movie star sunglasses. No, I won't dance with you. Why are these ferns dead?"

"Botritus got 'em, boss."

"What?"

"It real bad, boss. It get de ferns and make 'em smell like ol' fish guts."

"Vicki, stop crying and tell me what happened."

"Botritus come in de window and get 'em. It wuz terrible. I jest be sittin' around chompin' on dis jelly roll when, all of de sudden, dere wuz de botritus asneakin' through de window, singin' de blues. I screamed, 'You all git out of dere. If de boss ketch you, she gonna kick yo' butts.' An' de botritus jest laugh in my face an' say, 'BOO!' You wanna know what I sez den, boss? Duz you? Duz you?"

"Yes, I duz. . . . I mean, yes, I do."

"I sez, 'I'm gonna get my little silver clippers and cut yo' peaties off."

"Peaties."

"Yeah, peaties," says BIG VICKI, who then turns on little debbie, and reveals what's really in her heart, the heart knowing more than the eyes can see. "Just like I'm gonna cut yours off iffen you don't make things better around here!"

"Oh," says little debbie, "I'm so sorry you have negative feelings about your job, Vicki. Is there anything I can do to make working conditions more pleasant for you, dear?"

"I ain't no dear!" screams BIG VICKI. "An' if you wants to make workin' conditions mo' pleasant, you kin water de ferns by yo' damn self!"

"Alright, Vicki. I'll do what I can, though one day, you may try my patience."

BIG VICKI waddles away, thinking her triumph a major one. Oh, but little debbie did not get where she is by forgetting the insults of fat women. Little by little, BIG VICKI'S plants begin to die.

"WHATCHOU DUN TO MY PLANTS? WOMAN, I AST YOU A QUESTION. ANSWER ME, GIRL."

"Vicki, our records show that profits have dropped drastically since your employment here."

"Dat's a fuckin' lie, itch! BIG VICKI'S plants is de prettiest, healthiest plants here!"

"Vicki, I will not tolerate obscene language from my employees."

"Well then, missy, will you 'tolerate'," cackles BIG VICKI, who always laughs at big words, "a kick in yo' skinny butt?"

"Vicki, you've pushed me too far. Jorge? Adelmo? I need you."

Upon little debbie's crisply issued command, two heavily muscled illegal aliens come forward.

"KILL HER, BOYS!" screams little debbie, at last showing signs of a long-repressed passion.

Adelmo and Jorge, who, in moments, will be turned over to immigration officials by little debbie herself, hack BIG VICKI into little pieces with common garden tools.

Before she dies, BIG VICKI screams, "You gonna pay fo' dis one, slut!"

"Obscenity to the last . . . such a powerful woman . . . how magnificent in her wrath . . . the only one I ever really loved! You set me on fire, BIG VICKI!"

A few months later, all the plants have died, and little debbie has grown dangerously thin.

"One of these days," remarked Cross-Eyed Pete, the maintenance man, "that little gal's just gonna' dry up and blow away."

And one day, she did.

Did you like my little story? Did I go too far, or not far enough? Are you ashamed of me using a phony Negro dialect and drawing on every cheap linguistic trick in the book? Would you like copies for your friends at Williamstown? Do you have any friends? Am I turning into a fat black woman named Big Vicki?

Well, babe. I hope all is going well for you and that you have won the respect and approval of your peer group, back in summer-theater land. I remember it well, although I'm glad I didn't "re-up" at Mo Ranch again

this summer. I needed to do something with people who aren't crazy. (Although I keep having the feeling I left something behind there and must return to find it.)

In an effort to keep myself from really turning into BIG VICKI, I have decided to apply for VISTA, and be a little Volunteer in Service to America . . . with a preference for placement in the Boston area. (No reason I should be stuck in the sticks while serving!) Tomorrow, I send off my completed application. It looks like the next stop will involve much red tape and my invocation of that age-old virtue, Patience. And what can we do with those age-old virtues? ROAST 'EM!! HEH!! HEH!! HEH!!

Carrie called this afternoon; she seems sort of bored and disappointed with the new Mo Ranch crowd. I don't think I would be, but that's a road not taken, isn't it? I hope to visit them in late July. I will bathe in the river and shine in the sun, minus some of last summer's smoky melancholy, and try to figure out how to be a writer. Maybe these letters are a start. And when I am not there, I will sit on a cool porch somewhere and speak the truth gently, with the people I love, like you.

Tim

⌒

"See, he said it, right there. 'I *hope to visit.*' And that other place he says it," Stan flipped back through the letters, "'Although I keep having the feeling I left something behind there and must return to find it.' I rest my case."

He drew an exclamation point in the air with his forefinger.

I drew one back and thumped him on the side of the head with it, like Porky used to do when we misbehaved.

"That's one letter, one *sentence*—"

"Two," he interrupted.

"*Two* then, out of . . . how many? And it was, what, seven years ago? He went a million other places . . . Louisville, New York. Why not hide out there? You up to driving to Kentucky?"

Stan—suddenly the expert on my twin brother—wouldn't be deterred. "You just gotta know what to look for. Pay attention to what's important, and ignore the rest. So there."

Another exclamation point, drawn in the air.

I had never heard life summed up better, and from a kid. Pay attention to what's important, and ignore the rest. Maybe that was my problem: I had done them both, and at the same time: paid attention to everything, *ignored* everything.

For all my talk about hate . . . now, at least . . . Tim and I had loved each other back then. We were all we had, clutching each other as desperately at age twenty-one as we had in the womb. Those letters testified to that love; our anger from our last semester in college had mysteriously come and gone, or at least gone into hibernation.

I would never again, until almost five years later, see Tim for any period longer than a week or so at Christmas, or on a few other scattered visits. The letters that survived that fall are the only reminders I have of the greatest period of transition in our lives, when I fell in love with Jess at Williamstown, and moved to New York to live with him, and Tim stayed in McKinney, trying to figure out a future. I had Tim box up my things and ship them to New York, and say my hellos and good-byes for me. It was the time we had both known would come one day: when our paths would diverge, whether in a yellow wood or elsewhere, and take us separately into the future.

In the Big Apple, I wouldn't be a star anymore, getting awards at honors convocations, getting leads in plays, but selling subscriptions to *TV Guide.*

"Remember, Kim," the interviewer earnestly told me, "energy and personality, that's what makes a sale."

"Yes, sir, I'll do my best."

To hang on to the past those first few months in New York, I bought books I had read and loved as a child—*A Wrinkle in Time, From the Mixed-Up Files of Mrs. Basil E. Frankweiler*—and read them to Jess, as my fourth-grade teacher had done, my little head resting on my desk after lunch.

I read books from my childhood, when I didn't even know how to use the subway.

Read books about childhood, just as Tim had before his breakdown.

⌒

Dear Kim,

In the midst of all these witty letters and urbane telephone calls, I keep forgetting to tell you how much I miss you. Oh, I do.

Work ends on Sunday, and I'm facing this last week with high hopes, because nothing could ever be as bad as it was two nights ago. Joe asked me to stay late and spray one of the greenhouses. I looked as I did most days during the summer—covered with mud, dead leaves caught in my hair, baggy shorts, and mismatched tube socks. A vision. When the sun started going down, the greenhouses began to look like Cambodia. Steam, poisoned gases from the fogger, and water. Every little while, a stretch of bad electrical cord would drag through a puddle and sparks would fly, sometimes shocking me. I would throw the fogger across a row of ferns and scream obscenities in the darkness.

The next day, I came to work to find puddles full of all the dead worms in the world. No longer could they harm the ferns that I had

almost killed with too much fertilizer. Too much? Or not enough? Two very good questions.

Should another question be put, I am happy. I finally got an official offer from VISTA: yes, little brother is going to Louisville, Kentucky. Not exactly the cultural hot spot of my dreams as New York or Boston would have been, nor the sun and sand I had imagined in Florida. But above all, I need a fresh start, and I'll take it wherever I can.

Enclosed is the continuing saga of BIG VICKI, who has been resurrected from the dead and found peace of mind—at least for now—as she travels back in time, to when she was a little (and I use the word advisedly) girl:

Austin College Alumni News

The worlds of science and religion were shocked today when Tim Powers, a twenty-two-year-old white college graduate, turned into a fat, eleven-year-old black girl.

Insisting his name was "BIG VICKI," Powers boarded a Greyhound bus headed for Hunt, Texas, a small farming community near the Guadalupe River. Mr. J. T. "Happy" Peters, a local farmer, found Powers wandering around the bus depot and took him/her home for a hot meal and a bath, until authorities could be notified.

"We don' know where she come from," replied Peters, "but she 'bout the cutest li'l ol' gal we ever seen. She didn' have nuffin' in her suitcase but a pair o' movie star sunglasses. She say she want to ride on a tractor, and swim in the river. I jes' laughed, thinkin' she been in de sun too long. I jes' don' know."

Powers' friends and relatives remembered him as a high-strung but intelligent boy, whose clothes never fit properly.

"His pants just used to hang on him," recalled a tearful Altha Robinson, Powers' aunt. "I don't think he had much patience in clothing stores."

Dr. Gerald Hinkle, Powers's college advisor, remembered him as a bright student who excelled in metaphysics.

"You could ask him, 'Why?' and he'd answer, 'Why not!' He was quick," cackled Hinkle.

Later in the evening, after a bath and a change into knee-high boots and a flowered print, Powers answered some questions raised by the mysterious transformation.

"What do you remember, Vicki?"

"Nuthin'."

"Does that make you sad?"

"No."

"Do you think you'll miss your life as a white college graduate?"

"No, suh. It wuz too hard."

"Vicki, I have just one last question. Do you feel at all trapped within this Kafkaesque nightmare?"

"No," answered Vicki with a broad grin, "it's kinda like bein' in de cartoons."

"Now, BIG VICKI, you li'l sugar punkin, how 'bout dat swim?"

The world sleeps a bit more fretfully tonight but knows of one little East Texas girl who went to bed with a smile.

"See! I told you . . . it's right there, in black and white," Stan said, building his case. "BIG BLACK VICKI!" he couldn't resist adding. "A swim, that's what he wanted, that's what he's going for, back to Mo."

"He also wanted a tractor ride. You wanna stop at every farm between here and there?" That was my contribution.

"I'm just trying to help," Stan said, as little and defeated as little debbie.

"I know. I'm sorry."

"It's just . . . the river . . . that's what keeps coming up, in every one of these letters. Don't you think he. . . ."

"You might be right," I said, hoping he *was* right. "But there's all this other stuff. He went to Louisville, lived there three, four years." Just saying it made my head hurt. I didn't want to think about any of it; I just wanted to rest, to close my eyes, and melt into the starry, starry night that enveloped me.

But Stan wouldn't let up with his Nancy Drew act. "Well, at least I know we're heading in the right direction. He's definitely not at AC, or McKinney. This letter . . . it's beautiful, but it's such a good-bye. No, he's moving on, that's for sure."

How many hellos and good-byes had we said in our young lives? Too many, that was for sure.

~~

Captain, my Captain,

The sky tonight is that shade of Buena Vista blue that ushered in so many Saturday evenings at Austin College. I have slept in your bed the past week, pretending I had a brother who was going to Kentucky tomorrow, to begin serving humanity. My dreams have been fitful. I've been looking at McKinney with the eyes of an exile, that first step toward my gypsy fate. I feel strong, capable, sad, and scared these days, like the end of Cabaret—ghosts and headlights outside the railway car, singing and dancing up a storm.

This is the eve of my departure and I am filled with good-byes. Like all of our days of departure, this one has been spent running—hot and cold—between Wal-Mart, the Library, the Square downtown, Church Street, and the fruit stand around the corner for milk.

Ah, these days of departure! There is such anonymity about that whirl through the airport, to the luggage counter, through the bomb detector, down the ramp, and into the plane. Always I say, "Protect us, Mary, now, and at

the hour of our deaths." Such a spring takes over these clunky Earth shoes. I waft, yes, waft and bounce on my entrance to the plane. It ascends, one thinks of life. I listen to voices, inflections, accents. I always eat everything on my tray during in-flight breakfast, lunch, or dinner. And ALWAYS drink more of that wretched coffee than is good for me. Oh, to be wired when I land. My flight for Louisville leaves at four-twenty tomorrow morning. Gathering the darkness around me like a banner, I will hum a rousing departure hymn, an anthem to survival.

I bought warm, fleece-lined gloves and will walk cold streets tomorrow night, perhaps with a new friend, perhaps alone. Charlott wrote me a letter about her cousin Sarah who lives in Berea, Kentucky, and knits sweaters and scarves. She told me about Christmas there and eating Christmas dinner at a wonderful hamburger joint. The heart knowing more than the eye can see, I will try to find the very place.

Don't know what I'll eat. Don't know where I'll stay. Don't know what I'll do. But, you know, I'm planning on having a wonderful time.

Tim

CHAPTER NINE

He might not know what *he'll* eat, but I sure do. I'm starvin', Marvin! I sez, 'PULL OVER!'" Stan snapped at himself, in the thrall of BIG VICKI.

Had Tim created a monster?

I pulled off the highway to a gas station/McDonald's, its huge, football fieldlike parking lot lit by tall vapor lights, landscaped with dots of greenery planted in wood chips. We got out of the car to stretch our legs, before we went inside for food. Too much travel and too much memory can cramp you up. I needed the stretch.

Stan said, "I can see why he'd wanna go back. The river. It's beautiful."

His switch in conversation should have taken me by surprise, but it didn't. The river. It was the only thing that had been on my mind the whole time in the car, no matter where Tim had taken us with

his letters. I didn't need Stan to read them aloud; I practically knew them by heart, having read and reread them so many times over the years.

"Talk to me about it."

"You've never been?"

"Uh-uh. That was his. Everybody thought I'd go, the little drama star, but I never did. Williamstown was mine. If I hadn't gone, I never would have met Jess. Just like if Tim hadn't gone to Mo Ranch, he never would have—"

"Had a breakdown?"

"Who knows."

I had a second—no, a third, fourth, fifth bout—of thinking I'd lost my mind. I was standing in the middle of a cavernous parking lot with a Day-Glo McDonald's in the distance, the fluorescent vapor lights giving everything the look of perpetual daylight, like an Alaska where there was no day or night. It was too late to turn back now, but did I seriously think Tim could have gone to Mo Ranch? Or was I just killing time—an unfortunate turn of phrase—because I didn't know what else to do? I was the one who always rode to the rescue, fixed every situation, but now, I was fresh out of ideas.

Mindlessly driving was a lot easier than thinking.

Stan brought me back to the journey at hand, asking the very question I'd been trying to answer for the last seven years: "What happened to him?" He asked it differently, not like the other hopped-up, too innocent questions he'd asked until now. He asked it like somebody who'd seen things, knew things.

"Whatta ya mean?" I said, almost afraid, vamping for time. I knew exactly what he meant; I just didn't know how to answer.

"I mean . . . he's not crazy, you keep saying that. You can't be crazy and write letters like that. Even I know that. I've taken courses. No,

I mean . . ." and I knew what he was going to say before he said it, because it was the same thing I'd been asking myself for days now: "What happened between you? Why are you so mad at him? Why do you hate him so much?"

Did he actually say it, or did I just imagine the words, needing to hear them, needing to answer them, for myself?

I could hear the buzz of the vapor lights; time locked, and the buzz started in my head, and I thought I was going to faint.

"He wrote you great letters. He loves you. He cares."

How could I sum up umpteen years, a complete history, a mythology, to a stranger? Anything I said would sound so petty, but I said it anyway.

"He didn't care enough to keep my letters to him. He kept the stuff he wrote, just not my stuff to him."

"Well, maybe he just lost 'em. Sounds like he's a messy person. I'd hate you to see *my* room. You can't blame people for being what they aren't. He's not a maid."

This wasn't going to be so easy to explain; I didn't know if I could explain it even to myself.

"He's not crazy, you're right there."

What, *what* then?

"He's a drunk. Maybe that's what it comes down to. Our father's a drunk, so why did Tim become one too, after he saw what it did?"

"It's genetic. He can't help it. I've taken courses."

"If it's genetic, why didn't I get it? Take a course in that, then we'll talk."

"I'm just asking."

"I know."

The only person I had to talk to anymore, a stranger, someone that ten hours earlier, I'd never seen before in my life, and I was

trying to figure out twenty-eight years of existence with him, quick, before I ate Chicken McNuggets.

"I really am trying to figure this out. It's not just because he's a drunk. That's stupid. You're right, that's too easy." I said this when I couldn't think what else to say. "He's so unhappy."

"And that's a reason to be mad at somebody? Because he's unhappy? Who isn't?"

"So unhappy you wanna die?"

"Sometimes."

Thank God it was night.

I could only say these things, think these things, at night.

"Christmas. The first Christmas he moves to New York after Louisville. We're supposed to fly home together. I call him and call him to make plans to get to the airport, he never answers. I can't find him, and he ends up missing the flight. Now, I hate myself for it, I think. I actually left, without knowing where he was. I call him when I get to Dallas, *finally* get him, he's just getting up from a blackout, he'd passed out, didn't have the money to get to the airport. He barely knows where he is. From Texas, *Texas,* I call a friend back in New York to take him the money. Porky and I pick him up at the airport in Dallas the next day, and he's got a black eye and his glasses are broken and he doesn't know how . . ."

I stopped my recital, but Stan looked at me, wanting more.

"We fought the whole time on that trip, except when we went to our mother's grave. That finally shut us up. That's the only thing that's ever shut us up."

That's the thing that caused all this, Our Mother Who Art in Heaven.

I had to change the subject fast.

"And going to a gay bar together, so he could drink some

more. That shut us up too. That actually made us laugh . . . the three of us."

Maybe that's the other thing that caused all this.

"So Tim's gay now?" Stan asked.

That took me unawares; I hadn't really thought about it, but, yeah, Tim "was gay now," by the time we saw each other that first Christmas after college, back in Texas.

No big talk about it; I just inferred it, from references in his letters. Just as there was no big talk about it when Tim and Porky and I went to a gay bar in Dallas that Christmas, after escaping the house on Christmas Eve for our ritual of a movie in Dallas. We were quite the novelty; we got a round of free drinks.

Amazing; we never really talked about it, and Tim never really apologized for his behavior when I tried to start the gay organization on campus. Tim wasn't the only one who should apologize; Porky would later say he had deliberately withdrawn from us during a certain point when we were in college, so we would "make our own decisions" and not be influenced by his life.

Translation: so we would decide whether or not we were fags, and not "do it" just because our precious, revered Older Brother had.

He had left us—just as Tim had left me—at the time we needed him most.

It all wore me out.

My fucking family, too afraid to talk, too afraid to help one another.

I shook my head; Stan didn't know all the reasons. "I can't take it anymore. No more. This is the last trip. It really is. Whatever happens."

I let the thought disappear into the night air and walked around, toeing up wood chips.

I didn't think it was possible to miss someone so much, someone I thought I hated.

Stan guided me into the driver's seat of the car, the door open, my feet still out on the parking lot. Whether it was hunger or exhaustion or absolute despair, I couldn't stand anymore.

He took over. "Here. Listen to this letter. It'll make you like him again. People should like their brothers."

Both of them; except he didn't know he was referring to that.

Oh, Precious for the New Year,

I'm so glad I found you at home, in your palatial Upper West Side apartment, early New Year's morning. Your talk of giant puppets in Central Park filled me with visions of some ancient struggle between life and death. The images of those puppets, their struggle, warmed difficult sleep that morning. My housemates and fellow "VISTAS," Joe and Maxine, were sad that night. A party we had counted on fell through, so I poured glasses of red wine for them and pretended to be a café singer in Paris. "I will now sing ze sad, sad song, written for me by Edith Piaf. Maestro?" Give the old girl a hand.

I'm pretty certain it's one of those times for soul making, as we understand it in this world. Already, I've had to realize we're all here to help, including the various girls who carry around paperbacks about Kent State, talk about wanting to save the world, and are aggressively rude to people who smoke:

"Hey, like, could you, as the chairperson of the task force, ask the smokers to get the fuck out of the room before they kill us all?"

Many of them have Biblical names and wear down-filled parkas.

I have no real office space yet and wander around the city between appointments. I've begun to feel senseless, meeting with all these people who wonder, along with me, what I'm doing there. "Tell me all about yourselves, darling." This mood has something to do with the weather. It's just started

*snowing and it's too cold to walk the city streets. I find myself on corners,
singing gospel songs about "vales of tears" and "resting in someone's bosom."
How I would like to rest in someone's bosom on these cold days! I get very
lonely from time to time and go into the kitchen to bang around on pots and
pans until the sadness subsides. Sometimes it does, sometimes it doesn't.*

*I've spent much of the last year thinking about my "time at home" our
senior year. I know I've never told you and hardly acted like it at the time,
but your visits and calls helped me to "bear the beams of love." (That's from
one of my favorite William Blake quotes, "And we are put on earth a little
space, That we may learn to bear the beams of love.") The world seemed
almost unbearably harsh then. Most light seemed so blinding on those afternoons. I took communion in the form of Valium (and yes, I always knew
you took it) in the tiny kitchen where our father found our mother's body.*

*I've thought more about death than ever lately. Not my own, though: I
cannot seriously say I've ever considered suicide. Joseph LaFace once asked our
Heritage 21 class to raise our hands if we had ever thought about suicide. Cam
Willis was disturbed by the whole thing; I can't remember if this was before or
after her "weekend in hell" (when some boyfriend spurned her and she started
smoking because it looked "so good" with her long red fingernails).*

*Knowing Doug Maguire, someone I met very early on here, has been a
reminder that people can die more easily than most of us ever imagine. He's
doing well now; spontaneous bleeding from his hemophilia has stopped and
his platelet count is steady without steroids. The other night he gave me a
scare when he announced he was going off his medicine because he was tired
of all the effort. I don't cry very often, but I screamed that evening as if life
depended upon it: "I don't want you to die."*

*The following afternoon—a rare, warmish day—we walked in Cherokee
Park together. Whenever the weather is nice, the faggots come in droves to
the park to talk, wash their cars, and suck each other's dicks in the bushes.
For all Doug's "Auntie Mame-ness," he has an acute sense of the outdoors.*

He knows where to pick golden raspberries in a secluded part of the park and where certain catfish come year after year, spring after spring, to breed and die. In the sun, his glasses turn dark, and in a trench coat, he looks like Garbo coming, somewhat painfully, out of retirement. Whether we resolved any questions from the night before I do not know. The walk was quiet; the shadows were cool when we walked into them from the sun. I felt very still, and that, at last and at least, felt good.

For a long time I've felt the need to get down to business, to get to work and out of the garden, where I've been fucking around too long. Where all that leads is unknown. But it has started: the time to try again. I want to be a writer, and a writer writes. Period. And not just letters. I've fooled myself before with quicksilver cure-alls and such. Mo Ranch cleared away a lot of sloppiness for me. That place worked its changes and forced me to see in new ways. It would be nice to find another Mo Ranch.

Maybe I will find it here in Louisville, maybe I won't. I just know I've been pretending for too long, finding people and things that have given me a sense of motion, but have really just had me spinning my wheels. You and I have talked about art and work and the paralysis of being afraid that you will not be good enough. The fear of failing outweighs the belief in trying; you end up doing nothing instead. I want to write and will have to work at it.

But once again, it's mine—it's ours—to do.

Tim

"See? Mo Ranch . . . finding another one. . . ."

Stan was like a dog with a bone about fucking Mo Ranch— where the fuck did that name even come from?—reading those letters like the road maps that would get us there.

And I was like . . . what? He had said that letter would make me feel better, but it made me feel worse: Tim writing that he had never seriously considered suicide. Maybe he hadn't back then, but that would change in the years to come, and it would be all he thought about. Not just thought about, but *did*.

That's what this whole trip was about.

Thinking he had done it for good this time.

That's why we had to hurry up.

But I couldn't think he really had.

To die.

To not be.

To hate life and yourself so much you just wanted to disappear.

To hate me so much he never wanted to see me again.

It couldn't be.

That's why we had to hurry.

"C'mon. Let's get food and get outta here," I said, suddenly moving toward the McDonald's.

"Calm down. We've got all night."

No, we didn't.

He didn't see a yellow Oxford cloth shirt covered with blood.

He didn't hear someone drunk and disoriented say, "I just shined my shoes, I just shined my shoes."

No.

STOP IT.

I couldn't go back in that house, not yet.

"I should call home, check for messages first," I said, heading inside. First I couldn't wait to get out of here, now I didn't want to go, afraid to get to the end of the journey. "What you want? A burger, fried pie? My treat."

"Apple," Stan said. "And a shake. Chocolate. I'll meet you by the gas pumps. I gotta get all the dead bugs off the windshield."

I left him to his bugs and went inside to call Jess, who was still furious at me for leaving. But not so furious he didn't anxiously tell me this: there had been a message—a something—on our answering machine at home: breathing on the other end, labored breathing, almost like somebody was trying to make a sound, then the noise of a receiver banging at the hook, then nothing.

Tim.

Jess said bullshit, it was just a hang-up.

A telemarketer.

In the middle of the night?

A wrong number, then. Nobody.

"Where *are* you? You've gotta get back home."

"I'm still looking for him. Maybe that's a good sign, that hang-up, that he's . . ."

That he had been alive, at least at some point tonight?

That he was maybe still alive, but dying?

I had to hurry.

"I've gotta find him."

"He's not there."

"How do you know?"

"I don't, but you know Tim. He couldn't get to Texas."

"Do you think he's dead? Just . . . was that him, trying to say good-bye?"

"Don't talk like that. Of course not. He's just . . . he's on a bender again. Come *home*. We'll look for him together. I want you here, so I can take care of you. That's my job. We can look together. Everything'll be okay."

I loved this man so much.

"I've gotta go."

I hung up and went back to the car.

CHAPTER TEN

I came back out to the parking lot. Stan had driven the car over to the gas pumps and was studying a map he had laid out on the car hood.

"How much farther?" I asked.

"Where's my fried pie?" he asked at the same time.

"I forgot. Sorry."

"I need a sugar stimulus. I'm fading," he said, then left for the McDonald's. "Don't go anywhere without me."

"No, we don't have time. He called."

That stopped him in his tracks.

"Where. When."

They weren't even questions.

"Well, I *think* he called. Jess said somebody called. Back in New

York. There was a hang-up. Maybe it was Tim. Jess said the breathing didn't sound good. We've gotta hurry. C'mon, let's go. I'm driving. It's pedal to the metal time."

I was shaking as I got behind the wheel.

A call in the middle of the night.

I couldn't take another one.

I couldn't go in that room again.

Isn't that what Tim had said once, "I can't go in that room again"?

No, he had said, "I *won't* go in that room."

But there was no place else left to go, as the car headed in one direction, and I went somewhere else entirely.

Oh, yes, we've had this date from the beginning.

⌒

The thing I had dreaded for so long but never truly thought possible, began, like so many things in our history, with a phone call. It was Tim, just a few weeks ago, about five on a Saturday morning, saying he had just tried to kill himself by slashing his wrist. He was drunk and crying and there was blood everywhere and he didn't know where he was.

I ricocheted out of sleep, from dreams to def con in milliseconds, scrambling for words. I tried to stay calm, but the shakes and panic he must have felt carried through miles of buried phone cable to me. I squeezed the phone as hard as I could to keep from dropping it and tried to remember what to do when you're on fire:

Stop.

Drop.

Roll.

I did them:

My heart stopped.

I dropped through the sky.

I rolled through time, wondering if this is how, after everything else, it would all end.

"WHERE ARE YOU? D'YOU KNOW WHERE YOU ARE? STAY THERE. I'LL COME GET YOU."

I was screaming at a deaf man.

"Don't know . . . don't know where . . . come you . . . come house."

"NO! WHERE ARE YOU? STAY THERE. What's your phone number? LOOK AT THE PHONE. Give me the number . . . give it to me before time runs out."

The phone slipped from his hands, his bleeding hands, as I heard, "Don't get you, gonna die."

A scrambling sound, trying to find the hook for the phone, plastic banging at metal. . . .

"TIM . . . TIM . . . WAIT . . . YOU'LL NEVER MAKE IT. . . ."

Then the dial tone, same as a flat line.

I had just lost the only link to my twin brother, who was drunk and lost and bleeding to death.

I had started not to answer that phone.

That Saturday morning, I heard the jangle, squeezed my comfortable soft pillow tighter and whispered to Jess, "Don't get it." I knew it was Tim and I knew I didn't want to, or couldn't, save him anymore.

He needed money.

He needed a place to stay, another boyfriend having kicked him out.

He needed a job; did I know of anything?

He needed to stop drinking.

He needed a friend.

And I didn't need any of those things.

But sometimes there is God, so quickly.

A second before the answering machine picked up, I rolled over and grabbed the phone.

Seven years of knowing, and waiting, were finally over, but all I could do was wait some more, and remember the litany of good and bad that had happened since Tim had moved to New York two years ago, on the rebound from Louisville.

The bad: drunken phone calls late at night, berating me for some failing, some comfort I had that he didn't, that I had gone to Yale for grad school but he should have, because he was smarter than I was. Calls that would end with him slamming down the phone, just after he'd scream that his miserable life was all my fault.

The good: seeing Saturday matinees of plays together, Tim crying and saying they made him want to be a better person. His saying that made me want to be a better person, made me want to open my heart to the brother whose calls I used to welcome. One Christmas, we made stockings out of felt and glitter and hung them on my mantle in Brooklyn. They were the first stockings we'd had since we were kids.

Two years of life in the Big Apple, and a few plays and Christmas stockings were the only good things I could remember.

All that, flashing through my head, like the life review I'd have at Judgment Day.

I didn't think I'd pass.

Finally, Tim arrived at my apartment—minutes, hours, years later?—and stumbled out of a cab, as if pushed. (He *was* pushed, because he didn't have the money to pay.) Through the bay window in my living room, my eyes met his for a second before I ran to the front hallway to let him in.

His face was puffy and red, his hair abnormally short, as if he'd

tried to hack it off along with his hand. He was wearing black jeans and a yellow Oxford cloth shirt that was untucked; both were covered with blood—I could see it, rust-colored, even against the black of the jeans—and the stench of booze and cigarettes.

I pulled open the gate; metal scraped across the concrete floor. The dogs whined and pawed against Tim's blood-soaked legs. Still not saying anything, he held out his left arm to me, like Frankenstein slowly raising it to his master for the first time: "See what you have created." His fingers were smeared with blood; his skin was stuck to the sleeve of the shirt, but I could see where he had hacked into it: a V of skin, hanging loose, two slashes ending in a sharp point. I saw skin and blood and bone and muscle and snapped shut my eyes, just as I had done in the fourth grade, when I looked at my own broken arm and saw bone pierce skin.

Bone-pierce-skin; noun-verb-noun, it was that elemental, that primal, that unadorned, that horrible.

I said a quick prayer—Blessed Virgin Mary, save us miserable sinners, now, and at the hour of our deaths—and opened my eyes to find Tim staring at me with a dare. This was our contest: who could withstand the most pain. And he had won, hands down, hands cut off. He had gone to the mat, the bell had rung, the referee had held up his bleeding arm for victory, skin flapping in the breeze.

He had hurt the most and won.

He could burst into tears, now that he had been declared the champ.

Standing there, crying, he rocked back and forth on his heels, looking down at his shoes. "I just shined my shoes, I just shined my shoes," he kept intoning. He was wearing shiny black loafers, so shiny I could see my face in them, and I could imagine how nice his outfit must have looked at the beginning of the evening: the shirt clean and pressed, its sleeves rolled up and cuffed a perfect three

times; the jeans fresh, with a just-ironed crease down the front; a modest haircut that might have looked neat and trim in another light, but which now made him look like one of the lunatics we had played in *Marat/Sade* in college.

I moved him into the living room and sat him down on the couch, as he switched to saying, "I would have died if you hadn't been here."

I had been seconds—less—away from not answering that phone.

But sometimes there is God, so quickly.

I tried to distract him from his pain, and mine, while I figured out what to do; we had to get his arm sewn up. Most of the blood was dried up but a little was still seeping; if the loss of blood didn't kill him, I thought, massive infection would. To vamp for time, I was grabbing at straws, saying anything. "Look at the new rocker Jess just bought. We got it from an antique store in the neighborhood. Jess recovered the seat. See how much Opie and Franny love you?" Franny was trying to sneak her head onto Tim's knee, her favorite spot with visitors. I started asking—Tim, Jess, God, anybody who would answer—if we should take him to the hospital. Jess had been quiet, brought Tim water, but now started asking, too. Tim went back to rocking back and forth and saying he had just shined his shoes; he didn't want to go to the hospital.

It is no time/to make your brothers cry, shined shoes or not.

Jess went into the bedroom to find something for a bandage, and I followed, trying to be quiet so Tim wouldn't hear. It would have been funny if it weren't so damn serious, a movie scene where someone slaps a hysterical person to shut them up. Jess didn't slap me, but he should have; I clutched my stomach and wailed, "He's going to die," soft at first, then uncontrollably loud. I didn't care who heard me; I couldn't keep it in anymore.

He was going to die.

He was going to die.

Where had I heard that before?

Jess hissed that he *was* going to die if we didn't get him to a hospital; there wasn't any "Does he want to go?" about it. The cut was deep, and it was still bleeding. It had to be sewn up. Jess gathered a clean white tube sock with a red band around the top and some tape to patch it up temporarily. We went back to the living room, to hell with whatever Tim had heard. Jess, whose life had been so carefree and steady and uninterrupted before he met me, wrapped the wound.

Without warning, without even knowing I was going to do it, I grabbed Tim and whispered that everything was going to be okay, then guided him off the couch and out of the apartment, even as he held back and said he didn't want to go. Jess took his other side and we kept walking; there was no turning back. We moved outdoors like the characters in the final scene of *The Birds*: our avengers were gathering, ready to attack, but all we could do was leave. We couldn't stay in that house anymore. We gathered the dawn around us like a battle hymn, an anthem to survival, as Tim had once written, and began walking to the hospital, seven or eight blocks away.

We supported Tim on either side; he wasn't just cut and bleeding, but drunk. We hadn't changed his blood-soaked shirt—that would have meant unpeeling it from the wound—so the few people who were out so early stared at us. We walked in silence, nobody daring to ask what had happened, or where or when. I was looking for the mundane, the practical, like "a few hours ago, at my apartment"; Tim, the poet, the philosopher, the truth-teller, would have answered, "Twenty-one years ago, the day Our Mother died . . . seven years ago, at Mo Ranch, when I couldn't decide who to love . . . but neither wound has ever stopped bleeding."

Street lamps flashed by on either side of the highway, as Stan said something to me again. He had been saying it for a while; I just hadn't heard. "You sent him the same thing?"

"What?"

Stan had been reading more of the letters, and I had been remembering my brother with his hand cut off, and the family that had handed him the knife.

"This letter . . . it says you sent each other the same book for your birthday."

"Wait." I shook my head, to try and clear it. "What are you talking about?"

"I don't know where you've been, but I've been reading these letters. His letters. The one about the birthday, where you both sent each other the same book."

"Oh. Yeah. We did that a lot . . . the same thing . . . same book. We even had the same nervous breakdown."

"Huh?" Stan asked. "Now I'm confused. Which one of you had the nervous breakdown?"

"We both did," I said, focusing carefully on each word, so I wouldn't have to focus on drunkenness, or a long walk to a hospital, holding up my drunken brother, or a wrist that was cut and wouldn't stop bleeding.

"Read something, make noise," I practically begged Stan. "Make it go away."

"Make what go away?"

"The pictures in my head. Make the pictures go away."

So he read.

To little Peatie on his Birthday:

I bet the old woman who made our jelly-bean cakes is dead now, but if I could bring her back, just this once, I would, and you could eat jelly-bean cake with all your little friends. Would Little Peatie like that?

Enclosed is your birthday present: The Habit of Being *has been one of my constant companions for the last month or so, and I believe you'll enjoy Flannery O'Connor's letters. In a very strong way, they remind me of the letters from Mother to Porky we used to sneak into his room to read. Porky told me something very interesting during my visit to him in D.C. this 4th of July. We were sitting in his kitchen on a Saturday afternoon, drinking something called Lilet (it had won prizes, like A-1 Sauce). I was telling him about* The Habit of Being *(what a brilliant title) when he asked me if he had ever told me about Indira Gandhi. Of all the things we had talked about, that was not one of them. In a very quiet, humble voice—something rare from Porky—he said she was just like Mother. He talked of his surprise at flying halfway around the world to find a woman who looked, acted, and treated him like Mother would have. (Mother and the three gay Powers boys. What was in that water we drank as children? I think we should offer ourselves up—for a sizeable cash advance, of course—to any scientists who would care to study us.)*

Just as I was getting ready to mail this yesterday—obviously, I haven't made it to the post office yet—I got your birthday present to me, a copy of The Habit of Being. *Somehow, I'm not at all surprised we sent each other the same thing; are we the same person, I often wonder? That would not be such a bad thing. I love you more than life itself; you are my very habit of being.*

My heart goes out to you, during your rough summer in the sticks, bringing art to the masses—even if it is in the form of The Man Who

Came to Dinner. *(Are you the man who came to dinner?) And if you had a nervous breakdown while trying to make art, well, art hurts. So do break-downs. When we next see one another—will we ever see one another again, I ask?—we can compare and contrast them, the way we might be asked to do on an 11th grade English quiz. We can compare and contrast the effects of Valium on our little bodies, compare and contrast falling in love with the wrong people, compare and contrast going screaming into the night, as we have each done. Will we ever write our stories, the stories of our separation, so that we will know what happened to each other? In them, we can compare and contrast life itself versus—what? Maybe that's the problem in a nutshell, that I can't think of what to compare and contrast it to. Maybe we both missed that class.*

I face the day with a bourbon on the rocks in a chic little downtown bar, before my lowly collection job at the bank. I've only had one drink, not a third of the way through, and my lips are tingling.

Word is out now that First National Bank, where I work, now that my VISTA tenure is over, discriminates against queers. (Me, working in a bank: the irony. Me, the new gay activist: the irony.) Do you remember my telling you about Sam Dorr, who was fired by the bank when they found out he was gay? I have been in a rage for two days over it. When Sarah was raped in college, I wrote a pointed letter to John D. Mosely, our esteemed college president, full of sound and fury. He passed it on to Howard F. (didn't that stand for Fuckface?) Starr, the dean of students. There are times when you speak and wait and look and watch for some spark of recognition to strike in the other's face.

RAGE, RAGE AGAINST THE ABSENCE OF THE LIGHT.
Lord, give us the ability to rage correctly.
                    —Litany that rage will not drive men to madness—

And there are times when that recognition does not strike; it didn't with Howard. I left his office tired and worn. In such a way now I have walked in rage and weariness about Sam Dorr. Sherry Jeffries, my boss, the former beautician who turned in her Dippity-do to swim in the financial cesspool here, told me Sam's "being that way" didn't bother her, because "that's his problem." I laughed and said something funny. (Don't the Powers twins always do that when they don't know what else to do?)

Oh, well, oh, hell, I still don't think I've learned to live in the real world. I promise I won't turn into a martyr about this. One more thing—I feel like a raging drunk in a bar late at night, just before closing time, except this bar has just opened—it was my fantasy in high school, seriously, to save my friends—women, mostly—from ever marrying the wrong people. I wanted to save Sarah in college; I couldn't. I was going to save Ellen in high school; I didn't, and look what happened. I never told you that Ellen sent me a letter a week before she married saying she needed to talk to me very much. We never talked. She got married.

Draw your own conclusions.

Does all of this make you want to cry? Are you crying now? I've had too much coffee—and just the right amount of booze—to cry now. It will have to be a different season before I cry again, but I will cry.

I promise you that.

Timmy

He kept his promise.

He did cry again.

Happy fucking birthday.

"What's a breakdown like?" Stan begged. "I think I had one, too."

"You'll know when it happens."

I knew, because that's what happened to me, the summer I spent

as publicity director at Millbrook Playhouse in Pennsylvania, before I went to Yale. That summer, I fell in love with a straight boy, and he didn't love me back. I went crazy over him; I went running into the woods to scream about it. I started hallucinating as I watched a big dance number in the middle of *Stop the World, I Want to Get Off*, because I wanted off. I watched *The Shining* and thought it was my life. I read *Sophie's Choice* and thought I had it worse.

That's how bad it was.

I tried to go swimming in a nearby pond to get over the stress but couldn't, because I was afraid of the water.

That's what a nervous breakdown is like, in case you want to compare and contrast.

Stan was staring at me.

Had I said any of that aloud?

I don't know.

That's what a nervous breakdown is like, not knowing whether the white noise in your head is coming out, not being able to stop all the white noise of memory, not being able to forget Tim begging for help in a hospital.

The pictures were coming back, and I couldn't stop them.

"Was he working heavy machinery?"

Blood was seeping through Tim's makeshift bandage, but all the lady at the hospital's front desk cared about was his insurance and work address.

She was looking down at her silly forms.

I kept saying, "He cut himself."

She kept thinking I meant accidentally.

"He cut himself, he cut himself," I kept saying, not able to say the truth myself, "He cut himself *deliberately*; he tried to *kill* himself." I could only give the polite version; even Tim, mad at me for answering for him, would only say, "I cut myself."

"He *cut himself.*"

Finally, the light dawned in her eyes. It was the first time she looked up from her paperwork. "You shouldn't have done that," she said and seemed to slow down even more. I begged, then yelled at her, to call a doctor. When she wouldn't, I grabbed Tim as my human shield and pushed him through swinging doors into the real emergency area.

We came upon a clump of doctors, young and tired-looking, but at least they weren't hiding behind the protocol of forms to fill out. "How did he do this? Was he drinking?" One whiff and they knew. One doctor took over and unwrapped our sock bandage. "That's pretty nasty," he said, in front of Tim. "Whatcha use on yourself?"

"A bottle," Tim said.

"You drink it first? That's pretty dumb." He was the first person that morning to express any anger to Tim's face. This tired, busy doctor was too tired and busy for the special handling of twins.

Good.

We could have used him—both of us—years ago.

He told me to wait outside while he took stitches, just like when we were children and Tim's head was gaping open. This time, there was no nearby phone booth to hide in.

By the time they let me back in, I'd expected that Tim would have been changed into a hospital gown, but he was still wearing the black jeans and yellow shirt. His right arm was still caked with blood, but the cut forearm, his left—*sinister* in Latin, that's the one other thing I remember from four years of studying a dead language, besides

"odi et amo"—his *sinister* left arm was glistening and gleaming white from a tub of disinfectant the doctor bathed it in. The water was now rust brown.

Tim must have been given pain shots, but he still winced as the doctor sewed his hand back on with heavy black thread. Tim was Humpty Dumpty all over again, just as he had been, had wanted to be, in college, now literally being sewn back together.

When he had finished, the doctor brought me out of the room to tell me he wanted to keep Tim overnight for observation. They would try to get him into the psychiatric ward of the hospital rather than the closest facility, which he told me was a real snakepit. That's when it hit me: this was bigger than the Powers twins doing whatever they wanted to, damn the consequences. We had—fuck it, *Tim* had—crossed a line, and "authorities" had taken over. As much as I wanted someone else to take over, I was scared. Could they do what they wanted, or did Tim or I have any say?

No, we didn't.

The doctor left, and I went in to see Tim again, sitting in a side room on a gurney. He reached out to hug me, crying and saying, "Please don't leave me," and I pulled away. I pulled away like I did that night in college, when he wanted to "hold hands like European men" and dance across a dew-covered lawn in the early morning, and I wanted to have things my way.

Then, he hadn't felt me pull away.

Now, he did, because I wanted him to.

I wanted to make him mad for all those times he had made me mad.

It worked: he lashed out at me, as he had done so many times before. "Okay, be that way. Fine. Just get out of here. Leave me alone."

But I refused; I wanted another pound of flesh. "Make me. Just try. You're too weak to fight. Just try to get me out of here."

I swear to God I said that.

(I light a match to my skin now, to feel the flames of hell I know are waiting for me.)

He tried to hit me with his good hand, but he lost his balance and tipped over on the gurney because he couldn't put weight on the bad arm, bandaged up to the fingers in white gauze.

I laughed at him; I dared him to try again to hit me.

(I move the match to the delicate skin under my left bicep and think this is what hell will feel like. The pain is unimaginable.)

Tim started crying. "What have I done? My life is ruined. My life is a disaster. I could have died."

I told him I *might* come back to visit him that afternoon and left.

(I move the match to the hair under my arms and smell the curly singe.)

Outside the hospital, the promise that had been in the air that morning had turned into reality. It was a bright, beautiful day. The flea market was in full swing, people were in jogging suits, couples were picking up orange juice and bagels. I crumpled over into the chain link of a parking lot fence; Jess pulled me up and supported me all the way home, the way we had supported Tim.

⌒⌒

"Pull over, pull over, grab the wheel. . . ."

I thought I was having a heart attack, or a brain attack. I felt like I was going to die if I had to remember one more horrible thing I had done.

Stan reached over me to grab the steering wheel and swerve us to the side of the road. I managed to cut the engine; a crunch of gravel, a sudden stop, and we both banged into the dashboard.

"What's wrong? You okay? What happened?"

You don't wanna know.

You don't wanna ever find anybody cut up and dying.

You don't wanna ever deny your brother.

That's what's wrong.

I got out of the car and sat on the still-warm hood of the car. It was cool and dark outside, about five in the morning, and the warmth of the engine was the best thing I'd felt in days.

Tim and I used to sit on the hood of our car back home and talk about the future. They were the best, and scariest, times we'd ever had.

"Are you cracking up on me?" Stan ventured.

"You tell me. I'm too tired to think anymore."

I thought about my brother and curled into a fetal position on the warm car hood, under the limitless Texas sky that was just turning into morning.

I could die right then and there, and it would feel wonderful, and I would never have to think about my brother in a hospital ever again, waiting for me with his hand hanging on by a heavy black thread.

But even on the warm hood of that car, it's all I could think about.

～～

Back at our apartment, I took a shower and put on clean clothes, to get the hospital off me. Jess plunged into sketching; I languished on the bed in my robe, my skin still damp, not certain what to do or who to call.

Of course, I called Porky, as I did whenever disaster struck. A Saturday morning, calling him early at home, and I was afraid of disturbing him by telling him our brother was in the nuthouse with his arm hanging by a literal thread.

"Something bad happened. Everything's okay now, but Tim tried to kill himself this morning."

He said a quick, "Oh my God."

"He's in the hospital now and has to stay overnight."

I flashed back to the first conversation like this I had ever had with Porky, seven years earlier, when Tim had his breakdown, and I made a collect call to Big Brother, in my bare feet, from my dorm. The triangle was still the same: Tim, the one in trouble; me, the bearer of bad news, but almost apologetic about it; and Porky, the one who could fix any situation, mend any problem, with the same practical questions as always: was Tim's insurance paid up? Was there a convenient shuttle to take?

He told me to call him after I had seen Tim that afternoon, that he would come to New York the next day if I needed him to.

I didn't tell him I might not see Tim, because I already knew I would. I had known I would the second I told Tim I might not.

That afternoon, I put together a change of clothes and some magazines for Tim; packing them reminded me of Anne Frank, taking her few belongings with her in a little sack. The worst had happened; at least now we could live in hope.

Tim had been placed in the last available bed in the geriatric wing of the psych ward. For all the elaborate sign-in procedures downstairs—you had to carry a big wooden visitation pass, visible at all times—chaos reigned upstairs on the ward. Patients walked around at liberty, some wearing hospital shifts, others wearing regular clothes. It was difficult to tell the patients from their visitors, who seemed just as worn out and drawn from their visits as the patients did their incarceration. That's where those big wooden passes came in handy. Us versus them, they said; here but for the grace of God, they also said. A man shuffled up to me in broken-down house

slippers and asked if I had come to see him; another asked if I was from Long Island.

You have seen broken men, I am sure.

It was the phrase Tim had written in the letter to his friend Roy, describing the day and night of his breakdown in college, a phrase that conjured up the absolute depths to which Tim had fallen, from which seemingly nothing could lift him. And it was a perfect description of this place he was in now, a psych ward full of broken men, and the equally broken people who came to visit them.

Us, and them.

Tim had finally taken off his bloodstained clothes, wadded them up on a Naugahyde chair in his single room, and put on a hospital gown. His pale, spindly legs poked out from underneath the hem; how desperately I wanted him to have a summer tan on those legs, as if that would have prevented all this.

We stared at each other, then tears filled his eyes as he told me he had just prayed as hard as he could, a very real prayer, for me to come.

He looked at me with those pained eyes, no dare in them now, and asked, "Will you forgive me?"

Before I could say anything, he began talking.

"I've never told you this, but back in college, right before my breakdown, I had a dream. I had the same dream again just the other night. Maybe that's why this happened."

I still said nothing, so he began telling the story like a monologue from a play, as if he had already rehearsed it time and again. Maybe he had, so it would never leave him.

I know it hasn't left me, and never will.

"I said it was a dream, but I don't know. I think it was real."

He took a deep breath and started.

"We were back at home, and we were . . . it's like we were grown up and little at the same time, like we kept switching back and forth. It was after dinner and the streetlights were on. I was playing in the front yard and I looked up to see Mother walking down the street toward me, carrying a suitcase, that old blue cardboard thing we used to have. I said, 'I thought you died.' She smiled, like it was a joke or something, and said she couldn't stay. I was so mad at her for dying, just when I needed her, that I yelled at her.

"'Get out of here. Now!'

"But she didn't.

"It's like she looked right through me and said, 'Will you forgive me?'

"I wanted so bad to say no, but I couldn't.

"She said it again. 'Will you forgive me?' and this time . . . it's like . . . something inside broke or something, and I said, 'Yes.' And she held me and she was so warm, it's like I'd never felt anything that warm, and we were playing in the front yard and having so much fun I forgot what time it was and she said, 'I have to go now.'

"And I knew I couldn't go with her.

"She kissed me and told me she'd always be with me. Then she said good-bye and walked down the street. I watched her, harder than I've ever watched anything in my life, but, I don't know . . . a bird flew or a dog barked or something, and I looked away, just for a second. Just for a second . . . and she was gone. Maybe that's why I had a breakdown.

"Maybe that's why I cut my hand off.

"Because I didn't see her leave.

"I looked away.

"So . . . will you forgive me?"

He asked me again, the same question our mother had asked him in the dream.

I didn't answer, not exactly, but pulled from an even deeper place than the heart—oh, biology doesn't begin to teach us of these other places, other rooms, where the real business of life goes on—and asked, "Will *you* forgive *me*?"

Us versus them.

Broken men.

We held each other and cried.

He tried to tell me what had happened, how he cut his wrist, but he couldn't remember. All he knew is that he felt as if he had been asleep and filled with rage ever since our senior year in college, when he went home; so filled with sound and fury he thought he could literally uproot lightpoles from the ground. He would stare at them, close his eyes so tight he shook, and try to levitate them into the air. When that didn't happen, he turned the fury on himself; he could at least uproot his hand from his body, make it fly around and do his bidding. He dug into his arm the same way he would dig into the ground with a garden spade; he wanted to get to the root of the anger, which had spread and wouldn't let him go. And when he found that the "ground" of his skin was too hard, he started hacking into it, hard, sharp, with no concern about what the final result would look like, just that he had been able to break through.

And that's why I saw skin and bone and muscle and cartilage and veins and blood when he showed up at my apartment.

Now the anger had been leeched, at least for a little while, and there was nothing to do but try to live, and even laugh, until it returned. And make no mistake about it. It could, and would, return. So we laughed: about the "Nurse Ratched" who tried to get Tim to join "therapy"; about hatching a plot to break Tim out; about his joke in college that he was going to end up locked away in a nuthouse with a bunch of crazy old women who thought they were the Brontë sisters.

It wasn't a joke anymore, it had come to pass, but we still laughed at it.

We were the twins, sitting on Porky's bed once again, wondering what life would be like. The twins: one with his arm nearly slashed off, the other bearing gifts of toothbrush and magazines and clean clothes.

The blood was gone, for now.

I stayed at the hospital through the afternoon and into the evening, through the meal with plastic utensils and no sharp edges that was brought into Tim, until the announcement came that visiting hours were over. I left with the prayer that I had given him enough strength to face the night, to not be afraid of its newness, its darkness.

I left with the prayer that I would be given that same strength.

Outside, it was a perfect Indian summer evening, warm and cool at the same time. Now, I thought, I am a man, I have survived this day, and I would probably survive many more to come. As Tim had once written, I couldn't imagine anything more terrifying.

Back home from the hospital that night, I called Porky, already afraid of losing that special connection I had felt with Tim, of Big Brother taking over. But he seemed to sense that and knew to be gentle. "Don't worry, little brother. Everything will be okay now."

How I loved it when he called me little brother; it brought back the times when I truly was a little brother, rolling around, reading his letters on his bed with Tim, wishing and dreaming, crying and whispering, listening to ghosts. And safe. Always safe, like the lock was on the inside of the room as well as the outside.

But when Porky arrived the next day, he was in his no-nonsense business mode, honed through years of cutting through red tape and bullshit in Washington. Instead of good memories of New Year's Eve

and Shangri-la, another memory came to mind: him dragging us, hand in hand, to a trash can in our backyard, pungent with the smell of rust and ash, and the sight of sparks warring against the darkness, to make us burn our pacifiers, long after our friends had discarded theirs. It wasn't enough that we had to toss them in; Porky had to hold us up, one by one, over the lip of the can, our faces seared by the flames, so we could see the plastic and rubber melt.

He wanted to make us grow up by looking into the flames; oh, I was grown up now, I wanted to tell him. How many flames had I looked into since then?

"Well, what happened?" he asked, point-blank, as much what did *you* do as what did *Tim* do.

How should I answer? Should I go back to that night in college when I wasn't there to save Tim, when he threw an alarm clock across the street, its breaking glass the only sound he heard as he cried and screamed? Should I go back to the funeral of our mother, which Porky wouldn't let us attend? Go back to him holding us over a trash can alive with flames, watching our childhoods melt?

Should I go back to the time Porky himself had spent at home, a sick young man who might not live, when I heard our mother cry out, "He's going to die. He can't make it. *I* can't make it." Should I tell Porky that I—and maybe even Tim—had heard that, and carried that time bomb with us for years, that our whole family could go at any minute?

Should I tell him how Tim and I had both witnessed our sainted mother beat our drunken father with a frying pan, saying with clenched teeth that "the Great Apostle Paul told me to do this" and knowing she was insane, and that the same fate might befall us as well?

No, I didn't tell Porky any of those things; he wouldn't understand. To his question "Well, what happened?" I told him, "I don't know."

As we walked to the hospital, we passed a junky souvenir shop that had T-shirts in the window; Porky's eye was caught by one that said, "Because I'm the Daddy, that's why." He was the "daddy" in his relationship with Steve and said for me to remind him to buy it on our way back from the hospital. We were about to visit our brother who had just tried to cut off his hand, and Porky was thinking about cute T-shirts. But I went along, agreeing how funny the T-shirt was, how much Steve would love it, because I wanted Porky to love me. The walk was exactly like the one Jess and I had taken with Tim the previous morning to the hospital, talking, or not talking, about everything but the thing at hand:

Tim's hand.

With his assured, steady politician's voice, Porky got our clunky wooden guest passes, the ones that said we were "normal." On the elevator ride up to the ward, Porky said he would have a one-on-one with Tim, while I dealt with getting him released. But from the minute Porky and I walked into Tim's room together, just as I had known when Porky walked into my apartment, I knew there would be no more honesty, no more laughing and crying, but sullenness, defensiveness, silence, and fear: Porky bullying, Tim the same in return. Porky stayed behind as I signed a form accepting responsibility for Tim, formalizing what I had been doing most of my life. It was amazingly easy and only took a few seconds. As eager as they had been to get Tim into the place, now they wanted him out.

Must have had another patient on the way.

The heartfelt one-on-one between Porky and Tim did not take long; I don't know what was said, except that Porky was all business when I came back, ten or so minutes later, telling me to wait outside while Tim changed his clothes.

Not a lot was said as we took that now familiar path back home.

I tried to tell stories to break the tension, of the man who asked if I was from Long Island, but it was too sad to be funny, although Tim and I, by ourselves, could have gotten a laugh out of it. Porky had lost his sense of humor, of fun, of mystery, somewhere in the process of growing up. When he was a child, he had taken delight in believing he had seen a flying saucer; he had ridden the courthouse elevator (the only one in town) up and down just for fun on Saturday afternoons, when he had been a boy like us. But he had probably forgotten that boy or forced himself to forget him.

I couldn't forget anything, that was my problem.

Neither could Tim.

Porky was a boy no longer; he was a "Daddy," as the T-shirt he bought testified. He was already rushing to get home; if he did this and that, he could make the next shuttle back to Washington. It was like when our mother died; we made plans—or plans were made for us—but we didn't talk about what had happened.

Porky made sure I would take Tim back to his apartment, too afraid to face the truth, whatever physical evidence Tim had left behind: a shard of glass, the lost ring of keys, the blood. He left, in and out in all of three hours.

Although I offered for Tim to spend the night at our place, he grimly wanted to get back to his sublet, to try and solve the mystery of what had happened, because he had no memory of it. We took the subway together to his sublet on the Upper West Side, only for him to realize he no longer had his keys—they had been lost somewhere along the way.

He had to buzz a stranger to get into his very own building.

When we got to his apartment, the door was unlocked, but not broken into; his keys weren't in the lock. There was no blood inside, no broken glass, just the usual mess of his life, his green trash bags,

filled with all the pieces of writing and plays he was trying to turn into a life.

Where, and how, he had cut his wrist would remain a mystery.

⌒

I felt arms around me.

"Are you cold, tiny baby?"

They were the words Tim used to say to me, at our best, most tender times together.

I imagined he was whispering them to me now.

I opened my eyes; I was still curled up on the hood of the car, and Stan was wrapping me in a blanket from the trunk.

"We're almost there."

"Where?" I asked, shaking myself out of my reverie, knowing that that was the right question to ask, but having no clue as to where we were. I had been lost to everything but looking for blood, and a sharp knife or jagged piece of glass, for the last leg of the journey.

"There. Mo Ranch. I didn't realize we were so close. The fog cleared, and I saw it. See?" He pointed off in the distance. "Like Brigadoon. We did that in high school. I ran the light board."

It was just like Tim had described it, once upon a time—the gates of Mo Ranch, a wooden cross up on the hill in one direction, and a shimmering river in the other.

Stan magically whipped a bottle of orange baby aspirin from his pocket and spoonfed me a few of the chalky tablets. "I've been thinking. Maybe this isn't such a good idea. Not every one I have is. Maybe we should go back."

"But we're already here. I wanna see the sunrise. Tim used to say he'd get up early in the morning there, just to see it come up over the river."

"Yeah, but you . . . are you feeling okay? You seem kinda . . . sick. Upset."

"Let's just keep going. A few more miles isn't gonna make a difference. We've gotta find out if he's here or not. We can't stop now."

"I guess, yeah, but no more letters. I think they're kinda depressing you. Just funny stories the rest of the way. Or 'Ninety-nine Bottles of Beer on the Wall.'"

He got me off the hood of the car and put me in the passenger's seat. "I'll drive the rest of the way. You just look, or sleep. Don't read. I'm taking the letters away."

That's what he thought.

They may have been in the back seat, but I didn't need them in hand to remember what they said.

Didn't he know that by now?

He said it one last time before he turned the engine back on. "See, I told you it was beautiful."

And it was.

A hint of orangy violet in the sky, a tease of rising sun: the beautiful place where my brother fell apart.

BOOK THREE
SUNDAY

CHAPTER ELEVEN

We were there.

"God." I got out of the car. "The river. It's like you said. It's beautiful."

Below us the still-rising sun hit the surface of the Guadalupe and shot the brackish brown with streaks of gold and silver and early-morning pink. Canyonlike walls studded with stubby little trees channeled the river, which snaked into a patch of little eddies as the water sloshed over rocks. A gigantic metal-and-wood slide poured down into it.

"That *view.*"

Stan stood behind me.

"Told ya. This is where *I'd* come if I was running away." He pointed to the slide. "We'd go down that every morning just to wake up, hit the cold water. Some days I wouldn't even shower."

Just like I hadn't, that . . . when was it now? Yesterday morning? Yesterday morning I'd woken up in New York, wondering how and where I'd begin the search for my brother. An hour or two after that, I was on a plane to Dallas. An hour or two after that, I was wandering the grounds of my old college. A few hours after that, I was hooking up with a kid who'd magically take both of us on an all-night "Road Trip!" we'd be too cowardly to take by ourselves. All of that, in a little over twenty-four hours. Twenty-four hours, or seven years; take your pick how much time had actually passed, as it all swam together in my head.

Anchored by a stone fence of sorts, a sturdy iron gate formed the entrance to Mo Ranch—named after a Mr. Moran, I'd actually learned from Stan during the course of the drive—but the gates were swung open.

"Look, it's open. Maybe that means he's here. He drove in and didn't close it."

"Not necessarily. They keep it open nearly all the time."

Did he want Tim to be here or not?

Did *I* want him to be here?

"The camp mostly closes down after the summer. A few groups on the weekend, I think, stuff like that, but—Let's drive down to the barn. It's just a few minutes more."

"Are we gonna get in trouble?"

All night on the road, and suddenly I'm afraid of trouble.

Stan had a dubious answer. "If anybody asks, I'll tell 'em I left my watch here last summer, and I'm looking for it."

"*I'll* tell 'em Tim left his heart here; we're looking for that, too. Plus the person that belongs to the heart."

His heart, split in two. He couldn't save Sarah, so he moved on to Carrie. When he knew he couldn't love her, he moved on to Gil.

I was suddenly afraid to be here.

This was real.

This was Tim's, not mine.

I was the intruder.

Stan read my mind. "You okay? You okay with this? I can go first."

First, my big black angel on the 911 call. . . .

. . . then Sean and Dave, my hunky policemen. . . .

. . . and now skinny little Stanley Kowalski.

My angels came in every shape and color and size.

I wasn't okay with this; I wasn't ready, but none of them had to know that:

"Yeah, I'm ready."

("But are ye able?" asked the Master.

I couldn't answer.)

"Where should we start?"

"The barn. It's not far."

He drove the rest of the way in and stopped when I saw something I had only read about before.

"Oh my God, there it is . . . there's the heart . . . the one Tim wrote about."

A giant heart, carved from rock, was set above the entrance to the long narrow barn, with the tall pitched roof. Tim had discovered it on one of his last days there, when rains, which would soon turn into floods, washed away the dust that had hidden it all summer. A perfect metaphor for his time there: only when he was leaving, almost too late, did he discover his heart. I half expected that if I could climb up to take a closer look, the name "Tim" would be carved into half of it, bisected by an arrow, and the name—whose? Carrie's or Gil's?—would be carved into the other half.

⌒

I only found out the truth after the summer, after the breakdown, when I found a love letter Tim had written to Gil, stuffed in that same bedside cubbyhole at home that held Tim's asthma inhaler and Valium, the Valium I stole. A love letter written one hot and sticky night at Mo Ranch, when the air was filled with the conversations of cicadas.

My Precious Gil—

It was a Friday night on the verge of Saturday when Mo Ranch decided to play its one disco tape, Village People, and transform its concrete stage into Disco Barn. The centipedes hid under the painted revival chairs, and the mirror ball shook. All was complete, but wait! Was that not Young Tim in the corner, with a bit of melancholy in his heart? "Where is Paul? Where is Sondra?" he asked plaintively, dancing from couple to couple, remembering the two Tim and Gil had met on one of their first dates in Dallas. Through the din of Donna Summer and Smoke (get it?), Tim remembered Sondra's sordid confession: "Yes, Tim and Gil, a year ago, I was a boring person. Yes, I know you find that hard to believe." And Tim did find it hard to believe. The boys, glowing from a few times on the dance floor and from the general enchantment of the evening, refused Sondra and Paul's offer of artificial stimulants, opting instead for delights of their own imagination. And Tim, still remembering the cool of the air conditioner against his face and the delight of Gil near him, continued his search, trying to separate the dancer from the dance.

On several occasions so far, I have played the "underground game" first thing in the morning. It involves mental geometry of a complicated sort. I awaken at Mo Ranch every morning without fail, but with a little jiggling

of the memory, I end up on a dance floor, or at the Bagatelle Lounge with Nancy Paris and a gin and tonic.

And you are always there, oh Precious, always there.

Precious is what he used to call me.

The letters were coming back, and I wasn't holding a thing in my hands.

Just in my head.

⌣

Glass shattered.

"Oops."

Gentle, delicate Stan had just committed an act of vandalism for me, trying to open a stuck window at the barn/theater.

"I thought I could just wedge it open. I couldn't."

"Are you okay?"

"Yeah."

He gingerly cleared out the rest of the glass, looking around to make sure no one had seen him.

"Gimme a boost."

I cupped my hands for him to step into, and he lifted himself through the window.

"Don't cut yourself."

Don't cut yourself. If only someone had said those three little words to Tim.

Stan pulled himself up on his belly and plopped down on the other side.

"Wait there. I'll go around to the front and open it."

I waited and saw Tim's hand smashing through a plate-glass window, a Superman "POW!" with an uppercut, and then—no Superman powers had he. He bled just like anyone else.

A big weathered wooden door began sliding open on a track, Stan pushing it from the inside. The light from outside filtered in, its shadow lengthening as the door opened wider and wider.

"If it's all locked up, Tim couldn't have gotten in," I said.

"Not really. I saw another smashed window on the other side. He could've done that."

My heart pounded faster, thinking Tim might actually be here.

"You okay?"

This time it was Stan asking it.

"Would everybody quit asking that? I'm *fine*. He's my *brother*. It's my *job*."

I am my brother's keeper.

I am my brother's keeperkeeperkeeper. . . .

If I said it enough, maybe I'd start believing it.

He wasn't here. He couldn't be.

He'd've heard us.

He'd've come out already.

Game's over.

I started shaking again and grabbed on to the side of the barn, the bleached flagstone cool in the early morning.

"You okay?" Stan asked, one last time.

"Just *go*."

I followed him inside the barn, directly into the V-shaped wedge of light cast onto the stage from the open sliding door. "The Barn" was a misnomer; it was a name that had stuck from a prior life. It was now a full-fledged little theater in the three-quarters round, Dub's preferred style of staging. Audience platforms, with creaky old

movie house chairs, were set up on three sides; the stage was the concrete floor in the middle.

All of a sudden, Stan ran to a circular staircase, the top of which disappeared into a balcony.

"STELLA!"

Such a big sound, coming from such a little boy.

"Dub says I've gotta work on owning the stage, so . . . 'STELLA!'"

He shook the staircase.

"I don't know. It's more like I'm renting it. God, I had so much fun here last summer."

Maybe that's why he was here, pure and simple: a return to a place where he'd had so much fun. How many places like that did we actually ever have in our lives? I couldn't blame him for wanting to relive the good times.

"Here. You try."

He guided my hands onto the staircase and shook it, his hands on top of mine.

"Scream 'STELLA!!!' It'll be good for you. Get it out of your system."

"Get what out?"

"Whatever."

I couldn't.

"C'mon. Nobody's here. Let loose."

I tried, but a weak-willed "Tim!" came out instead.

He didn't know what to say. "Let me check the rooms."

He headed up the circular staircase, leading up to dorm-style rooms on the second level.

I wasn't up to being my brother's keeper; I wasn't up to being his finder, either.

Stan saw me steady myself on the staircase, take an extra breath, look down.

"You're right. Wait there. I'll check 'em out first."

I heard doors opening; Sean and Dave, opening doors.

"It's okay. He's not here. I mean, it's not okay, but whatever. He's not here," Stan reported.

"Then I'll come up."

I went up the stairs to the balcony as he flipped a switch. A small spotlight shot its beam directly onto a mirrored ball hanging over the stage, the lone remnant from Disco Barn all those years ago. Some of the mirrored panels had cracked or fallen off; the few remaining cast a watery shimmer over the stage.

It looked like we were inside a swimming pool.

"Disco Barn," escaped from my lips.

"How'd you know that? We did that too. 'It's Raining Men.' 'I Will Survive.'"

No, I wouldn't. I didn't want to be in a swimming pool, or a disco.

"Turn the spot off. I feel like I'm drowning."

He did; now we just had the light from outdoors again, as he led me into one of the rooms.

"This is where the boys stayed. I had the top bunk over there, and . . ."

He kept on talking, but I heard none of it. I was too busy looking at a room full of people, a room that had been empty just a moment ago. Now it was filled with the people who had been here Tim's summer: Casey and Ray Stell and Gil and Roy coming to visit and Kent Johnson bringing drugs and McNabb in her kimono and good Laura Vargas who stayed out of every fight and Sarah and Carrie and Tim, not knowing where to turn; Tim, wearing Dr. Johnny's white ice cream suit; Tim, wearing yellow greasepaint as the Chinese stage manager; Tim, waking up in this very room in one of the bunk beds, just like the ones we had when we were little, and a very empty room was suddenly

much too crowded for me, and I knew that's how it had looked to Tim, that summer before his breakdown.

I had never been there, had never seen it, but I knew.

I stood perfectly still, trying to hear the room, trying to hear Tim through his adventures in time and space, trying to hear him give me any clue he could manage about where he was, a letter or a phone call. . . .

I would settle for crumbs.

⌒

My dearest Kim,

The stage was set for what I hoped would be a wonderful visit: you were coming to Louisville to the New Play Festival at Actors Theatre as a VIP, representing the Second Stage in New York. You had an official literary manager name tag and everything. I had nothing, or at least that's the way I felt, maybe the way I've felt ever since Mother died. I wanted to be a more "official" part of everything than I was, instead of just a lowly little play reader. I wanted a real-life job, a decent job, for once, like you had. I wanted to have a stuffed avocado waiting for me, in my fancy little brown bag, just the way you did, instead of wondering if there would be any leftovers for me. From childhood on, I have stood by, waiting for leftovers, waiting to see if there was any mother "left over" for me when she was done with everything else, instead of having the confidence, the birthright, to demand my due. We just weren't raised that way. We were too goddamn polite; maybe things would have worked out better if Porky had never taught us those manners.

You looked so elegant, so sophisticated, all in black, when you jetted into Louisville the night before the festival. I was so proud to show you off to my friends that night. Proud of your job at Second Stage, proud of your being at Yale, and not so proud of myself. I introduced you to my new best friend

Amy, who called me Timmy, just as you had done in the past. She had become my muse here; I had finally begun writing because of her, writing plays for her. Maybe, I thought, that would make you proud of me, my writing. My doing something, finally.

It was late, and we went to Zena's, the country-and-western bar behind the theater. That was probably our first mistake, after drinking so much at the Starving Artist Cafe at the theater. Oh, make no mistake about it; most of our problems (and I'm talking the universal We here, not just the Powers twins, or this Powers twin) begin when we drink too much. I can send you an inventory of every disaster I've experienced here in Louisville, and there will be a hefty bar bill to accompany each one.

After yet more drinking, we started fighting oh, so easily. All that booze loosens tongues; we should have learned that from our father. I was drunk and nervous; you were showing off, maybe equally nervous. You made a joke, with some unusually bad comic timing, I thought, about Mary Lou Owens, the costume shop manager, having had a nervous breakdown. Having had one myself, and I thought you had as well, I do not think nervous break-downs are things to joke about, but hey, maybe that's just me.

In that unbearably noisy bar, I'm not sure how many people heard us yelling at one another, but I will never forget your telling me you would never talk to me again. All the noise in the world couldn't drown that out. You smiled as you said it, and I think you believed it, at least for that moment. Thank God Amy was there to come to the rescue, and drive us home. You walked behind me with her, but I still heard her say, "Poor Timmy." Poor Timmy, the son of a drunk, and a mother who died because she didn't love her children enough to stay behind and take care of them.

I was too embarrassed to have you see my hovel of an apartment, so my neighbor Jerry let us stay at his nice big house across the street. Up that tall and winding staircase we walked. (How many lonely, drunken walks up staircases have I made? Too many.)

It was cold there, but even colder at my own apartment across the street, where I said I would go to be away from you. Where I said I would go to freeze to death, because there was no heat at all there. (Are you crying now? I am, even though that was not my intention.) I told you I had gone to a doctor who said I might have AIDS; I told you I was terrified of dying. At least, and at last, that got us to quit fighting. I'm sorry it took that much.

I started crying, then, as now, and you held me. I wish that's where we could have begun, and just skipped the middle part. When we awoke from our fevered and troubled sleep in the morning (did either of us really sleep, I wonder?) you dressed me in some of your beautiful clothes and everything was alright again.

We continued crying for the rest of the weekend, but at least it was the plays making us cry, not each other. You came out of seeing The Value of Names, *one of my favorites this year, and quoted the last line to me: "It's not enough," and we both cried some more. There are some things that can't be forgotten, even though you can try to forgive them.*

"It's not enough," no matter what you do.

At the bank where I work, we send out coupons to tell people they are "overdue" on a payment. Consider this letter one of those coupons; we are "overdue" on a nice visit. I owe you one.

Actually, we owe each other.

Your brother

⌒

There were too many words in my head.

There were too many memories.

There were too many people who weren't there, and they were all I could see.

Stan and I were halfway down the rickety circular staircase when I stopped. I wanted to cut into my arm or my head with a shard of glass, as Tim had done, and let all the words and memories and people from my past come gushing out.

But I couldn't.

It wasn't mine to do.

People weren't supposed to take their own lives.

A summer by a beautiful river wasn't supposed to make somebody go crazy.

Not knowing who, or what, to love wasn't supposed to make you go crazy either; having so many choices was supposed to make you happy.

But people did go crazy, all the time.

I couldn't move.

Yes, I could. I could run away from it all, just as Tim had. I could quit saving Tim, and just try to save myself.

Or not.

I wasn't worth saving.

I let everybody down.

I let people have breakdowns and didn't know how to save them.

I let people die because I wore the wrong clothes.

I let God down because he told me I was supposed to be my brother's keeper and I'd turned away for a few minutes and now my brother was missing.

I could run away to the river and throw myself in the current, dash my head on the rocks that jutted out of the rapids and . . .

Bleed.

Drown.

Die.

Not have to do anything anymore.

Just not be.

So that's what I did.

I ran past Stan, down that shaky circular staircase and onto the stage floor. Glass from the broken windows mixed with the panels that had fallen off the mirrored ball; they picked up the light from outdoors and sent even more watery waves over the place.

I was drowning; water was covering me, even though I was bone dry.

Stanley wanted a "Stella!!" from me; I'd give him one he'd never forget.

I picked up a nice big juicy shard of glass and, yelling "STELLA!!!" as if my very life depended on it, ran outside to the river, to wash away my sins.

⌒

Alas, Babylon:

I will have talked to you by now with the bad, but liberating, news of get-ting fired from Actors—and to imagine, I just got the job! When Julie, my boss, and I had our talk, it began like a scene out of Streetcar. We looked in vain in the theater for a place to talk and decided on the balcony of the big auditorium. Walking up those circular stairs, I needed a nice outfit with a bunch of artificial violets and a seahorse pin, someone to scrub and talcum me for the leave-taking. (I've been unusually cheerful today and I think it bothers them all. Good.) Julie found a nice dark spot. At first, I did not want to be in any kind of darkness with her. (Save it for her husband, please.) In some ways, she was very good: promising wonderful recommendations and references when needed. I guess most of it boils down to group chemistry.

It's Tuesday now. I've weathered the storm better than I expected. In some ways, it's easier to get out of bed now than it has been in months. I've cleaned

everything out of the office and just have a few loose ends here. It was hard going back in there—like Masha's "I won't go in there. I don't go in that house anymore," from The Three Sisters. *(Could they make a play about us, and call it* The Three Brothers?*) It is the empty garden there and I'd best make my way slightly east of Eden.*

I spoke last night to a library group across the river in Indiana and got paid fifty dollars. I told them, believe it or not, about listening to Babar the Elephant stories at the McKinney Library when we were children, when it was still in that old house across the street from the First Baptist Church. Do you remember Mrs. Finch and her retarded daughter Paula who always seemed to have a cold, who lived next door to the library? Are they still living there, do you suppose? Are they still living, period? I spoke of Stanley Green's The World of Musical Comedy, *which we repeatedly checked out as well. Was our childhood more absurd than our peers, spending all of our free time in libraries and checking out books about musicals? Or does it just seem that way now?*

Don't know what I'll eat. Don't know where I'll stay. Don't know what I'll do. But, you know, I'm planning on having a wonderful time. Didn't I write that to you when I left McKinney for Louisville, a million years ago? It seems fitting that I write it again, as I prepare for my departure to ports unknown.

Tim

I was standing at the bluff, with a shard of glass in my hand, about to slice away; Stan was yelling at me to stop: "Don't cut yourself!" Fool that he was, would that stop *anybody*??? The sky was alive with magic-hour pinks and purples and oranges, just as it had been the morning Tim awoke to have a nervous breakdown, and . . .

. . . there he was.

Tim, in the river.

He'd been there the whole time, swimming; the rising sun had blinded me to him.

Back and forth, as if the river had lanes, and he was doing laps. He'd get to a certain point and pivot down and back around, like a champion.

From up above, I could see his back, tan and muscular, V-shaped, his hair as blond as it had been when we were children.

I had found him!

I could stop running.

I could start breathing.

I could believe in God again. He would forgive me, because now I'd found my brother, whose care had been entrusted to me.

There he was, Tim, at the one obvious place.

He had written "swimming" on his calendar, so that's what he had done, gone back swimming to a place of such joy and heartache.

Why hadn't I believed him?

He was so beautiful down in that water, a fish, the incredible Mr. Limpett, I didn't want to disturb him.

I'd never seen anything more beautiful.

He flipped over, backstroke now instead of breaststroke, and my eyes adjusted even more to the play of sun and shadow on the river. A cloud passed over the sun, and it was suddenly fall again, chilly; a breeze rustled the pampas grass we were standing in, and I thought, he's going to freeze, and . . .

. . . everything fell away, and it wasn't Tim.

It wasn't anybody, no matter how much I wanted it to be.

It was a phantom I had created from all the stories I had been told of Mo Ranch, a young man who was strong and muscular and golden and blond and young and . . .

. . . not Tim.

The phantom of someone trying to relive the past, trying to make believe the chill of autumn could be a hot summer's day.

This time, I didn't even cry.

I just sliced.

⌣

My Kimmy:

It's a bright Saturday morning in McKinney, Texas, where I have taken refuge until I figure out what to do with my life. Already today, I've seen a young mother with three-year-old triplet sons in Wal-Mart. Each wore a green Izod shirt and a short haircut. I stopped and said, as much to you and Jesus as to anyone else in earshot, "Triplets!? Not tiny look-alike boys dressed in green? Not three tiny boys, No!" I explained our twinhood to the young mother and she said, "Were you like this?" The boys had taken tiny toy machine guns and were stalking the store. Did they demand the justice and beauty denied them in a fallen world?

I'm trying to turn it all into a big game, much the way Melba Davenport attempted to teach nouns and verbs to the Negroes at J. L. Greer, when we were in the sixth grade.

"There's a big fat noun hiding somewhere in that sentence. Pretend it's a shiny red apple. Juicy and delicious. Find the apple! Find the apple!"

"Ain't no fuckin' apple here," said Omie Earle Smith.

Hearing the words "big" and "fat"—she would later know them as "adjectives"—Omie had her mind set on "dick" and was pissed off to find it was only an apple. And not really even that. A noun. The first in a series of cruel jokes life would play on Omie Earle Smith.

My being back home is another cruel joke, although my spirit is surprisingly high, given the lowly job I've found with the Parks and Recreation Department. Didn't I have a low-level job in a greenhouse, four years ago?

I guess I haven't advanced much, but there are still pleasures to be had here. I'm still amazed at how much sky there is, and how hot. There's chance for purification here, given the flesh and spirit in cooperation.

In a fit of anxiety, I walked to the Holiday Inn the other day and joined Lauren's, the private club there. Little private clubs, with booze (one even hears rumor of topless waitresses in some), have sprung up all over McKinney. Lauren's is a rather cheesy affair. An effeminate Mexican named Joe tends bar in this particular corner of Hell. A DJ gone to pot spins country and western tunes for the cowboys and fat women who are patrons. During DJ breaks, Joe turns on a Dallas disco station that plays "Girls Just Wanna Have Fuh-un" and "Let's Hear It for the Boy." ("But what he does/he does so well/makes me wanna Yell!") The girls at Lauren's just make me wanna yell, "Lose weight!"

I take refuge from everyone by swimming, a pleasure I've rediscovered for the first time since my summer at Mo Ranch, or That Certain Summer, as I've now taken to calling it. Here's something I wrote the other day, about this second rebirth of mine, in the water:

The whistle, signaling the end of swimming, blew early.

"Get out of the water," said one of the more callused female guards, "It's over." (I hear they end sex the same way.)

I dried off with the dignity of Bette Davis at the end of Hush, Hush, Sweet Charlotte. *No one was there, however, to give me a corsage or a thick letter absolving me of my sins.*

"Get out of the water. It's over."

Chuck was there, though. The most gorgeous lifeguard who ever blew a whistle. I found out from someone that his name is Chuck, and that he will be a high school senior this fall. Oh, Precious. He looked at me and smiled a few times. More than once, I wanted to ask if he had any questions I might answer.

The other day, I did my biweekly, Parks Department–mandated cleaning

of the pool and its grounds, including the hallowed room where the lifeguards spend their free time. Did I blush and hope to find Chuck's Speedo, with my name on it? Or legal pads with "Chuck and Tim 4-ever" written in several handwriting styles?

Yes, I think I did hope to find those things.

I found, instead, several half-empty, half-full (the eternal pessimist/optimist dilemma) bottles of suntan lotion offering varying degrees of brown. I found, as well, a pair of mirrored sunglasses. Pretending they were Chuck's (the glasses he used to look at me, unbeknownst to the cruel eyes of those around him), I took them, like a bandit.

In the course of my various disappointments, I'm trying to take life into my own hands again, and to look at things I've been ignoring for too long. I used to wonder why Daddy drank so much, and I realized that drinking is a thing born of sadness. I'm looking at the way I've been acting and feel ashamed: I've gotten off track, lost sight and perspective, become too pretentious. BIG VICKI'S right: "You know what yo' problem is? You eats out too much." I'll try to listen to her better next time, and cook some of my own meals.

For boys who bury themselves in the water, and bask in the sun,

Tim

I held my cut arm above the river, trying to get my blood to flow into the stream.

"See, Tim? Now *I* win. I'm bleeding too. Now we're even."

People wanted us to be the same; so be it.

As it is on earth, so shall it be in heaven.

But the flow of blood was too slow, just drops, really, so I sliced a little bit harder, in exactly the same pattern as Tim's cut: a V-shape

on my left arm. But I was a sissy, afraid of pain, at least the physical kind, so I couldn't make it deep enough.

"Don't cut yourself anymore. *Please* put the glass down."

That phrase again, except now Stan added a please, with his voice, and his eyes; I could see them. But I could also see Tim, in my memory, at my front door, holding his handiwork up for me to see.

Share and share alike.

Bleeding in front of this beautiful young boy who had tried to help me find my brother . . . this muscular young mermaid I had seen swimming, and thought was Tim.

But it hadn't been him.

It hadn't been anybody, just somebody in my head.

Enough with living in my head; I wanted out of there, where every other thought was about Tim: how to help him, how to save him, how to fix him.

But now, I wanted to live in my body for once, and feel things, and let somebody else fix all the problems.

That's why my throbbing arm felt so good.

I could *feel* it, feel the nerves inside.

I could see it—the cut, the red—and know it wasn't just in my head anymore.

It was real.

Stan spoke up "Come on, put the glass down. You're scaring me. I'll help you. I'll get you whatever you need. We'll find help."

"But you can't find Tim. That's what you promised. You said he'd be here, and he's not. He's not here, he's not anywhere, and I can't go on without him."

There, I'd said it.

The truth, the hard nutshell of my life: I couldn't live without him, no matter how much I hated him.

I loved him more.

Odi et amo.

I hated and loved, each more than humanly possible.

"I've gotta keep cutting till I can count the rings inside. There must be hundreds of 'em, just since I've come here. I'm twenty-eight, but I feel like a hundred. I'm a sequoia. Tim made me age faster, he's gonna kill me, gonna make me get old and die. Maybe I can cut the rings out, let 'em flow out, be young again, then I won't die. I don't know what else to do."

Except not fight anymore, just give in, the way Tim had, just let go.

Let the water carry me away.

Wash me away, just as it had washed Tim clean that summer.

So I threw the glass down and shimmied up the stairs of the big slide that swooshed down into the water, like the little slide in our backyard that swooshed down to the wading pool in which Tim had broken his leg. Maybe I would break my leg, on top of breaking my skin.

I didn't care.

I looked like Quasimodo, scuttling up those steps, my left arm tucked against my side, a little blossom of red against my shirt, all the weight on my right side.

At the top of the slide there was a stack of pads to make the descent easier. I shuffled one into position with my foot, then looked down at the beautiful river below me, just as Tim had looked out from his dorm window to see the school for the sham it was, seconds before his breakdown.

Everything I saw, Tim had already seen.

It was like having your life flash before you, only the life that flashed before my eyes was Tim's, not mine.

Fuck him.

I couldn't have anything just to myself.

I wasn't going to be afraid of the water anymore.

I was going to get baptized again.

I sat down on the pallet—

Whoa!

That baby was greased.

It almost slid out from underneath me, throwing both arms over my head, banging them on the lip of the slide. Now I'd have a broken wrist in addition to a cut arm.

My "WHOA" rang out over the river, bouncing back from the cliff on the other side.

It mixed with the sounds of Stan screaming at me—or with me? (Laughing at me, or with me? Half full, or half empty?) I couldn't tell the difference anymore, as I plopped into the water and couldn't hear anything, the water that went over my head instantly obliterating any sound. Two shocks: from screams to silence, and the incredible cold: my lungs closed up as I went into slo-mo beneath the water.

Even when my head popped back up, I couldn't grab a breath; my lungs were paralyzed from the cold. A fast poke of sound came flying at me: Stan yelling at me (yes, it was *at* me, that was clear now) from shore. But there was no time to take in the sound: the little eddies grabbed me and carried me along.

The water was God.

I saw Stan start to wade in, but my eyes were stung by water and blinded as I went by him.

This was a really dumb idea.

There was just time for that one quick thought.

I had been in control of cutting my wrist—I had done it, even if some crazy chatterbox in my head was telling me to—but I was not in control of this river. It was going to do with me what it would. Is

this what had happened to Tim? He had controlled his actions to a
certain degree, and then his "river," his particular chain of events, just
took over, leaving his free will out of the picture entirely. I don't
think he had actively wanted to hurt me; we had hurt all our lives,
he knew what that felt like. He had just done it and got caught up
in the rushing tide, with very little time to think about how it would
affect me.

I was on the verge of understanding and forgiving Tim—one
thought was all I had time for, as I tried to gulp some air and not
water—when I hit a rock and FUCK, IT HURT, and now my head
was throbbing and the water suddenly felt warm and enveloping and
God is there so quickly and Stan was there, so quickly, dragging me
onto shore and I was chucking up water and he was beating on my
back and . . .

"That was a dumb thing to do," he said, the same as the doctor at
the emergency ward had told Tim.

Along with the burbles of water that came out of my mouth were
the strangled sounds, "I'm sorry, I'm sorry."

Stan was looking at my arm, wiping off the blood. "Scare me to
death, but you can't even cut your arm right. It's just a scratch. But
you're gonnna be lucky if it doesn't get infected from all the pee-pee
and poo-poo in that water."

Pee-pee and poo-poo; my good-bye to the world, and it had
come to this.

It wasn't a deep cut, just a beaded bracelet of blood drops. I hadn't
really wanted to die, just like Tim hadn't, but his resolve had been
stronger than mine. He had dug deeper; I had just imitated the outward pattern.

Tim had won, after all.

I must have said that aloud, because Stan suddenly snapped.

"Would you get over it? I don't care how fucked up your brother is. You're as fucked up as he is to do something like that!"

He put both arms straight out and knocked me in the chest, so much fury only now finding release. "Why'd you do that?! Why'd you DO that! WHY'D YOU WANNA HURT ME!?? I DIDN'T DO ANYTHING TO YOU. You don't even KNOW me! You could at least THANK me! I SAVED YOUR FUCKING LIFE!!!"

He started crying, standing above me.

He'd said what I'd wanted to say to Tim, but never had.

"Could somebody just say 'thank you' to me for once in my fucking life?"

Maybe that's what this trip had come down to for Stan: he'd just wanted somebody to notice him, to say thank you.

I took a deep breath, trying to decide what to say next, to apologize or not, and in that breath, that moment of consciousness, I looked at the things around me: a bleeding arm, a stranger reading me the truth of my life, wet clothes clinging to me, Halloween in the air, Tim not here, and . . .

. . . it was time for me to go.

Just like that; I knew.

I'd gone nuts, for no good reason. Maybe there was *never* any good reason. I'd disrupted enough lives; I'd disrupted my own life enough, and . . .

It was time to go.

That dunk in the water had cleared out my head and made me realize what I'd been doing: running away from all the anxiety and panic that Tim caused me in New York—maybe as much as Tim had run away—and hiding out in the Hill Country of Texas, with a young boy who had briefly and conveniently allowed me to revisit my youth, which was a comfortable place to be, because I knew everything that

was going to happen there. But I couldn't stay there anymore, with
or without my brother; I couldn't take refuge in any more young
boys, who let me hide from my life, from my responsibilities with Jess,
who let me pretend to be older and wiser, when I wasn't.

"I've got to go."

Stan's eyes widened, even if he did temporarily hate me. "But we
haven't found him yet."

"He's not here. We both know that. I don't know where he is, but
you're right. I'm sorry I didn't thank you. You did save my life.
Really. I'd probably have frozen to death in that water."

"But where you gonna go? Where is he?"

"I don't know. I just know he's not down here. He might be dead,
I don't know. I just know I have to get back to New York. I'll keep
looking, maybe something's turned up, or . . ."

Or what?

"Or I'll bury him. I don't know."

Now Stan turned from seeming to want never to see me again, to
desperate that I was going. "But I can still help. I owe you. After all,
I dragged you here, which was probably a really dumb idea."

"At least I got to see it." I was trying to cheer him up, this kid who
now seemed be falling apart, after having been the strong one all night
long. "I always wanted to see it. Now I have, and it was fun meeting you."

Now *I* sounded like the idiot: "fun meeting you." If that's the best
I could come up with, the only way I could sum up what we'd just
gone through. I knew I had to go, and I didn't want to leave him,
both at the same time.

"I don't mean that. Fun's so stupid, I mean . . ."

For the first time, I touched him, when words wouldn't do, or
come. I pulled him to me and hugged him, feeling his face, his
breath, and somebody's tears.

Mine or his, ours; I couldn't tell.

"Don't go back."

In the hours since he'd first suggested coming here, and in the few, ever-dwindling conversations we'd have in the years to come, it is the closest he would ever dare to answering why he'd needed this journey in the first place, and it was no answer at all, just three loaded words for me to interpret.

"Don't go back."

Did that mean "Don't go back, I'm in love with you?"

"Don't go back, I never get parts at school?"

"Don't go back, I have no friends?"

"Don't go back, I'll be all alone?"

I never asked more specifically, and he never said. It was too private to bring out into the light of day.

For me, "Don't go back" meant "You're breaking my heart." This kid whom I'd come to love, after all of one long night. This kid was me seven years ago, facing his future, desperate to find love, as I had been. What could I say to him, without sounding like even more of an idiot?

"You don't have anything to be sorry for. We tried, Tim tried. It's not his fault. It just is. Things are what they are."

I couldn't hurt him.

I couldn't hurt myself anymore.

"At least I went swimming. You got me back in the water."

"It almost killed you."

"But I did it. It's stupid to be afraid of it anymore. That's something . . . that's something."

I had swum again, for the first time since childhood.

It was around ten on Sunday morning and we were at the airport in San Antonio; I'm not even sure how we got there. I just know I opened my eyes and I was in the car with a Happy Meal in my hands, a makeshift bandage around one wrist, and a slightly damp blanket around my shoulders, covering up a shirt that had a watery red stain of blood on it.

I looked great for the flight back home.

Stan led me out of the car and over to the ticket counter, where I pulled a nearly maxed-out credit card out of a soggy wallet and plopped it down.

He talked for me.

And then I was standing at a gate and telling him to take my rental car back to Dallas. I was crying as he said, "Promise you won't forget?"

"That's never been my problem."

I wanted to give him Tim's letters, I really did. I carried them in my heart and head; I didn't need to hold them in my hands any longer. But I just couldn't let go, not yet. They might be all I had left of Tim.

I cried even harder and wouldn't look at him. But he forced me to; he was now the adult, and I was the child. He said my name, with such understanding. . . .

"Kim."

. . . that he forced me to turn around and see him, to hug him, to say good-bye. There was perfect clarity in his expression, through his tears, the same way Tim looked swimming, in my head.

Now I wanted to be the one to say, "Don't go back," but I knew I couldn't.

And then he was gone.

⌒⌒

"Are you okay? Sir?"

I was on the plane, and the flight attendant was talking to me.

Maybe she thought I was afraid of flying.

She had come to offer a beverage but realized she had to offer sympathy as well.

I looked at her; I opened my mouth but nothing came out except tears.

"Should I call somebody?"

"There's nobody left to call."

Okay. She didn't freak out.

They taught them not to freak out.

"That blanket's wet." They taught her not to ask what passengers were doing with wet blankets wrapped around their shoulders.

"Would you like another one? A dry one?"

I nodded my head yes.

I was going home, but angels were watching over me.

"Blessed Virgin Mary, protect us now, and at the hour of our deaths."

She brought me a fresh blanket, and I took a deep breath.

I was going home, to find Tim, or not.

CHAPTER TWELVE

I t was Halloween, and I was home.

Sort of.

I was back in New York around three on Sunday afternoon, but instead of going to my apartment I was going directly to the police station and my old buddies Sean and Dave, the police who'd last seen me make a fool of myself as I hopped into a cab that would take me to Texas, where I had just left a part of my heart, and some of my blood.

"Guess what, guys? It didn't pan out. Except I cut my wrist a little and almost drowned and had a nervous breakdown (another one) and still didn't find my brother, so you think you guys could take over from here? I'm kinda worn out."

I didn't know what else to do.

More than forty-eight hours had passed since I first got the call that Tim was missing. I had no more money; I hadn't showered in days—except for my dunk in the Guadalupe; I had abandoned my boyfriend; I had been taught some life lessons by a complete stranger and, I didn't know what else to do.

As I got out of the subway a few blocks from the police station, a group of children in Halloween costumes came barreling down on me, their voices so high and squealing, my hands flew to protect my ears. I was swallowed up in that sea of costumes, mermaids and pirates and witches and devils, going from store to store in the neighborhood in their late Sunday afternoon hunt for candy.

A little boy in a devil's costume and pitchfork jabbed me, but I didn't jump. I was too hypnotized seeing myself in him, from a time long ago when I had been a little boy dressed up like a devil, trying to scare away the bad things.

Devil costumes: the last Halloween costumes our mother would ever see us wear, in the third grade, five months before her death. For some reason that year, she had let us splurge on Halloween and get real costumes, not those scratchy nylon things that were squeezed into black-and-orange cardboard boxes with cellophane windows. She had taken us to the nicest clothing store in town, to pick out a pattern from the Butterick catalog for our neighborhood babysitter/seamstress to make for us.

Standing on our tiptoes to page through that catalog, high up on a counter, Tim and I settled on devil costumes because we loved the appendages that stuck out of them: cotton-stuffed horns atop a little skullcap, a forked tail, and the best feature of all, a large fluffy

cape with a ruffled collar. Our mother bought the pattern and took us through the store for material: bolts of red fabric, a spool or two of matching thread, and her own playful addition, red fabric with white polka dots to line the skullcap.

That fated Halloween of our devil costumes, after we had gone trick-or-treating, our father took us to his Lion's Club carnival, on the parking lot of McKinney's first shopping mall. In the costume contest, a "fashion lady," as we called her, flamboyant by McKinney's standards, pulled us out of the line-up, fluffed out our capes for all to see, to admire the handiwork herself. We were awarded third place and given two separate but equal five dollar bills. Our father drove us home after our big win, then went back to the carnival with the excuse—half legitimate, half not—of helping to tear down the rides when the carnival was over. He had started drinking earlier that evening; I heard my mother tell him not to bother coming home that night, and he didn't. I wore my devil costume to bed that night—horns, tail, cap, and everything—to stretch out the excitement of winning, to protect myself from any bad dreams that would come during the night.

That was our mother's last Halloween.

I would wear that costume for the next several Halloweens, long past the time I was too old to go trick or treating; I wore it to try and bring my mother back from the dead. By my last Halloween, in the sixth grade, the costume was sad and forlorn from my sleeping in it; the red had faded to dingy pink, the horns sagged, the cape was torn. But I wore it anyway, up and down the street by myself; it was my armor, coated with special alloys to make me invulnerable to pain. When one neighbor told me I was too old for candy, I finally went home, to Tim's "I told you so."

After that, I combined Tim's devil cape with mine, put them

together to make a skirt I could wear whenever I played damsel in distress, wanting to be saved on some dark, velvet-jeweled night.

That cape would literally save my mother, but not me.

But not yet, not yet. That story must wait.

I have to save Tim first.

⌒

I went back to the police station, even though I thought Tim was dead. Friday, Saturday, Sunday afternoon; three days and nothing. He had never disappeared for that long with no word.

The *word* was dead.

Sean and Dave were all I had, but I had the feeling they wouldn't know what else to do either. They had already broken into his apartment. I had done all the detective work they would normally do— called Tim's friends, checked out the places he had last been seen or heard from, flown to and from halfway across the country—but now I just wanted to sit and do nothing. I could sit on one of those wooden benches in the police station as easily as any other grieving family member.

On my way to the station, I stopped at a pay phone and checked back home for messages, but there were none. ("I don't suppose there's anything in that bag of tricks for me," Dorothy Gale had asked, after the Wizard had given out all he had to her fellow travelers. "No," he answered sadly, knowing how much the answer would upset her, knowing he wasn't a wizard, but just an old man who had gotten as lost as she had.)

This time, there was a woman at the station's front desk, not a male clerk; she told me to wait. This time, I didn't want to push ahead, insist on my importance, as I had in the ER, but just stop and

let *them* come to *me*. I took my place on her long wooden bench, and watched the officers go in and out, no one paying me any mind: women wearing horrible polyester pants, men so loaded with accoutrements—gun, bullets, billy club, summons book—they waddled as they walked. It was like the ER, where Tim's hand had been sewn back on: life went on with its jokes and banter, despite whatever the cat dragged in.

An arm.

A leg.

Whatever.

A pay phone was across from the bench. Using it would just be killing time, I knew; I had already called home and Tim's apartment so much, nothing would have changed. But I decided to call anyway, something to be active, so I wouldn't look like a victim or a suspect, sitting on that bench.

I called Tim's apartment.

Nothing.

I called my apartment.

Something.

The staticky sound of the tape rewinding let me know that someone had called. I pressed the buttons that would play back the message and turn the static white noise into words.

They were words I hadn't ever expected to hear again, from the voice I had been waiting for all weekend: Tim's. Tired, drugged, telling me he was—what? I want to be exact here—not "okay," but just . . . was.

Alive.

That's not the word he used, but it's the only one I can think of right now.

Alive.

Speaking into the phone.

Leaving wherever he was to go back to his apartment.

Tim.

It was Tim.

It was.

Tim.

I suddenly understood Gertrude Stein.

Yes and no, both at the same time. The word hasn't been invented to describe what I felt; only gestures and angry scratches and blood would do.

I understood Jackson Pollock now, too, a million colors splattered on a canvas to turn it into one big angry blob.

My heart stopped.

It started again and ricocheted out of my body, banging against walls, leaving blood and tissue everywhere.

My brother was back from the dead.

The relief lasted a millisecond; the fury was . . .

AAAHHHHHH . . .

I HATED HIM.

I slid down the wall and folded over into a fetal position, shaking, epileptic, because of a phone call no one else had heard.

I wanted the police, the woman at the desk, Dave and Sean, the junkies and whores, to see how mad I was, that this wasn't a joke. I wanted them to see that I had just heard Lazarus had risen from the dead, something that hadn't happened in over two thousand years.

I had just heard a miracle.

The woman at the front desk came running to me; even one of the whores sitting on the bench came to help, smelling of musk. The one fragrance I had ever worn in my life, Jovan Musk, that I hadn't

smelled since high school, and there it was on her, on her dangly gold earrings and short rabbit skin jacket, and . . .

NO.

The woman at the desk didn't come to me.

A whore sat on the bench, but she didn't come to me either.

I didn't slide down the wall, although I wanted to; I calmly put the receiver back on the hook and betrayed nothing of what I had just heard.

Tim's drugged-out voice, after a disappearance of three days, saying he was going home: that's the only thing that was true.

The whore did wear Jovan Musk, though; I smelled it. And I did wear it in high school.

(I don't even know that she was a whore.)

That much is true.

I started walking toward the desk, wondering if I should just walk on by, or tell them I was going. No one would miss me if I left; clearly no one would miss me at all. Tim hadn't. But I didn't have to decide. The desk woman said Sean and Dave were on their way back to the station.

I said, "It's okay, I just got a message that my brother's okay."

I walked out as quickly as I could.

That's the truth.

I couldn't be alone.

That's the truth, too.

My brother was alive.

That's the truth.

After all my searching, he had been found, but I hadn't found him. He had just found himself.

I could have been asleep all weekend, not going anywhere, not breaking my heart, maybe breaking someone else's, and the outcome would have been the same.

He would have found himself.

I called my friend Brett, who had dutifully stood by me on so many occasions, whom I had called on Friday to tell what had happened. He would be waiting for me, at his apartment on the Upper West Side, the wheelchair and ambulance ready as the plane pulled onto the runway.

I stopped at a Korean vegetable market, with its fruit salads in plastic containers and fresh flowers hidden by bamboo curtains, and bought the cheapest pack of gum—Juicy Fruit, still just a quarter for a foil-sealed pack—to get change for phone calls. I called Porky first, and told him that at least Tim was alive; I didn't know anything else, not yet. I wanted him to shout with me, to shout at Tim, to match my anger, but he didn't. I called Frank, Tim's boss. He told me that everything was going to be okay, that we'd get it all worked out.

No, we wouldn't.

That was the truth.

Porky, Frank . . . they didn't get it.

They hadn't buried Tim in their dreams.

They hadn't heard the music that would be played at his funeral— "A Quiet Place," from the record album we had made in high school, to finance our church choir trip to Puerto Rico. The song that Tim had told me, way back then, he had wanted played at his funeral.

They hadn't known that *I* had died, that I had lost myself and wondered if I would ever be found, that I was Tim and Kim at the same time, that I had seen and mourned my own death, because I couldn't go on living if Tim wasn't here.

They hadn't seen that.

They hadn't seen me in my coffin.

They hadn't known.

They couldn't.

Nobody could know but me.

If Tim was dead, then so was I; my reason for living would be gone, and I would just fade away, whether I did it by my own hand or not.

The sad truth.

I took a cab across town to Brett, flopped down on his trundle bed that was already pulled out, as if waiting for my collapse.

I called Tim's apartment; he picked up the phone in the same drugged, sad voice, telling me he had just set up an emergency session with his shrink and couldn't see me yet. He was more worried about what Frank had said, about losing his job, than seeing me. I was the expendable one; I would survive. Well, fuck you, Gloria Gaynor, I wouldn't. I screamed at him that I didn't know what Frank was going to do; I wanted him to be afraid, to be in as much pain as I had been.

I wanted to kill him, now that he was found.

I screamed did he know what it was like to go through old pictures for a missing person's poster.

I screamed at him did he know what it was like to hold your breath as a policeman opened a bathroom door, because you're sure a dead body's going to be on the other side.

I screamed at him: "Why'd you do that?! Why'd you DO that! WHY'D YOU WANNA HURT ME!?? I DIDN'T DO ANY-THING TO YOU. You could at least THANK me! I SAVED YOUR FUCKING LIFE!!!"

I screamed at him what I had stolen from Stan, what he had screamed at me, back on a bluff overlooking a river in Texas.

I screamed at him that the worst thing a person could ever do was kill himself and make someone else witness it, and be left alone, as he had left me.

I screamed at him I hate you I hate you I hate you before I slammed the phone down, and tears burned my face with heat and salt.

You may have seen broken men, but you have never seen a broken man like me.

They were the words Tim had used to describe his nervous breakdown, but now they fit me, more than they ever fit him:

YOU HAVE NEVER SEEN A BROKEN MAN LIKE ME.

I washed my face at Brett's house and went home.

⟋⟍

Tim called near dusk that Sunday night, after a three-hour session with his shrink. He didn't remember much of what had happened, except that he had woken up on a bench in Central Park. He had gotten drunk Thursday night, at Peter's apartment and afterward, at Uncle Charlie's, knowing it was the anniversary of his breakdown, knowing he was going to have to pack up and leave for yet another new home the next day. He had planned to go to Texas, to escape, but hadn't; he had called a car service that he never met. How he had passed the days to Sunday he didn't know—and he would never remember, or tell me, at least—except that he had gone from man to man, stranger to stranger. He woke up shivering on a bench in the park, covered by wet fall leaves.

Halloween had come; red and gold leaves had fallen and covered him, maybe the one bit of protection he had, hiding him so no one could kill him, except himself.

In my mind, I had seen him covered by leaves.

Somehow, I had known where he was.

On the phone, he told me his story, and I told him mine: I had walked on eggshells around him, waiting for the bomb to go off, ever

since college. The bomb *had* gone off, so many times, and I just stood there, letting the shrapnel fly into me, time after time. But the wounds kept getting covered over with scar tissue, always healing over and hardening even more.

But there would be no more.

My skin couldn't take it.

I couldn't take it.

And yet, I would—after threatening that I wouldn't help him move to New Jersey that evening, our last chance to use Jess's car before he had to take it out of town the next day.

I threatened him but knew I would help. It went to the very core of our twin DNA; no matter what I said, it was the one unchange-able thread. I knew I couldn't keep my promise never to help again. I made my first promise in the womb—to come out first—and I knew I would continue making promises, and keeping them, until I died.

I might hate him, but I would still help him.

I might hate *myself* for it, but I would do it, because it was easier than the gnawing worry I would go through about what would happen to him if I *didn't* help. The relief that he was okay, for now, had completely disappeared, in the anger of riding to the rescue yet again. We were back to our old pattern, however much I might have told myself "just this one last time."

I told him I would be there to pick him up and he'd better be ready.

Several hours later, around eight or nine that Sunday evening, I drove Jess's car from Brooklyn to the Upper East Side, such a foreign land until the past few days. I pretended the minor dips in the road were the hills and valleys of San Francisco; I forced myself to think about cable cars and Rice-a-Roni. As I gunned the car and bounced

up and down, I thought about driving until I ran out of gas; let Tim come and find me then, go through what I had gone through.

I parked in front of the apartment complex in exactly the same spot the police had two days before, Friday afternoon, a million years ago. The old car had sputtered on the way here; now I wondered if I could get it to start again. We would have to hurry. Walking across the courtyard, I looked around furtively for the super, wondering if he had set up watch to capture the escaping twins, get them before they could climb over the Alps, out of danger. (That's it, Kim, make it all a game; use some metaphor, some movie reference, instead of digging into your own heart to see how you really feel.)

What did I really feel?

Nothing.

But really, everything. So much going on it was like one of those canvases that just looked black but was really the accumulation of every color. The same thing I felt when Tim told me how our mother died, and I writhed on the kitchen floor, the same way she had. I could describe what I saw, but not how I felt.

And what I saw, as I opened the door on that fourth-floor landing and saw my twin brother for the first time in days: a face as red and puffy as mine from all the crying. We certainly looked enough alike to be brothers, but at that moment, we looked identical: our faces had the same redness and puffiness and tiny little blood vessels popping out in our eyes. We looked like we had been on the same trip, with the same deprivations: no shaving or face-washing, hair mussed and greasy, clothes rumpled and smelly, unchanged for days. For two boys who had always looked different enough to be thought of as the little brother and the big brother, we finally looked like mirror images, our faces young and old and weighted down by history, all at once. And all the same. And even though one look said he'd gone

through hell this weekend, the same as me, I couldn't let it go, I couldn't, or wouldn't, feel for him.

Just myself.

As we silently glared at each other, daring the other to speak first, this is what I saw, that wouldn't let it go: our patented stare, the stare that had started as far back as the womb, saying, "You go first."

The stare from Tim's suicide attempt, saying, "I win."

The stare from his hospital room, saying "Do you forgive me?"

But I couldn't forgive him.

I couldn't even look at him.

If it was a big reunion scene I wanted, or expected, or even needed, it wouldn't be happening; I could already tell. It wouldn't happen, because I wouldn't let it.

I barged into the apartment, barely saying anything, just grabbing stuff, the inevitable green trash bags that would stretch and go translucent as I carried them down the stairs, bouncing out in front of my knees. They were the perfect metaphor for his life: stretching and ripping and tearing, but never quite spilling all the way open, because of all he pushed inside, so malleable you could stuff them anywhere.

He did try to break the silence: "Please don't be this way. Please don't act this way." But the words didn't have any energy, or real pleading, left in them; they were just exhausted, taking all the breath, the little effort he had left, just to get out. His emergency session with his shrink had used up all the words he had. And when I didn't even acknowledge them, the few words that were left, but just kept moving green trash bags, he gave up trying to say anything more.

I didn't care.

All the desperation I had felt earlier to know where he'd been,

how he'd spent every minute of some seventy-two-odd hours, missing in action, was gone. I didn't want to know anymore. Earlier, on the phone, he'd said the best he could remember, he'd spent it in the park, drunk and drinking more, moving from man to man.

He'd spent the time running away.

So had I.

We were the same, after all: I'd spent the time with a young boy I barely knew.

I hadn't been drinking, we didn't have sex—although I probably wanted to—but wasn't it the same?

Maybe that's why I was so angry, and silent, and ashamed.

We were the same, after all.

When I finally did speak, it was to ask Tim a question about his mattress, the very last thing of his left in the room, and whether he wanted to take it.

"Well, do you or don't you need it? What are you going to sleep on tonight? Another park bench?"

(Only my nose and eyes were still above ground.—I was gasping for air as the devil pulled me deeper into hell and poured more venom into my mouth.)

Tim said his sleeping bag; he'd buy another mattress later on.

"With what?" I said, the venom almost gagging me.

(Now my nose was in the flames; only my eyes were left in the cool earth above, and already my eyelashes were getting singed.)

"Because I'm not going to buy it for you this time. I'm not going to do *anything* else for you."

(My head was in flames, my hair screaming with fire. There was no more saving me.)

Without a word, he grabbed the mattress and half walked, half slid it down those four flights of stairs, throwing it over the banister the

last flight. With twine I had remembered to bring, we strapped it to the roof of the car.

There was no fond farewell to the apartment, no good-bye note for Liz.

There had been no good-bye note for me.

Tim refused to sit in the front seat with me.

He screwed up the directions to Casey's house in New Jersey—our college friend Casey, who had called out of the blue to offer sanctuary because he needed a roommate, and Tim needed another place to run to—telling me to go way downtown to the Holland Tunnel instead of the Lincoln Tunnel near the Port Authority. We drove through the tunnel in silence, our arms stuck out the windows on either side of the car, to keep the mattress from blowing off.

We got to the other side, to New Jersey, and I gunned the car to the side of the road so I could rest my arm, just as the car stalled out.

Just like me.

"We can't go on like this," I said.

"I know," Tim answered.

We sat in silence, until I put my head down on the steering wheel.

"No good-bye note. That's how much you think of me. No note, no letter. Not when you disappeared this time, not when you cut your hand off, not when you disappeared in college. That's all I ever wanted. A fucking good-bye. A thank you. Something to let me know you were thinking about me when you left, just like I think of you every fucking hour of every fucking day. And believe it or not, most of those times, I love you."

"I love you, too."

"I even tried to pretend that's what all your letters over the years were, one long good-bye note, one long love letter, but they weren't. That was just me making up stuff, looking for what wasn't there."

I could see he had started crying, even though we didn't look at one another.

"You think you're the only one who's had it bad. About mother, about everything, that you were the one with the most pain. You wanna know about pain? I'll tell you about pain. I'll tell you about the first time I didn't get a good-bye note, just so you'll know what that's like. Just so you'll know neither one of us won."

I heard my own voice, in that stalled-out car on the side of a New Jersey road, with a mattress flapping overhead in the October wind, tell my most painful story yet to Tim.

⌒

Saturday afternoon.

Third grade.

Just weeks before Our Mother died, whether by her own hand or not, we would never know.

Months after we wore our devil costumes for the very first time.

I was across the street from our house, playacting with Jim Poston and Mike Willis, the boys I would later jump across the ravine to impress. My arm not yet broken, we played capture the castle, the two giant bushes with purplish-blue berries in Mike's backyard as our hiding places, our parapets. I nominated myself the damsel who needed saving and even volunteered a costume: my red cape from Halloween, which I would combine with Tim's to wrap around my waist to make into a medieval skirt.

I ran home to get it, throwing open the door to Porky's room, where I had secreted my treasure trove of disguises.

There, on Porky's bed, the same bed where Tim and I would pretend we were in the womb as we read his letters, the same bed where

we would see her attended by a doctor, and not understand why, lay our mother, perfectly still.

A plastic clothes bag was tied around her head.

I stopped, not understanding.

I stopped, dropped, and rolled, for the first time in my life.

I was seven years old.

Inside the see-through bag, her closed eyes popped open, but she didn't move.

Neither of us did.

Then her hand reached up to tear the plastic off her face.

She gulped for air, silent for a few seconds, then said—oh, what a fast thinker she was, just like the clever twins she had given painful birth to—that this was how to get rid of a cold.

She never thought her impressionable little boy might try it himself, the next time he had a cold.

She told me not to tell my father what I had seen.

What I had seen, what I remembered as I told the story, a very real story, for the very first time, to Tim: the small white printed warnings of suffocation flaking off the blue transparent bag; her nose, red, when she pulled the bag off; and what she used to keep the bag on, fastened around her neck: the madras print belt that matched the plaid Easter jackets she had just bought us.

"Oh, Kim."

"Oh, Kim" is right, even though "Oh, shit," or "Oh, God" would have said more.

"Why didn't you ever tell me?

Tim said it, bringing me back to the present, and New Jersey, and two little twins left to their own devices, by the side of the road.

My eyes were dry now. I was looking at the past and present at the same time.

I needed clear eyes for that.

I would not cry again, as long as I lived.

I WOULD NOT FUCKING CRY AGAIN, AS LONG AS I LIVED.

"You know what, I just realized something. All these years, until this very *second,* it's always just been 'one of our belts' she used to tie that noose. One of our belts. But you know what? I just realized it, I just saw it in my head: it wasn't 'one of *our* belts,' it was *mine.* The belt around her neck was blue; that's the one that went with my jacket. My jacket was blue."

"And mine was gold," Tim said, as if he saw the same scene.

"That's right."

The one thing we had that wasn't the same.

We both looked straight ahead, not at each other, only at the past.

"She used *my* belt to try to kill herself. Does it matter? Did she think it out, decide which one of us she wanted to fuck with more? Maybe. Maybe she just reached in Porky's closet and grabbed the first belt she found. One more thing I did wrong, without ever knowing it. Almost caused her to die then. My belt. *Did* cause her to die, wearing those stupid hobo pants to school. *Did* cause you to have a nervous breakdown, even though I don't know how. Anything bad that happens, it's my fault."

"Jesus, Kim. . . ."

I stopped him. "But I *was* a good boy: I kept that promise, not to tell anybody how I'd found her. I did exactly what she asked. All these years. I never told Daddy, I never told you, I never told anybody. I just lived with it."

"Why?"

The answer came out immediately, although I had never thought it before.

"Because it was mine. Because it was the one thing I had all to myself. Because I didn't want to share, I didn't want to have to be a twin with it and share it with you. It was mine."

Silence, on that New Jersey roadside.

"I went back to that room later that night, even though I didn't really understand what I had seen, but I knew it was bad. I knew to look for a letter, just like all those letters she had written to Porky. Did she write one to us? No. No good-bye. That's why I kept being drawn to that room, looking for it, and keeping my secret. That's all I've ever wanted. Just a good-bye. From her. From you.

"I found her trying to kill herself, just weeks before she died.

"Then you tried to kill yourself, just weeks before. . . .

"This.

"So that's what I've always thought: if you try to die but don't succeed, try, try again. You do it for real a few weeks later.

"I thought that's what had happened to you."

Silence, on that New Jersey roadside.

Silence, after our mother died in the third grade. But I couldn't keep silent anymore.

"I kept reading your letters, all weekend, just so I'd have a map to get to wherever you were, a treasure map. I could find you, when nobody else could."

I couldn't go on.

"Oh, Kim. I've fucked us up so bad."

"I've gone through life thinking everything's my fault. *That's* fucked up. I know it's not my fault, not really, but the night you had your breakdown in college, did you try to find me? I would've done anything to help you."

I still couldn't look at him.

He couldn't look at me either, but he could talk, finally. He could finally solve the mystery of that night.

"I was ashamed. My head was out of control. I started thinking about Mother, about the summer, about Carrie, about Gil. I didn't know who to love the most. Sarah, I loved her, too. But I didn't save her. You would've saved her. You wouldn't have had a breakdown. Maybe that's why I had mine, so I'd have something all to myself, too. And then, this weekend. I . . . wherever I was, if it was in a bar or the park, I don't know, I just kept thinking, just praying, that if I closed my eyes and pictured you, you'd come get me. And you did."

"No I didn't. You called me."

"No, you did. The pictures in my head . . . you made me call you. You made me get out of the park. I was covered with leaves."

"Like Rip Van Winkle," I said, somehow allowing myself to see something beautiful from something so sad: my twin, covered with fall leaves, old before his time.

I had seen that.

"How are we gonna fix ourselves? How are we gonna fix all this?"

It didn't matter which one of us said that; we both felt it. It was the apology we offered at the same time.

"Double trouble. The Powers twins."

We laughed—no, but at least we smiled, oh, so ruefully—to keep from crying. It was so true: double trouble. The trouble we'd caused ourselves, the trouble we'd caused each other, without ever meaning to. Maybe I'd just realized it for the first time: that we were both in pain. That we hadn't intended malice. That we were doing the best we could. That as angry, and scared, and lost as I had been this weekend, Tim had been, too, maybe even more so. That we would need to work together to recover.

It wouldn't be easy. There would be starts and stops, backs and forths, but our forgiveness had to start then and there, or we might as well just get out of the car and walk into the traffic.

And somehow, it *wasn't* the same as before, it wasn't just going

back to the same old pattern of forgive and forget. There's no way we could ever forget this weekend. And some parts of it, some things that had been thought, and said, would probably never be forgiven. But something was different; we both felt it.

We both had scars now.

Tim would begin the act of contrition, with an offer to take over the wheel. "Let me drive the rest of the way to Casey's. I owe you."

It's as if he were making up for his stubbornness in the womb all those years ago, when he'd refused to "come out" first.

I smiled, thinking that something like that could almost be true.

He got out the passenger side of the car and came around to where I was in front; I scooted over inside the car.

"I'll get us there. I'll get us the rest of the way there. I won't fuck up this time. I promise."

And he drove us the rest of the way to Casey's house and found the key above the doorjamb, where Casey had said it would be.

We quickly moved in Tim's things, among Casey's favorite colors of purple and orange and black, the colors of UT Austin, where he'd gone to grad school.

Orange and black.

Halloween.

"You wanna come back to our house and give out candy tonight? It'll be fun. Just till things settle down."

I asked it simply, but the world was in it: apology, forgiveness, sorrow, a promise to do—to try to do—better.

He answered the same way.

"Yeah. That would be nice."

The house in New Jersey would still be there when he was ready for it.

Halloween.

It had been our favorite holiday once, a time for dress-up, a time when devils were just make-believe, not real, a time when falling leaves were a miracle, not something to cover a body.

Maybe it could be again.

We got back in the car and left New Jersey, making up stories about the new world there, about the bluffs in Tim's backyard that he could jump off, to swim to Manhattan.

Oh, how wonderful it would be, to swim together once again.

We sat in the front seat together this time, and looked out the window to say a prayer, a very real prayer: "Blessed Virgin Mary, protect us now, and at the hour of our deaths"—as we made our way back through that narrow tunnel, as we had done so many years ago.

AFTERWORD

I broke my promise.

I said I wouldn't cry again, as long as I lived.

But I would cry again, several more times, although not as much as before, and not only for sad reasons.

I would cry with pride as Tim took me to his AA meeting, on the anniversary of his not drinking for one year. It would be close to eight months after his "lost weekend" in the park that he started AA, eight months during which the "crash and burn" notations that still peppered his Day-At-A-Glance calendar gradually gave way to numbers I couldn't interpret at first. Later, I realized they marked when he started "counting days" as part of the program.

At that one-year anniversary that had been so hard won, I would cry as he stood up to applause and gave his qualification and introduced me to his new friends over coffee afterward.

I would cry with happiness, some six months after that, when he shyly told me he had just met a wonderful new man named David.

Another six months after that I would cry again—but just for a second, before I pulled myself together—when Tim called me from a pay phone on the street and said he had just been to a doctor who told him the horrible cough and cold he could not shake might be AIDS.

I would cry in the TV room of Mount Sinai Hospital three days later, when I told Tim we would beat it, together.

The first Christmas after Tim's diagnosis in the fall, all three brothers spent the holiday together. As a gift, I had put together some old 8-millimeter home movies on a VHS; they showed the little twins—a year old, two, three—opening presents, at picnics, playing with Porky's dog, Cutie, crawling around in our crib. I thought it was the best present I had ever come up with.

Porky's first words when he tore off the wrapping paper: "This is the last thing I need."

He wouldn't even watch the tape until the next day.

Later, we would learn that that Christmas trip was when Porky had planned to tell us that he, too, had AIDS, but couldn't. The weight of the past, watching us grow up on that tape, was too much.

Over the two years we had left with him, things would soften between us; we knew we didn't have much time left. On one of the best times, which began as one of the worst, I had gone by myself to Washington to visit. As I waited at Porky's front door, not having seen him in months, I remembered what I had heard our mother cry out, late one night, when she thought we were asleep: "I don't know how much longer Porky has to live. I don't know how much more of this I can take."

Then my mother's words came true, because Porky looked like he was already dead as he opened the door for me. Kaposi's sarcoma lesions covered his face, chest, arms, and legs. His hair was matted and thinning. He had lost a lot of weight, and what was left just hung off him, revealing the outline of the bone underneath. He was incoherent. He didn't know who I was, or why I was there.

"I don't know what you're doing here," he kept repeating as he made his way back to the bedroom, walking ahead of me as if he had

already forgotten I was there. He got back into bed, and I began to brush his hair. It was the only thing I could think of to do; small talk was out of the question. He must have been doing it when I rang the bell, because the brush was out on the bed. The hairbrush—it looked like one my grandfather might have used, like grandfathers were *supposed* to use—was ballast. Careful not to press too hard, I murmured about making his hair look nice. "If you're going to brush it, then brush it," he blurted out, and I increased the pressure. My eyes filled with tears, first for his anger, then for his death. Then he forgot he was mad at me and just lay there, letting his little brother, as he so often called me, brush his hair.

After a while, he seemed to refocus and said, "I might as well make myself look decent for you." He reached into a drawer beside the bed and pulled out a small bottle of liquid makeup, the same color as his skin. Without any hesitation or thought, still in the moment, I took the bottle from him—"Here, let me"—and began covering the KS lesions on his face. He didn't resist.

I sat next to him and dabbed streaks of the oily makeup on his nose, cheeks, and forehead, then spread it outward, my fingertips automatically falling into the same position and rhythm they had when I was an actor in high school and college and put on makeup for plays, those times in turn reminding me of when I had sneaked into my mother's bedroom as a child and put on her cosmetics. After our mother died and I could get to her makeup more easily—all under the guise of using it for Cub Scout skits—I overheard our babysitter say to someone, "He watched his mama put on her makeup. He knows how to do it." I took that as a compliment. Only later did I understand that it was a skill I was not supposed to have, that would brand me as different.

All of that—a life, certainly a childhood—came back to me from

the roar of that greasepaint on my fingers, touching the purple patches on Porky's face, some slightly raised, almost scabrous, others so smooth it seemed that almost no skin separated me from his blood. He allowed his face to go slack, knowing that I was the expert here.

We didn't say much as I blended the mask over his face, but he held my hand that wasn't working. His touch—I can almost still feel it: soft, cool, a child's hands again. Innocent. Porky's hands, his fingers, had never been childlike or innocent. They had always been big and threatening, thumping me on the forehead as punishment whenever I popped my knuckles or did something wrong. But now they were newborn, just like when they came into the world, reaching at anything that came near them for comfort and security. I hope I gave it to him.

When I was through with the makeup, I closed the bottle and picked up his hairbrush again, pulling it through his thinning hair as he must have through mine when I was a newborn baby, saying goo-gaw things about how life would be. I finished brushing Porky's hair, said, "I love you, brother," and kissed him on the forehead.

"I love you too, brother," he whispered.

It felt like the first time he had ever said it, and it was near the last. A few months later, he went into the hospital; his body had stopped making blood. I sat next to him in that bed, too, held that soft, sweet hand one last time, and prayed, "Flights of angels sing thee to thy rest."

Before he died, he selected a favorite photo to be placed on top of his coffin at his funeral in McKinney: of him standing, healthy and happy, in front of the hot-air balloon he had just stepped out of, on the African veldt. An adventurer. That is how he wanted to be remembered, and that is how he would be, in the grave next to our mother's.

By then, Tim had moved to a new apartment in New York, the first he could truly call a room of his own. I was with him when he found it. We met for coffee as he nervously held the *Village Voice* that listed the apartment, a block from David's, in the Hell's Kitchen section of Manhattan. Was he ready to do it? Could he afford it? Could I help him out with the deposit? What if they found out he was sick and wouldn't rent to him? What if his student loan problems came up on the credit check? There was a huge litany of "what ifs," but an even greater sense that life had started, was going, and that he had to stake his claim now.

He wanted to make his first, and last, home.

The apartment was tiny, a fifth-floor walk-up, but the wide floorboards were painted blue, a deep, rich blue like the ocean. That did it for Tim; it was the only apartment he looked at. It could be the beach house he had always wanted. He and David found a poster they loved, a Hockney print from the exhibit at the Met—a boy on a diving board, rippling panels of lilac and turquoise and ocean blue underneath him—and they designed everything in the apartment around those colors, that mood. A turquoise wash over the wooden bed frame. Mauve walls. Aquatic posters and objets d'art. Flea market bamboo chairs covered with South Sea island prints. Sheets that would take Tim away to the ocean every night, to the cooler, friendlier places he'd been to with David—Fire Island, Key West, Barbados, Provincetown.

From childhood on, through college and now in New York, Tim had tried to find and make a home for himself. It was the one ongoing search in his life, but something kept getting in the way. Orpha Shurley, the postmistress who was his work-study boss at

college, told him, "You look like you think you belong in a trash can, the way you look all the time." At Actors Theatre of Louisville, the artistic director, Jon Jory, his first father figure in an ongoing line of father figures, told him that *Food From Trash,* the play he so loved and understood, was about someone learning to clean up their room and start living. At the end of Tim's own play, the beautiful play he was never able to finish, a boy who has lost everything and gone through hell and back to find a reason to keep living starts cleaning up his apartment, ready to go on with—or start for the first time— his life. A clean room meant a lot. It said something about your soul.

Tim tried, he really did, but the apartment didn't stay clean for long. Maybe I'm making too much of it; maybe it wasn't a metaphor, maybe it was just a mess, nothing more. He used to get mad at me when I would putter around his apartment picking up things instead of focusing on him. I did it to keep things clean, but was it also to express some kind of anger, however unconscious, at the way he lived, at how messy he was, at how he still couldn't pull himself together, even without the booze? Maybe I was so angry—at God for this disease being in the world, at life for just not working out— that I had to take it out on something.

During one of the especially bad times later, when he was really sick when I puttered and picked instead of really listening to Tim, he said, "You know, it's not my fault I can't clean up this place. I don't have the energy. I can barely breathe. So don't treat me like that." I didn't defend myself, didn't say anything snappy or mean, just looked at him, and he didn't look away. We both knew he was right.

He would have about two and a half years that were really good, before things started spiraling down. He never looked better: his new triple obsessions had become going to AA meetings, working on his plays, and working out, and it showed. Those first two years

of his illness, with David, he blossomed; he was strong, assured, happy; the golden, muscular, beautiful swimmer I thought I had seen at Mo Ranch.

But after that time, with Porky gone and Tim's relationship with David precarious, his inner core seemed to be dissipating. The strong, solid masthead he had become for a while was now peeling, weather-beaten, losing color day by day.

Still, he hung on and fought, in his quiet way. He would imitate Dr. Gaan, the gentle Asian doctor who gave injections directly into the lesions of Tim's expanding KS. "Oh, yes, it KS, but we take care of it right away." Somehow that gave Tim confidence. He would come to Monday night ACT-UP meetings after he got the shots and then we, or more accurately, he, would wait: the nervous smile on his face giving way to the aches and pains that would inevitably come from the chemo, the gradually building fever and sweat. It was the first time I really felt the gap between us. He had AIDS; I didn't. We were different now, and I could almost see it in his eyes—a good-bye of sorts—as he waited for the nausea to come.

Sometimes we would leave the meetings early and get a bite to eat; we joked that it was the meetings and its politics making Tim sick, not the chemo. At a nearby coffee shop, I would tell Tim about the dreams I had. Just the good ones, though; if something bad happened in one of them, I made myself forget it. I was willing to give the dreams some power, but not that much. In one of them—surely a sign of hope—we were lying on twin operating tables, and a siphon of blood was going from me into Tim. We were somewhere far away, on a mountaintop, and it was a secret operation, like something from the Great War. My blood saved him. Another time, at the same coffee shop, Tim told me a dream of his: the Virgin Mary had come to him as he walked across a craggy mountaintop. He had

fought his way through a labyrinth of rosebushes with thorns and he was scratched and bleeding, but he had made it to the top. He said I was there, too, and had helped save him. Our tears flowed when he told me that, as they had when I asked him for forgiveness when he was in the hospital that first time. I was sure these were omens, these dreams of rescue and renewal on a mountaintop.

We hunted down every new rumor, every whisper, to beat "this thing." That's all we ever called it. During the weekend Tim had disappeared, I'd done a "dress rehearsal" for what it would be like without him. It had been my own living hell, and I would fight as hard as I could to keep from reliving it. I just wouldn't accept that something final could happen to him. On my own, I ran around to psychics and New Age gurus, spent money I didn't have, to try and find answers and healing: for Tim, for both of us. I only heard good news from them: the psychic in California who told me he saw Tim sitting on a beach at sunset at age forty, after seeing me take more money out of a cash machine; the psychic in New York who told me Tim would be cured if only I confessed to him, the psychic, the worst thing I had ever done (the sad thing is I've done so many bad things one hardly seems worse than the other, until now, when I truly know the worst thing I've ever done: asking Tim why he was depressed, as he lay wasting away on my couch); the John Cazale lookalike at the Doral Inn, where you paid fifteen dollars and got fifteen minutes with the psychic of your choice, at the end of which a bell would ring and the crowd would shift, like speed-dating. He saw no illness at all around me and told me I was "goin' through the roof" in the next couple of years. Anything about a sick brother, I asked? No. I left, convinced he couldn't be legit. The guy who did "past life regressions," that I made the appointment with just because his ad picture was so cute.

During one of Tim's rare hospital stays, I went by his apartment to pick up mail and other things he needed. I loved being there by myself, living for just a while in his world, eavesdropping on his life, finding out his secrets and making myself a part of them, just as I had in Porky's bedroom way back when, reading his letters from our mother.

In Tim's apartment, I came across a letter I thought, at first, someone else had written to him. In a way, someone else had. It was a letter he had written to himself.

Dear Tim,

It was so nice being with you last night, like visiting an old friend and forgetting how much fun it was to be together.

Somewhere along the way, I've forgotten who I am. I've stopped listening to the music I like, I've adopted a persona that has little to do with who I am. I've pretended for so long to be somebody else that I've let go of the person I once was. Some of that's good, I suppose. I'm not a drunk anymore. That's really something to be proud of. But I've lost track of the man who delighted in what he could do. Who delighted in waking up in the morning.

Last night, I felt high in the most marvelous way. I felt like I was driving a car down the Texas highway at 100 mph. I felt marvelous and alone— powerful in my exploration of the world around me. Oh, what a sky I saw on some of those nights. Nights that were so filled with possibility for the future.

That's something I've forgotten; thinking of a bright, exciting future. I've become so obsessed with visions of decay and ruin—my body not supporting me anymore, turning into a scarecrow without a mind. Into something fright-ening to look at, something helpless.

But it doesn't have to be that way. I take charge of my life once again, with the help of a benevolent, loving higher power. I don't want to be dependent and afraid anymore. I want to be brave and to live boldly.

Oh, Tim, it's all possible.

My apartment provides the opportunity for a whole new way of living. I want to make a home for myself before I die—a place that is uniquely my own. A clean place where I can invite friends and David. A place where I can cook and learn to take care of myself properly for the first time in my life.

I keep thinking about driving today, about the freedom of riding in a fast car. I miss that. Remember that night Elton John's "Ticking" played on the car radio and you were vibrantly alive with a sense of life and wonder? Remember Thursday nights in high school? Friday afternoons before a football game? All that wonder, all that excitement is still there for you if you choose to embrace it.

Whatever my destiny, it is mine. Mine to enjoy and delight in. Life isn't drudgery. It's the excitable gift, it's sitting in the football stadium, watching the sunrise at the end of my junior year. Having defined "romanticism" in Carol Daeley's term paper. It's dressing in my Zorba the Greek pants, belted with a red tie, ready for action with Gil or whatever came along.

All those years weren't a total waste. I lost my way, but on the way to the wreckage, I sailed high and brightly, from time to time. I don't want to lose track of who I am, of all these experiences that have created me to the present moment. Keep remembering. Keep coming out. Write. Live. Love. It's yours to do.

Putting that letter back down, Tim left me shamed by how much time we—how much time I—had wasted.

Tim swore a new start, a new life, after that Easter hospital stay. I look at his daily planner, and it's full. Appointment with his trainer— "Start light, build back up." Plays he had seen with boys I had never heard of. But then the appointments trailed off, and there was no more writing in his daybook, except for doctor's appointments. He more or less came to live with us, although we never called it that.

He was just staying with us until his strength built back up, and he could manage his fifth-floor walk-up again.

At our apartment, I don't know if he was in pain, but he slept most of the day or stayed on the couch and read. He read a lot—the masters he never got around to in college, when he was nervous but brilliant—Jane Austen, Dickens, Virginia Woolf, Eudora Welty, stories about southern people standing around deathbeds, waiting. He even started Proust and laughed about it. He said all he had was time, and remembrance.

Sometimes I looked forward to coming home at night, to see his beautiful smile, to tell him silly, funny stories about what had gone on in my silly, funny office during the day. I'd bring home dinner, or sometimes he'd surprise me by having made something—spaghetti, his standard, or once, the most delicious meatloaf I have ever had. We were getting better at it, the habit of being: sometimes we could just be with each other, without having to do anything. Other times, it was like a flashback to some of our worst times: I dreaded coming home—racing, tired and sweaty, my two dogs and people to walk and feed and entertain, putting on my happy face as I put the keys in the door.

Sometimes the nights were hard, and I couldn't sleep. Jess and I would hold each other, and in the pacing of my breath I would tell him, without words, how scared I was, how I couldn't go on. Half awake, half asleep, I would hear if Tim lost control of his bowels in the night, would hear the angry, disappointed "shit" he'd utter, would smell the sweet, sickly smell. From my bed in the next room, I would ask if he needed help.

"I'm sorry I woke you up."

"That's okay."

And I would get up, get out the clean pair of pajamas and set of

sheets. I'd bring him a warm, wet washcloth to clean himself with, and take his dirty things to the bathroom to rinse out and leave to dry. Sometimes he'd make it to the bathroom before he lost control. He'd spray the room with a deodorizer that was worse than the other smell.

Sometimes, afterward, we'd sit in the middle of the couch, or on the daybed halfway to the bathroom, if he needed to get his strength back. He wouldn't say much. I'd put his head in my lap, or just hold on to him, sitting up. Sometimes we'd pray, or I'd do my healing work: my hands over his lungs, his stomach, praying for golden light from God to go into his body.

"Oh, dear God, bless our Timmy, heal him and bring him wonderful peace and rest and comfort," I would say. To myself, silently, I would pray not to be resentful of or angry at him. Sometimes it worked. Sometimes I didn't beat up on myself so badly.

"Thank you," Tim would always say when I finished.

In those closing moments of the day, there was no pain, no fear, no need. I never felt closer to him than during those evening vespers.

But sometimes during those late-night visits, he talked about suicide, and that horrible weekend came flooding back. "I can't see any good that comes from being this sick anymore. I can't see God's purpose in it. Before I lose my sight, or have to have a catheter put in . . ." He had become so depressed that he started taking an antidepressant, but even with that he said he was barely able to get out of bed in the morning.

As scared as I was, I told him that I loved him and would support him in whatever he decided to do. He asked me to get him some books about accepting death, killing himself painlessly. It was hard for him to get out and around now, so I was the lifeline—to death—for him. Only I couldn't do it.

The books that were always there at A Different Light, the AIDS books next to the pinups, had disappeared. (Death and its opposite, desire, said our friend Tennessee Williams.) The books about accepting death, letting go, even killing yourself, that book that I had wondered about getting so much earlier, were gone, almost as if they weren't supposed to be there for me: it wasn't time yet. I ran around to the other bookstores in the neighborhood but I couldn't find anything at them either. I came back empty-handed.

Tim's disappointment showed, and I think he felt I hadn't looked hard enough, even though I told him all the stores I had gone to. He said, "Never mind," and that was that.

This is so hard, helping my brother die.

Later on—I don't know how—Tim found a book called *A Graceful Passage: Notes on the Freedom to Live or Die,* about a man who had spent most of his life in an iron lung, constantly thinking about suicide, but who had decided, finally, somehow, to live. (I still have the book, just as I have all the books Tim brought here to die with. I cannot get rid of them, but I cannot read them, either.) There was little talk about it until one night, he suddenly, and simply, said, "Even with all my fears, what I've gone through and might still go through, I've decided on the side of life. I'm going to try as hard as I can to stay alive. As much as I've tried not to believe in God, I can't *not* believe in Him, and in some purpose to my life."

And in my heart, and in my prayers, I thank them both for that.

Oh, God, give me strength. These sad, sad stories.

⌒

One Sunday, a few weeks after a second, debilitating hospital stay, we had a big fight. I started it, but I didn't mean to. At least I don't think

I did. I think I just wanted to say something to release the tension, the claustrophobia that had built up in the apartment.

"We have to talk about what we're going to do," I said calmly, but I didn't stay calm. Within seconds, it seems something in me came unleashed, the worst kind of cruelty. "Let's not pretend anymore. You can't go back to your apartment, you can't climb the stairs, it's boiling hot up there."

"Just shut up about something you don't know anything about. It isn't . . ."

"You don't even have an air conditioner. . . ."

". . . that hot."

"And you can't even climb the stairs. . . ."

"In a few days . . ."

"Don't you get it? GOD HAS LEFT US."

That was the point I had started out to make. God's the one I really wanted to fight with. I flew out of the rocking chair and toward the bathroom as Tim struggled off the couch. He began throwing his things into a bag. I kept ranting.

"Go ahead. DON'T listen to me, nobody ever listens to me. And put your stuff down. You're going to have to STAY HERE."

He tried to leave but couldn't. He couldn't even walk down the hall. He was paper thin, and his skin had turned a sort of sunburned orange, the blood so close to it, burned by chemo. (My brother, thirty-three years old, gettingw chemo. I cannot believe it.)

I begged him to stay. I begged for forgiveness, a truce.

"Why do we always fight?" he asked, so tired. "I don't have much time left. We can't go on like this."

I wouldn't have anybody if it weren't for you. All I have is gone. I look horrible. I can't take care of myself, I'm trapped here, I can't even walk up the steps to my house. If you didn't let me stay here I

don't know what I'd do. My life is over, and you've hated me for all of it. (I can't put it in quotes. I can't stand remembering he said it. I can't stand remembering I caused it, and yet I play it over and over in my head.)

It was the great mystery of our lives, how we loved, yet—at the worst times between us—hated each other so much.

"Why have our lives been so sad? Why has there been so much hate?" I asked, crying as quietly as I ever had.

"I don't know."

Questions asked, not looking at each other. I didn't know if we had the time left to answer them.

For our thirty-third birthday, the one I knew would be our last, Jess was out of town, so I had invited our friend Wayne to go out with us, thinking I needed a third person to help soak up the pain I was so afraid of on that night of all nights. But it was so horrible outside—heavy, purple clouds overcast with green, what I have always imagined the end of the world would look like—that Tim didn't want to go out. We would stay home and order in Chinese and make the best of it.

I had left work early that day to buy Tim his presents, paperback copies of Elizabeth Enright's *Gone-Away Lake,* and its sequel, *Return to Gone-Away,* books that had been our favorites as children. When he tore off the gift wrap and saw them, his eyes widened and he said, "How did you know I wanted these? I kept thinking about them when I was in the hospital." Maybe I had heard him say something, maybe I just knew, as I so often did with him. I inscribed them, "Timbo, my dearest brother, for our lives past and to come." I also got him a little homemade rag doll from a shop on Christopher Street, complete with a card that told her life story: "Hello, my name is Sarah and I come from the island of love. My favorite things are

to eat pasta and to write stories. I love people. Whenever you feel alone, I am here for you."

He got me a beautiful tie and bow tie from Camouflage, his favorite store. His final sacrifice. I don't know how he even had the strength to get out of the apartment to get them. The tie was red, with bold, colored shapes outlined in black. I wore it to work the next day. "I knew you could carry it off," he said as I kissed him good-bye. A week or so before his death, I wore the bow tie—black, with an explosion of colorful flowers, almost Japanese. I woke him up that morning just so he could see me wear it. He seemed so proud of it.

Despite these memories, or maybe because of them, it was a perfect night, our last birthday together.

And now, I have run out of stories, except for the last one. The one I don't want to tell, but know I must.

(Bless me, Tim, be with me now and always as you promised you would.)

⌣

That night, Wednesday, was like so many others. The summer heat, me coming home tired and sweaty from work. Tim was lying on the couch, a smile on his face despite some pain, reading one of the books from his last phase. There were always little piles of books around him.

He started feeling worse as the evening wore on—some tightness in his chest, a heaviness to his breathing. By nighttime, he wasn't feeling well at all but wanted to ride it out. He didn't want to give in to the pain or admit that something might be happening. If he didn't mention it, maybe it would go away.

He hadn't gone in for chemo in two weeks. Whether he saw that as just a respite or a much more permanent break, I don't know; we didn't talk much about his decision. He said he just wanted to get some of this strength back. He had come to dread the days it took to recover, only to start all over again. Later, I would wonder if his quitting for those two weeks brought on the final onslaught. I probably asked his doctor, but it was one of those meaningless questions. He had come as far as he could, and this last piece of life, if it was dependent on bad medicine, just wasn't worth it.

He thought maybe it was indigestion from dinner. He kept stretching out, arching his back, trying to free up more space in his lungs. I rubbed his back, mopped his forehead with a cold washcloth. He tried to focus on reading and get away from the pain but couldn't.

Did we call his doctor that night? There were other times when we had done that, but I can't sort them out now. I think we called; I think I talked to somebody at the other end of the line. Just try to get him through the night, they said. (Why is this night different from all others? Because your brother is dying.) I decided to call Neil, our doctor friend. Maybe he could help. I kept calling him, but his line was always busy.

"Damn," Tim said, his first anger of the evening. "He's always on the phone. He's a doctor—why doesn't he have call waiting?"

"Why don't we just try to sleep?" I said. "Maybe that will help." I fixed his couch bed for him, removing the back pillows and shaking out the sheets. I lay by myself in bed—Jess was out of town—and looked straight up at the noisy ceiling fan we still hadn't had fixed. I tried to breathe, I tried to pray, I tried everything, but no peace came. We were alone, he was getting sicker, and I was scared. He wasn't supposed to die in the middle of the week like this, out of the blue. He

was sick, but not that sick. I forced my eyes closed and all I could hear, even over the grating sound of the fan, was my poor brother trying to breathe.

"I'm sorry I'm making so much noise," he said. He knew I was awake; he knew I was scared.

"Tim, something's really wrong. What are we gonna do?"

He thought for a while. "Try Neil one more time." It wasn't really an answer, just a waiting game.

I tried to be calm as I had the operator break in on Neil's line, which was still busy. "It's not exactly an emergency," I said, not wanting to scare anyone else.

"Well, what is it, then?" she barked.

I made a decision. "It's an emergency. He's a doctor, and I need to talk to him."

Neil called me back a few minutes later.

"I'm sorry about getting you off the line." He was calm; maybe they teach them about breaking in on phone lines in med school. I described what was happening. "The fever's gone up a lot—it's about 104 and he can't breathe. What should we do?"

"Get an ambulance." He didn't say it sounded like the end, he just said we should get an ambulance as fast as we could. I hung up, still doing my smiling act for Tim, trying to stay calm. This can't be happening. I'm not ready.

The fear just wouldn't stop.

Tim had heard all of it, even what went on in my head. He thought the same thing. In these last few minutes, we both knew that things had gotten very serious. It had come over him like that.

I went over and sat on the couch. "Neil thinks we should call an ambulance and get you to the hospital." I was trying not to rush or scare him, but I was beginning to panic.

He didn't want to go. He wanted to die at home. He didn't want to die. He had gone into a kind of trance, his thought processes slowing down—because of fear, because of pain. "What am I gonna do? What should I do?" he kept asking.

My thirty-three-year-old twin brother was dying in front of me.

"I'll do whatever you want. I'll make you as comfortable as I can, but I think we should get you to the hospital." Then I said the scariest words I have ever said: "I think you're gonna die if we don't. At least they can you give you some oxygen to make your breathing easier."

Silence. "What do you want me to do?" he asked again, as if he hadn't heard anything I had said.

I thought of when we were born, my feeling that he was supposed to come out first but changed his mind at the last minute. "What do you want me to do?" he had asked then, too.

"Okay. Let's call the ambulance." It was a decision to get us to the next decision, whatever that would be.

I had never called an ambulance before, and I suddenly thought of the men in my life, my forebears, who had had to call them in a line before me. My father on his lunch break, when he found my mother dead on the kitchen floor; Steve, as Porky lay hallucinating. I thought of the kindly woman who had taken my 911 call years ago when Tim was missing: was this the same woman I talked to now, our guardian angel?

She told me the ambulance was on its way, and I came back to sit by Tim on the couch. "Hold me, rub my back," he said, his face and eyes white with pain. He was trying to ration his breaths just to keep going, talking as little as he needed to get from one to the next. My right hand rubbed his pitifully thin back, my left hand gripped his knee. "Say a prayer with me," he asked, a look of wild panic, of

searching, in his eyes, and from somewhere I remembered something
I hadn't said since I was a child:

> The Lord is my shepherd;
> I shall not want.
> He maketh me to lie down in green pastures:
> he leadeth me beside the still waters.
> He restoreth my soul:
> he leadeth me in the paths of righteousness
> for his name's sake.
> Yea, though I walk through the valley
> of the shadow of death,
> I will fear no evil:
> For thou art with me;
> thy rod and thy staff they comfort me.
> Thou preparest a feast before me in
> the presence of mine enemies:
> thou anointest my head with oil;
> my cup runneth over.
> Surely goodness and mercy shall follow me
> all the days of my life:
> and I will dwell in the house of the Lord
> forever.

We were more scared than we had ever been in our lives, but
when Tim opened his eyes from the prayer, they had settled on some
sort of acceptance, an absolute knowing. Whatever this meant, these
moments, this life, we were together, as he had written in his play:
"We stood in the middle of a graveyard and loved each other. We
didn't run."

"Whatever happens to me, remember: I will always be with you," he said. Those were essentially the last words he ever said to me, before the paramedics arrived and shutdown began. "Whatever happens to me, remember: I will always be with you."

We stood in the middle of a graveyard and loved each other. We didn't run.

⌒

In the ER at St. Vincent's, they put Tim in a cubicle and rushed to take X-rays, stripping his clothes off and laying him flat on photographic plates, the cold metal against his protruding backbones, his lungs now so close to the skin because there was no cushioning layer of fat or muscle. They wadded his clothes up—a pair of jeans, a blue-and-white striped shirt—and stuck them under the portable bed.

For some reason they had to take off the portable oxygen mask, and that caused the first moment of absolute panic. "I CAN'T BREATHE," he screamed between gasps, and his face broke out in a sweat. Is this what death is like? When you can't get your next breath? He started crying, his eyes pleading with me.

I spun around, shaking, paralyzed. I ran to a nurse and said he can't breathe, as frantically as Tim had. "Somebody help," I cried, but what if there wasn't anything else to do? What if he was dying right there in front of us? I was shaking so much I could hardly walk or talk.

A young male doctor, concerned, earnest, put an oxygen mask on Tim, who gulped down the air.

He then brought me to the front desk and said—was this the first time he ever had to say these words, to look at someone the way he looked at me?—"Do you know how sick he is?"

"Yes, he has pulmonary KS; he stopped treatment a few weeks

ago." I wouldn't tell him how sick I really knew Tim was; I would make him tell me. Maybe if I didn't say anything, he wouldn't either, and everything would get better.

A pause. He was deciding how to tell me the rest. "I don't think there's anything else we can do. His lungs are gone, they're completely white. I can show you the X-rays. There's no air in them. We can put a breathing tube in, but it will never come out, I guarantee you."

"NO," I almost shouted. It jumped out of me. "We talked about that. Don't resuscitate him." How did I know that big word—resuscitate? I was only twelve years old, and I was having to make an adult's decision. We had talked about it, but it was never going to go that far. It wasn't fair.

Was there a chance? Was I cutting him off too fast?

"No, this is it. He's not going to pull through. I promise you."

Silence. Tears came to my eyes; the grief had already started. The child I had become asked questions, polite, scared, halting. "Can you give him something for the pain?"

"We'll start him on morphine and make him as comfortable as we can. That's the best we can do. I'm sorry. You have to sign here."

And surprisingly, I remembered my name and signed the death warrant for my twin brother: me, the one who had come out of the womb first when he got cold feet; me, the one who had to come out of the closet first when he wouldn't own up; me, the one who always had to pick up the pieces; me, the one who loved him more than there are words to tell.

"They're going to give you something for the pain," I said to Tim, trying to sound optimistic, like everything was going to get better now, even though my eyes were full of tears. His were gigantic and scared behind the oxygen mask. I don't know if he knew what I meant, that this was good-bye.

Very quickly, it seemed, a young nurse gave him a small injection. Sweat started pouring off him almost immediately; his eyes rolled back into his head. I thought I saw him dying. I started playing out the scene from *Longtime Companion* that had so haunted us, of Bruce Davison saying good-bye to his lover, urging him to let go.

I thought it would happen quickly, but it didn't. I somehow thought the morphine itself would kill him, like putting a dog to sleep. I didn't realize it just knocked out the pain sensors so death could sneak in on its own. He hung on through the night. That same sweet nurse, a tissue in one hand for her tears, syringe in the other, kept saying, "He doesn't want to let go," as we watched his breath rate and pulse slow down on the overhead monitor.

I sat by him all night long. The staff went about its business, forgetting us, and despite the hustle and bustle, the place was quiet. At times, he would wake, his eyes open without knowledge, or maybe too much knowledge, blank. No emotion, no curiosity. What did he see in that fevered, waking sleep, the sweat pouring off his body as it tried to save itself?

Amazingly, there would be a deathwatch of a day and a half, before the end. I had time to call David, Tim's ex, to come be by his side, and mine. I hadn't wanted to wake Tim up; David did. He wanted Tim to know he was there. "Hello, baby," he said, not afraid. Tim's eyes opened slowly and he smiled, the first smile of the last many hours.

"I love you," David continued. Tim smiled even more beatifically.

At one point, an old woman approached me as I stood in Tim's cubicle. She gazed at me, then at Tim. Old as the hills herself, she asked if he were my father. Sadly, I smiled at her and said no, my brother.

"It's hard, isn't it?" she said, as if she really knew. I nodded my head yes.

"Do you want me to get you a Coke?" she asked, just like my

ancient Aunt Bonnie would have. I said that would be nice. She went away and came back quite a while later with the Coke. I drank as much of it as I could, more for her than for me. When I turned around to thank her, she was gone. Maybe she was the gentle spirit Tim and I had wondered about, sent to guide him home. No one else saw her. I'm sure if I checked the hospital records for her, they wouldn't know who I was talking about.

Around three that last afternoon, Tim seemed to resurrect himself for a while and started talking. Because of the oxygen mask and the morphine, though, his words were unintelligible. They came from a different place than I could interpret. I held on to his hand and put my ear up to his face to play out our good-bye scene.

"I love you, sweetheart. So much. You don't have to fight anymore. Just let go. It's okay. It's time to go now." I kept repeating those phrases over and over, like mantras, as Tim struggled to make himself understood.

"Yes," I said, nodding my head as if I understood. "I know you love me, too."

He shook his head in frustration—NO, it seemed to say. Even doped up and dying, he cut into me with a look that leveled all the anger and disappointment of his life right between my eyes. He kept shaking his head and trying to say something.

As the guard literally started pulling me out of the room, my ten minutes of visitation time used up, I finally understood what Tim had been trying to say: ICE. WATER. He was dehydrated; dying, literally, for a glass of water, and I hadn't understood. The one practical thing I could have done to help, and I was too busy playing out a scene from a movie to do it.

Just before I was taken out of the room, I yelled out to one of the nurses that he needed water. She looked like she understood, but I

will never know. Maybe it is better that way. I will make myself think she took him his water.

That is the last time I ever saw my brother awake, the last thing he ever said to me.

ICE.

WATER.

That evening, I went back in by myself, the room surprisingly quiet as dinnertime approached. The patients were settled in, not needing attention, not even Tim. He was just dying, and he could do that by himself. I crept up to his bedside. He was sleeping—peacefully, it seemed, if you didn't know, and maybe even then. I instinctively knew that it was the last time I would ever see him, but I couldn't bring myself to wake him up. I was afraid that I wouldn't be able to say good-bye to his face, so I did it in prayers, as I had so many times before, the same last words I had said to Porky, "Goodnight, sweet prince, and flights of angels sing thee to thy rest."

I touched him, kissed his brow, and left the room. That was the last time I ever saw him.

Around eight the next morning the phone rang, and I knew what it would be. It was the doctor who had admitted Tim to the emergency room thirty-two hours before, that kind, concerned man who hesitated, then asked me what my relationship was to Tim, as if he were following some sort of prescribed protocol.

I said I was his twin brother.

In that case, he said—and I have wondered about the strangeness of that phrase, that qualifier, ever since—"I regret to inform you that your brother passed away this morning."

I waited a beat, as if that were expected of me, although I didn't really need to pause then. "Did he feel any pain?" I asked in my little child's voice, knowing no one but Tim could answer that.

"We don't think so," the doctor said, for my sake. "I'm awfully sorry."

"So am I," I said. "So am I."

⌒

I had cried so much during those three years, and before, but I would not cry the day Tim died, when I ran into my ACT-UP friend Mark Fischer on my way home from the hospital, the hospital from which I had just called friends and the funeral home, to break the news.

Mark Fischer would see me walking home on that gloriously bright Friday morning, and, not knowing what had just happened, ask me, "How ya doing? How ya holding up? How's Tim?"

I would not cry when I said, "He's fine. He just died, but finally, I think he's fine."

Fine, because he wasn't suffering anymore and had finally gone home, to see the mother he had missed for so many years.

I would cry for myself, but no longer for Tim.

He was fine.

He was free.

I did not—would not—see Tim's body after he died; the funeral home had a door-to-door pickup policy, from the door of the hospital to the door of the funeral home. All I had to do was let my fingers do the walking; they did everything else. There were papers to sign and bills to pay, clothes to pick out for the cremation. David, still in shock—I don't think he ever thought Tim would actually die of this; neither did I, for that matter—volunteered to do that. He

brought over one of Tim's favorite outfits, a fancy blue work shirt and khaki pants, and a selection of ties. I can't remember which tie we picked out; I thought I could never forget.

Maybe that's a good sign, that I'm moving on.

Tim died on a Friday morning; I delivered the clothes to the funeral home on Saturday. I was early; nobody was out on the streets. There was a light rain, and it was gray outside. It was the kind of day I used to love in college, and later—get up early by myself, go outside and read, control the day. A fall day. I felt powerful then. Now I walked through the meat market to the funeral home a few blocks away, carrying this last outfit in a sheath of dry cleaner's plastic. I handed over the clothes to a stranger—a stranger who couldn't possibly understand how special, how perfect, how sad, these clothes that no longer fit were—no ceremony involved except for my trying to smile but shrugging instead, looking back one last time after he had already whisked the clothes away.

Later in the day, I realized I hadn't taken over any shoes. I remembered some story about people being buried without their shoes, but couldn't remember if that was a good or bad thing. I called the funeral home in a panic, and somebody said—this must have been the gist of what they said, not the exact words—"It's too late. It hardly matters anyway, does it?"

For the rest of the day, I braced myself, wondering if I would feel anything when Tim went into the flames.

In the week or so after Tim's death, I was drawn to Tim's apartment like a sleepwalker, unaware of where he's going but determined to get there, panic-stricken once he wakes up. (Our father used to sleepwalk after our mother died. He even got in the car once and started it up, all in his sleep. I used to think it was because he was drunk. Now I understand. He was looking for our mother.)

There was a hint of the last cleaning we had done, but not much. The apartment was a mess again. I don't know how Tim could have done it; he had barely been there in months. I picked up his mail every few days, got the books and clothes he wanted, and he called in to his machine for messages. The last set of them (the blinking red light the only light in the room) hadn't been checked since Wednesday, when I had taken him to the emergency room. I cleared a space on his bed, lay down, and pressed the button to listen to the people who had called him at the end, not knowing he was already gone: Michael Lane (now gone himself), Lynn Thompson, Bill Roberts, Cathy Cannon, Ron Mandelbaum, Beth Stapleton. I wrote their names down on a page from his journal—those bare, unfinished pages—knowing I would have to give them the bad news. That's when I saw this, the last entry he wrote:

Sunday Night

I've been so out of touch that I haven't written anything in months. Tonight, I'm just going to let my mind go. It's a muggy evening, poised at the beginning of summer, a time/season which once held such magic for me. Last night, Neil Theis reminded me how much I've let go—taking care of myself in other than medical, pharmaceutical ways. Our discussion of Tai Chi and writing did stir some hope in me—it's not all dead and neither am I. I expressed to him my desire to pull this summer out of the crapper before it's over or too late. I intend to do that.

I am angry that this has/is happening to me, but there has to be more to the picture than what I allow myself to see. And the biggest one of those components has to be my God-given imagination. I've simply stopped using it—I've stopped dreaming, stopped seeing myself in any other role than "sick" person. That's not all there is, though it sometimes seems that way. I am more than a sick person. That is what Beth means by seeing options and

choices for myself. This last hospitalization really kicked me—my spirit grew weak. How I long now for real nourishment—God grant me that. The kind of peace I want doesn't have to end with suicide or giving up.

My fantasy is always about traveling on a foggy night in early summer— taking a taxi ride where the air on my face is cool and refreshing, something that makes me feel good and lively again. I take a night train to a resort town on the Jersey shore. The train, my lodging, the ocean are all in walking distance of each other. I walk along the boardwalk and in the clearing sky see more stars than I dreamed possible. I feel my connection with them, with the love and mystery of the universe and I am at least in total peace. Everything is as it should be. I'm in harmony with God, who loves me without condition.

Help me to start living again, sweet Jesus. Give me the power and strength to fulfill my destiny here, wherever that leads me. You've told me I will not be given more burdens than I can handle. Give me the faith to believe that. Show me victory.

I sat on the bed and cried, stunned, empty, too full, these sheets he had sweated into, these things that were his, this room I had so begrudgingly trudged up the stairs to, delivering nourishment, I thought, I hoped, but probably only delivering bile. He had somehow found his way up those five flights of stairs for the last time and poured this letter out from his heart in a direct line to God.

I looked at the beauty of the sunset from his window and thought I had gotten it all wrong. I used to judge our separate views: mine large and expansive, his tiny and cramped, covered with bars. But now I thought our souls were the exact opposite of that: mine had been tiny and cramped and locked up for so long, looking out onto a brick wall, an easy target for thieves. His is the one that had looked out onto a river, taking in the rough waters and healing fog equally.

How I wept on that bed because I already missed him so, because I would never be him, my cramped handwriting of those final names no match for the life he had recorded in those pages.

When we finished cleaning the apartment the very last time, the wonderful Dick Larimer and I, the room was as bare and *possible* as it had been when Tim and I first walked into it, Tim nervous but determined to commit to a new life. That beautiful blue floor that convinced him to take the apartment, that made him think he was floating in the ocean, part of the kingdom of fish, was visible once more, awaiting the next sea-struck soul who would sail in.

Summer was sliding into fall, the leaves were changing; the ferries to Fire Island would soon be going out only once or twice a day. It was the last weekend of my summer share. I had ended up not going out that much because of Tim's being sick; now I needed to pick up my things. Sitting on the top deck of the ferry, the sea spray, the sun in my eyes, the loneliness, I was like the narrator in *Dancer from the Dance,* my introduction to Fire Island: he goes out alone to pack up the belongings of a dead boy who has walked into the ocean, once the season is over and fall has come.

The lesbians with the parrots were there when I arrived, but they soon left. I was the only one in the house; it seemed like I was the only one on the island. I liked it that way. I had brought a Stephen King book to scare myself, as if I needed it, and very little else, more empty space for the things I had to take back. Among the things I would leave behind: some of Tim's ashes, lovingly but ludicrously poured into a Tupperware container; the rest I had put in a little cube, painted with fish and moss and the sea, on my desk at home.

It had taken months (weeks, probably; days, in actuality; it just seemed like months) before I could tear the brown paper wrapping off the cardboard box the ashes came in; months after that (again, weeks; days, even—Tim had just been dead a month) before I could open the black plastic carrying case inside the cardboard box, very carefully, almost ritualistically following the instructions to use a "screwdriver or coin, such as a dime" to pry open the lid; and not until the morning of my last trip out to Fire Island could I tear open the clear plastic sack that actually held the ashes inside the black container. But I could only look at them as I poured them from parcel to parcel, amazed at their weight, portioning them out for friends—this many for David, that much for Charlott; I couldn't touch them yet. I couldn't feel Tim again.

Around sunset on Saturday I went to the beach, taking the ashes with me, prepared for but not certain of what I was going to do. I wore my outfit reserved for those foggy, cool Fire Island nights, jeans and an oversized sweatshirt, purchased on the island the first weekend we were there for twice what they would have cost in the city. A right on the boardwalk in front of our little house, a left on Tuna, across the Boulevard and down the steps onto the beach—I did it automatically. Without realizing where I was heading, I found myself in front of the house where we had spent Christmas several years earlier, the first Christmas of Tim's diagnosis, the Christmas when Porky wanted to tell us of his own diagnosis but couldn't. The sky was beautiful: orange, purple, blue; the beach was almost deserted. A couple with a dog walked far away in the ebb and flow of the tide.

The ocean seemed to go on forever.

For the first time—and I am given to portents and omens, metaphor and symbols, signs—I thought of Tim saying he wanted

to live in the sea, to become the incredible Mr. Limpett. Goofy, tall
Don Knotts, just like Tim, his Adam's apple bobbing away, not comfortable on land, somehow transporting himself beneath the waves
and finding happiness there. It was the first movie we ever cried at.
The summer of Tim's breakdown, all of his writing about the
kingdom of fish and how he'd never seen anything more beautiful.
A place to hide, or to find his true nature? It didn't matter. His last
journal entry, his visualizing taking a trip to the seashore on a foggy
night, walking along the boardwalk with the air cool and lovely on
his face. We were there now, on that trip. He had made it come true.

I reached into the container and actually touched the ashes for the
first time. They were flakier than sand, as coarse as shale. No bone frag-
ments, as I had imagined there would be; nothing that I could identify
as human, or Tim, and yet it was. I rubbed some of the ash between my
fingers, on the whorls of my fingertips, and then started applying it to
my face, like makeup; ritualistically, primitively, instinctually. The
powder I had purloined from my mother's drawer as a child. The
greasepaint I had used in school plays. The liquid with which I had
covered the KS on my older brother's face. A line from birth to the
grave, and beyond, as I made myself up with my twin brother's ashes,
outlined my lips as I had observed my mother doing, tracing my eyes,
rubbing the shale into my cheeks to bring the color back to them. I
closed my eyes and imagined literally becoming my brother, as his very
being—the only thing that was now physically left of him—became a
part of my face. I rubbed harder and harder, so a shard would pierce my
skin and draw blood, and my brother would truly become a part of me.

He had never been more real in my life.

I knew that it was the right time. I knew that Tim would always
be in that ocean, on that beach, in this world, and the next, with me.
I looked up into the sky and said a prayer.

I was ready.

I threw the rest of the ash into the waves, and they danced around my feet.

ACKNOWLEDGMENTS

I'd like to thank Jennifer Lyons, my agent, for selling the book; Don Weise, my editor, for buying the book; and Barbara Simon, my best friend and pretend wife, for helping me survive the book. I'd also like to thank Jeff Gumprecht and Milton Wainberg for keeping my body and mind intact enough to be around for what comes after. From the Austin College crowd, I'd like to thank Carrie McLarty, Casey McClellan, and Marc Daniel for knowing there's a good and bad part to nostalgia; ditto for Jennifer Wilson Davis in McKinney. And in New York, I thank so many good friends, for iced tea and sympathy along the way: Laura Zaccaro; Karen Compton; Tom Touchet; Andy Baseman and Mark Randall; Michael Becker and Tee Scatourchio; Patty Neger at GMA; Kate Edmunds, my "first responder;" and David Bromley for his cover painting. I thank David Elledge and Dick Larimer for being there when Tim needed you most, and I thank Jess Goldstein for being there, always, for me.